Turner's Britain

Turner's BRITAIN

James Hamilton

MERRELL
LONDON · NEW YORK

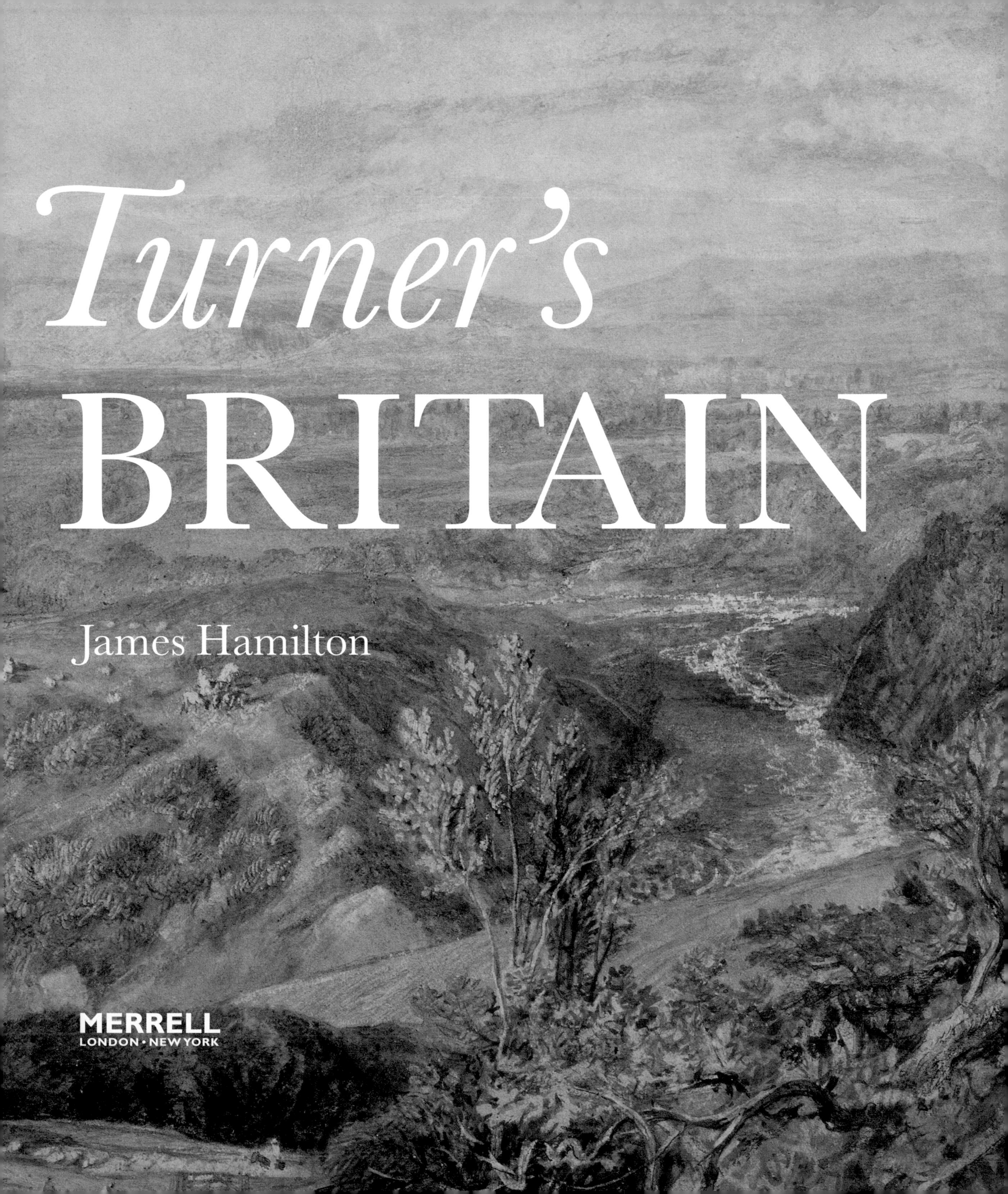

First published 2003 by
Merrell Publishers Limited

Head office:
42 Southwark Street
London SE1 1UN

New York office:
49 West 24th Street
New York, NY 10010
www.merrellpublishers.com

in association with

Birmingham Museums & Art Gallery
Chamberlain Square
Birmingham B3 3DH

Published on the occasion of the exhibition *Turner's Britain*
organized by Birmingham Museums & Art Gallery
7 November 2003 – 8 February 2004

This exhibition has been generously sponsored by
Ernst & Young

EY ERNST & YOUNG

ISBN 1 85894 211 X (hardback)
ISBN 1 85894 212 8 (paperback)

British Library Cataloguing-in-Publication Data:
Hamilton, James, 1948–
Turner's Britain
1.Turner, J. M. W. (Joseph Mallord William), 1775–1851 –
Journeys – Great Britain 2.Great Britain – In art 3.Great
Britain – Description and travel – Pictorial works
1.Title 11.Birmingham Museums & Art Gallery
759.2

Produced by Merrell Publishers
Designed by Matt Hervey
Edited by Sarah Yates
Indexed by Hilary Bird
Printed and bound in Italy

Front jacket/cover: *St Mary's Church, Warwick, from below
Hill Wootton*, ?1830, detail of pl. 125
Pages 2–3: *Crook of Lune, looking towards Hornby Castle*, c. 1817,
detail of plate 92

Contents

Sponsor's Foreword

Ernst & Young is delighted to sponsor *Turner's Britain*, Birmingham Museums & Art Gallery's major exhibition for 2003.

Birmingham Museums & Art Gallery inspires, informs and excites many thousands of visitors every year through its permanent collection. It owns a significant and comprehensive group of engravings after Turner. These, together with paintings, watercolours, drawings, prints and sketchbooks, including a number of highly important loans from Britain and the US, some of which have never been shown in public before, will ensure that it maintains these qualities through *Turner's Britain*.

Ernst & Young is proud to work with Birmingham Museums & Art Gallery on an exhibition of such high quality and one of great importance to the Midlands region. In Britain, there have been few major Turner exhibitions outside London, and it is appropriate that an exhibition that addresses Turner's expression of national identity should be held in Birmingham, one of the key centres of expansion and industrialization in the nineteenth century.

In the UK, this is the tenth year that Ernst & Young has been involved in supporting the visual arts. *Turner's Britain* is our ninth sponsorship and our second exhibition at Birmingham Museums & Art Gallery, and follows our highly successful sponsorship of the *Burne-Jones Centenary Exhibition* in 1998–99. Previous sponsorships include *Picasso* (1994); *Cézanne* (1996); *Bonnard* (1998), all at Tate Britain; *Monet* (1999) at the Royal Academy; *Vermeer & the Delft School* (2001) at the National Gallery; *Matisse Picasso* at Tate Modern; and *Art Deco 1910–1939* (2003) at the Victoria and Albert Museum.

As one of the world's largest business advisers, we welcome the opportunity to contribute to the cultural life of the countries and cities in which we operate. Sponsorship gives us the ability to do so. We hope you enjoy this unique exhibition and that this book provides a reminder of it for years to come.

Ronnie Bowker
BIRMINGHAM OFFICE MANAGING PARTNER
ERNST & YOUNG

Director's Foreword

Birmingham Museum's Gas Hall Exhibition Gallery opened ten years ago in 1993 with the acclaimed *Canaletto & England* exhibition, and it is with a conscious echo of that event that we present *Turner's Britain* in 2003.

No Turner exhibition on this scale would be possible without the collaboration of Tate Britain, which owns and manages the Turner Bequest. We are indebted to Stephen Deuchar and his colleagues, who have been exceptionally generous in their support. We are also indebted to the Trustees of the National Gallery for their willingness to lend the famous *Fighting 'Temeraire'*, which provides an apt centrepiece to the exhibition.

Numerous public and private lenders have responded warmly and generously to our requests and we would like to extend our grateful thanks. It is also an honour to collaborate with the Earl of Egremont and Nicholas Horton-Fawkes, both direct descendants of Turner's two great patrons, the 3rd Earl of Egremont and Walter Fawkes MP.

James Hamilton, author of this magnificent publication, has been our guest curator and selector. He has brought imagination and flair to the project and enabled us all to accompany Turner on his myriad journeys across Britain. It has been a great pleasure to collaborate again with Hugh Merrell and his colleagues at Merrell Publishers. This is also the second time that our sponsor Ernst & Young has entrusted its faith and financial support in Birmingham Museum – all the more laudable as the Museum is not nationally funded and not in London.

On my own staff, I would like to thank the many colleagues who have contributed to the realization of this major exhibition and, in particular, Jane Farrington, exhibition organizer, Elizabeth Smallwood, Tessa Sidey, Helen Moody, Colin Edmonds, Lee Handley, Carl Turner, David Bailey, David Rowan, Jill Fenwick, Julia Kirby, Carmel Girling and Guy Evans.

Graham Allen
HEAD OF BIRMINGHAM MUSEUMS

Author's Acknowledgements

The central idea that provided the seed for the exhibition at the Gas Hall in Birmingham and for this accompanying book was to demonstrate the depth and diversity of Turner's identification with Britain and the British through his painting, writing, business partnerships and friendships. The exhibition and the book aim together to show Turner's evolving breadth of purpose, and to examine the expression of his vocation to create a collective image of the nation and to disseminate this to all levels of society.

Bringing this idea into the reality of a powerful exhibition and what I hope is an entertaining, instructive and influential book has been the work of dozens of people. I have had a long and happy collaboration with Birmingham Museums & Art Gallery, and in particular with Graham Allen, and with Jane Farrington, Principal Curator, who has been the champion of the project from the start, and who led the team in Birmingham that turned the concept into its practical reality. Hugh Merrell and his staff, in particular Matt Hervey, Julian Honer, Anthea Snow, Kate Ward and Sam Wythe, gave the catalogue its beauty and allure. Barrie Trinder wrote the scene-setting and authoritative essay that introduces the book, and provides an insight into the historical context in which Turner found himself. If there is an identifiable Midlands bias to the book and exhibition, it is intentional.

The lenders to the exhibition have been warmly and properly thanked in the Director's and the Sponsor's forewords. I would like to add my deep gratitude, and also to thank in particular those whose contributions have in their different ways been crucial in ensuring that the exhibition would take place: Mikael Ahlund, Nicola Ayton, Caroline Bacon, Amy Barker, Timothy C. Baylis, Steve Bell, Susan Bourne, Julian Brooks, Peter Cannon-Brookes, David Brown, Pamela Clark, Ron Clarke, Catherine Clement, Sir Timothy Clifford, Ann Compton, Alan Cowie, James Cuno, James Dearden, Hattie Drummond, the Earl of Egremont, Oliver Fairclough, John Gingell, Richard Green, Antony Griffiths, Carolyn Hammond, Martin Hampson, Colin Harrison, Robert Holden, Nicholas Horton-Fawkes, Sarah Hyde, Nicky Ingram, David Jaffé, Adrian Jenkins, William Johnston, Vivien Knight, Alistair Laing, Victoria Lane, Andrew Loukes, Catherine McFarlane, Neil McGregor, Beth McIntyre, Francis Marshall, Corinne Miller, James Miller,

Charles Nugent, Julia Nurse, John O'Neill, Sarah Quayle, Joe Rishel, Fiona Salvesen, Peter Saunders, Eric Shanes, J.P. Sigmond, Susan Sloman, Alistair Smith, Christine Stevens, Miriam Stewart, Sheena Stoddard, Gordon Thomas, Katrina Thomson, Michael Tooby, Julian Treuherz, Alexandra Walker, Ian Warrell, Henry Wemyss, Catherine Willson, Tim Wilson, Andrew Wilton, Christopher Woodward, Andrew Wyld, and lenders who have asked to remain anonymous.

I am grateful also to my colleagues at the University of Birmingham, including David Allen, Clare Mullett, Dr Paul Spencer-Longhurst and Professor Richard Verdi, each of whom has given me the time, space and encouragement to embark on this project. Any writer on Turner owes deep gratitude to those living and dead who have contributed to our understanding of this beautiful and enigmatic man: those whose writings I have read with pleasure and instruction include David Brown, Martin Butlin, Judy Egerton, John Gage, Luke Herrmann, David Hill, the late Evelyn Joll, Cecilia Powell, Eric Shanes, Sam Smiles, Ian Warrell, and Andrew Wilton. Where their work has naturally enriched and enlivened my own, it has, I hope, has been properly and fully acknowledged. Finally, I would like to thank my wife, Kate, and our daughter, Marie, who have lived with Mr Turner for perhaps too long.

This exhibition, which runs in parallel in Birmingham with the exhibition 'The Sun Rising through Vapour': Turner's Early Seascapes at The Barber Institute, is one of an unprecedented alignment of Turner exhibitions in the British regions in 2003 and 2004. When I proposed Turner's Britain as long ago as 1998, I proposed also the idea for a quite different Turner exhibition, Turner's Late Seascapes, to the Clark Art Institute, Williamstown, Massachusetts, travelling on to the Manchester Art Gallery and the Burrell Collection, Glasgow. Expecting one proposal, at most, to be accepted, in the event they both were, with the happy result that for a few weeks in the autumn and winter of 2003 there will be three major Turner exhibitions on show outside London, a conjunction of a magnitude that has not happened before, and is unlikely ever to happen again. A further consequence, happy or not, is that the catalogues of both Turner's Late Seascapes and Turner's Britain were written in parallel and might properly be considered to be one work, to be read, perhaps, together. Threads of one have floated into the weaving of the other, enriching the colour of the whole without, I hope, distorting my account of the artist's purpose.

Two books require two dedicatees, and no two Turner scholars are woven more closely together through their work than Martin Butlin and the late Evelyn Joll. Their comprehensive catalogue, The Paintings of J.M.W. Turner, revolutionized Turner studies when it was first published by Yale University Press in 1977. I should like to dedicate this book to the memory of the late Evelyn Joll, and the catalogue of Turner's Late Seascapes to Martin Butlin.

James Hamilton
UNIVERSITY OF BIRMINGHAM
MAY 2003

Introduction

J.M.W. Turner enjoyed a long life centred on London, but he spent extensive lengths of time travelling, sketching and noting what he saw in other parts of Britain. His travels were motivated by the patronage of publishers, connoisseurs and landowners, and by his ambition to experience wider landscapes, to sharpen his skills with the pencil and brush, and to become a great artist. He did not set out to compile a documentary record of his times, but he was sensitive to the implications of what he saw in the landscape: to the political nuances in painting a ruin, Old Sarum, in Wiltshire (pl. 136; cat. 122), to the geological questions raised by sketching mountain scenery, to the tensions between the new world of canal aqueducts, steamships and recently built country houses and the inherited world of ruined castles, watermills and sailing vessels. His most valuable legacies to historians are the questions that arise from his works rather than the data conveyed in the images themselves. The insights that they can bring are best explored through an examination of the landscape of Turner's lifetime, and of the choices of subject he made on his travels.

Turner followed in the footsteps of the artist Paul Sandby (1725–1809) to mountainous regions: to the Lake District and North Wales in 1798, and to Scotland in 1801. Like his contemporaries the poets William Wordsworth (1770–1850), Samuel Taylor Coleridge (1772–1834) and Robert Southey (1774–1843) he regarded mountains as sources of awe and wonderment (*Kilchern Castle*; pl. 50; cat. 30). Turner was the contemporary of men who were seeking other kinds of enlightenment in the mountains. William Reynolds (1758–1803), the Shropshire ironmaster, was aware of the wealth that could be gained through geological knowledge: he displayed to visitors the carboniferous fossils found by his miners, and told his brother-in-law William Rathbone (1747–1809) that on a trip to Liverpool he "expected to get my pocket full of fossils, either sand from America or clay from Africa". Reynolds surveyed the lines of several canals; it was another canal surveyor, William Smith (1769–1839), whose interest in fossils found in excavations led him to establish the foundations of the science of stratigraphic geology. Turner was aware that views of mountains carried many implications – they represented new ways of interpreting natural scenery, they depicted rich sources of minerals, and potentially they offered new means of understanding the earth.[1]

The upland landscape of North Wales, for example, changed significantly during Turner's lifetime. In 1798 he made several drawings at Tygwyn on the shore of the estuary of Afon Dwyryd, looking south to Harlech Castle, and north towards Snowdonia, across the estuary over which a ferry plied to the shore. In that year William Alexander Madocks (1773–1828) began to purchase land there in the Treath Mawr, the great sands, at the mouth of the Afon Glaslyn. After obtaining authority through an Act of Parliament in 1803, Madocks started to drain the sands and to build the dam known as the Cob, across which part of the Festiniog Railway was laid down in 1836. He intended to create useful agricultural land by draining; to build a road to Porth Dinllaen, potentially a port for ships sailing to and from Ireland; to stimulate slate exports; and to construct an elegant town beneath the cliffs at Tremadog.[2] He followed the example of Richard Pennant (?1737–1808), first Baron Penrhyn, who from 1790 had rationalized the extraction of slate in the Ogwen Valley between the foot of Tryfan and the sea at Bangor. Pennant constructed railways and a harbour called Port Penrhyn to expedite slate exports, a 'factory' in which slates for schools were shaped, a model dairy, and a road that enabled tourists to reach a well-appointed inn at Capel Curig.[3]

The concept of 'improvement' also inspired developments in the lowlands. From 1791 the first Sir Robert Peel (1750–1820), in collaboration with Joseph Wilkes of Measham (a landowner and agricultural improver), purchased land at Fazeley alongside the River Tame, near the junction of the Birmingham and Fazeley and Coventry Canals. By creating a network of pools and channels they made many acres of farmland productive, created an ornamental setting of water and woodland for Peel's mansion, Drayton Manor, and replaced one ancient corn mill with four water-powered factories in which cotton was spun, woven, bleached and printed.[4] The textile industry at Fazeley lasted for just over two centuries. It emerged not merely from a decision to build factories, but from the same inspiration – to make land productive and to create employment – that lay behind the work of Penrhyn and Madocks.

Turner's journeys through the Midlands took him through other landscapes that were changed radically in his lifetime. Leicestershire, Northamptonshire, Warwickshire and Oxfordshire were classic areas affected by parliamentary enclosure, where in many parishes commissioners empowered by new legislation created patterns of neat, straight-sided fields, enclosed by hawthorn and blackthorn hedges, in place of open fields that had been cultivated in common. The commissioners laid out new local roads that ran straight for long distances and were lined with uniform verges. Many farmsteads were built among the newly enclosed fields. In more westerly parts of the Midlands patterns of enclosed fields had developed in earlier centuries, but in some areas the landscape was changed dramatically. Such areas included the sandy heaths of Prees and Moreton Say, enclosed in 1795; industrialized heathlands, such as the 400 acres (162 hectares) of common in West Bromwich enclosed in 1801–04; high hills, such as the Long Mynd, enclosed in 1795; and wetlands, for example the Fens or the Weald Moors in Shropshire.

Sentimental views of the English countryside emphasize those aspects of rural society that appear to have changed little over time, and suggest that there was a uniform pattern of social relationships in rural areas, but Turner passed through very varied communities. Joseph Ashby (1859–1919), the rural reformer, remarked that villages "had their own special ways and dispositions, as men do".[5] In recent decades historians have 'rediscovered' the distinction made in the nineteenth century between 'open' communities, where settlement was easy and social control slight and from which labour and skills were exported, and 'closed' villages, controlled by landowners, where settlement was discouraged and to which workers travelled daily. Some closed communities were model villages – showplaces created by landlords – such as Blaise near Bristol, designed by John Nash (1752–1835), or Hulcote, the early nineteenth-century village at the end of the drive leading to Easton Neston, near Towcester. Nuneham Courtenay, alongside the main road from Oxford to Henley, was built by the Harcourt family in 1755 when they destroyed the villagers' houses within sight of their mansion, an act commemorated by the writer Oliver Goldsmith (1728–1774) with the lines, "The man of wealth and pride takes up a space that many poor supplied … His seat, where solitary sports are seen, Indignant spurns the cottages from the green." Turner sketched the mansion from the River Thames, but not the village.[6]

Open villages looked very different. Thomas Mozley (1806–1893), a young High Churchman, became the incumbent of Moreton Pinckney in Northamptonshire in 1832, and found it 'a very rough place'. Cottages were built in an untidy fashion. Cottagers displayed little regard for authority, whether seigneurial or ecclesiastical, and kept pigs that hurtled through the parsonage garden.[7] Open communities included such contrasting places as Alstonefield, on the Staffordshire slopes of the Pennines, and Headington Quarry. In the former most of the inhabitants gained their livings by peddling in southern and eastern England the buttons produced locally, small wares obtained in Manchester and crockery from the Potteries;[8] the inhabitants of the latter provided laundry and other services for the University of Oxford.[9]

Some communities inspired by idealism grew up during Turner's lifetime. When he visited the Falls of Clyde, Turner would have passed through New Lanark, the cotton-spinning settlement made famous in the second decade of the nineteenth century by Robert Owen (1771–1858). However, Turner appears not to have sketched the tenements, Owen's innovative school or his Institution for the Formation of Character, where adults spent their leisure hours. Owen's socialist ideals inspired Queenswood, or Harmony Hall, a community established at Tytherley in Hampshire in 1839, but wound up less than a decade later, and the settlement on the site now called Colony Farm at Manea, Cambridgeshire. This was built in the shadow of the embanked Old Bedford River, with views beneath towering skies across the Fens to Ely Cathedral.[10] Protestant idealism was embodied in the school-centred settlements of Moravian Brethren at Fulneck near Leeds, Fairfield in east Manchester and Ockbrook near Derby. The villages created by the Chartist Land Company in the 1840s, at Heronsgate in Hertfordshire,

Minster Lovell in Oxfordshire, Snigs End and Lowbands in Gloucestershire, and Dodford near Bromsgrove, represented not a desire for communitarian living but a yearning for independence, for a return to a past when supposedly each family provided for itself from its own land.[11]

Turner and his contemporaries enjoyed an inheritance of antiquarian knowledge, so that he was aware (as travellers of the early eighteenth century were not) of the antiquities that he was likely to encounter. An early source for him was Henry Boswell's *Picturesque Views of the Antiquities of England and Wales* (1786; pl. 12; cat. 1), the engravings in which he coloured by hand aged eleven or twelve. Turner was sensitive to the fact that he lived in an old country, that he was passing through landscapes that had been peopled through countless generations. Ancient monuments, castles, churches and ruined abbeys, including Stonehenge and Salisbury Cathedral in Wiltshire, fill many pages in his early sketchbooks.

Turner lived at a time when most provincial towns were bursting their medieval bounds and spreading into the countryside. He saw towns almost in stratified terms; they rose from rivers lined with commercial wharves and crossed by ancient bridges, through busy streets up to hilltops crowned by castles and churches, as seen, for example, in Dudley, Nottingham and Stamford (pls. 115, 120, 134; cat. 99, 107, 124). He portrayed the distinction between towns and countryside in his distant views of Oxford (pl. 2; cat. 39), Chester and Carlisle (pls. 3, 21, 22, 105; cat. 7–9, 90). He also recorded in detail the bustle of urban life, in the medieval rows of Chester or the less celebrated 'piazzas' at Ross-on-Wye, and in Wrexham (pl. 23; cat. 10) and Wolverhampton. In many towns the pace of life was generally slow, as it was in the fictional Cowfold of Mark Rutherford (1831–1913),[12] where the shopkeeper's working day was long but generally unhurried, but it accelerated on market days and during fairs such as the ones Turner observed at Wolverhampton and Louth (pls. 24, 113; cat. 13, 98). Fairs drew in many of the wandering tribes of the early nineteenth century: horse, cattle and pig dealers; drovers; travelling comedians and ballad singers; German musicians; itinerant traders in many kinds of goods; and military recruiting parties (in *Wolverhampton*, for example).

Most towns had 'manufactures', trades involving the production of goods that were distributed nationally and even exported. In small towns manufactures were on a small scale, such as the whips produced at Daventry, the steel springs made at Pershore, or the iron hoops at Dudley, and did not involve the use of specialist premises. Most consumer goods, food, clothing, footwear and furniture were made by local craftsmen. Some towns became places of resort, where families defined by a newspaper in 1852 as "people who come to spend money not to make it"[13] settled in elegant thoroughfares; examples are Broad Street and Mill Street in Ludlow, or the newly built terraces beyond medieval town boundaries such as Rutland Terrace in Stamford or Holywell Terrace in Shrewsbury. Some towns subsisted almost entirely on the trade generated by wealthy residents. By 1775 Bath had long been the archetypal resort, and by then Cheltenham was growing rapidly. Leamington Spa expanded from humble beginnings around 1800 to become a substantial town with nearly 16,000 inhabitants in 1851.

2 *Oxford from the South Side of Heddington Hill*, 1803–04, pencil and watercolour, 31.6 × 44.8 cm (12¹⁄₂ × 17⁵⁄₈ in.), Oxford, Ashmolean Museum. Engraved for the 1808 *Oxford Almanack*

The new ploughing equipment to the left, as well as the smart stagecoach, bring modern improvements into this view of the historic skyline of Oxford. The positioning of the stagecoach and the long wall channels attention to the distant spires.

As Turner reached his sixties in the mid-1830s the nation was debating 'the condition of England', a discussion concerned above all with the growth of towns, although overshadowed by other questions, including an economic recession and demands for free trade and for an extension of the parliamentary franchise.[14] By 1831 about one quarter of the population of England and Wales lived in towns of more than 20,000 people. Birmingham then had 144,000 inhabitants and Leeds 123,000. Large towns were not uniform. To some extent Manchester was a city of cotton factories, although even in Turner's lifetime it was better defined as the commercial centre of the cotton trade. Leeds was the capital of the woollen manufacturing district of the West Riding, but also the principal centre of linen manufacture in England, the provincial town with the highest concentration of tanneries and the location of important engineering works. In comparison with Manchester, Birmingham has always been perceived as a city of workshops rather than factories, although Matthew Boulton (1728–1809), by centralizing the manufacture of metal wares in his Soho Manufactory, had set the pattern for the concentration of production.[15] Turner characterized his views of Birmingham by sketching the towers of St Philip's, St Martin's-in-the-Bullring, and St Paul's, Hockley (pls. 19, 124; cat. 14, 114). His painting of Leeds, however, shows an urban phenomenon that would have been familiar in several Midlands towns: the five- and six-storey flax mills of John Marshall (1765–1845) and the brothers Benyon

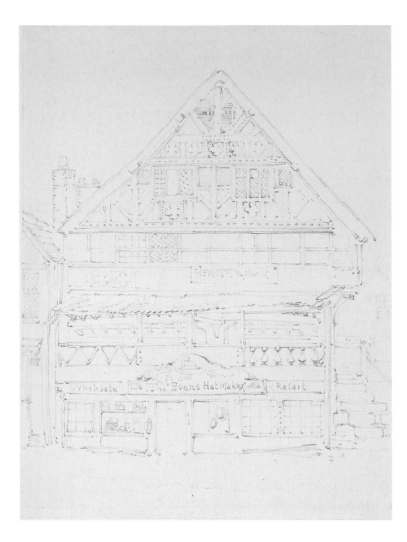

3 *Old Shops in Chester*, 1794, pencil,
27.1 × 20.3 cm (10⅝ × 8 in.),
Oxford, Ashmolean Museum

The long history of Chester is
reflected in the continuous use of
this group of medieval buildings
by generations of shopkeepers.
The displayed wares of the tailor
and hatmaker can just be made out
beneath the intricate carved beams.

towering above every building except the churches. A view of Shrewsbury between 1804 and
1835 would have shown mills of the same two companies dominating the town's northern suburbs;
one of them – Marshall's Ditherington flax mill, the first iron-framed building – still stands.[16]

Most visitors to Birmingham marvelled at the pace of the city's growth. In 1776 Arthur
Young (1741–1820) described it as a "region of Vulcans" and, on his return fifteen years later,
noted that villas were spreading in every direction along the road from Henley-in-Arden. He was
impressed by the canal wharf, the source of the coal that provided the city with cheap energy,
describing it as "a noble spectacle, with that prodigious animation, which the immense trade of
this place could alone give". He concluded that "It is now a very great city." Reflecting on economic growth, Young deplored "that dronish, sleepy and stupid indifference, that lazy negligence
which enchains men in the exact paths of their forefathers, without enquiry, without thought and
without ambition", and posed the question "In what path of life can a man be found that will not
animate his pursuits from seeing the steam engine of Watt?"[17]

Turner's career was influenced by wars between Britain and France that broke out when he was eighteen, and, with a brief interval in 1802, continued until he reached the age of forty. Awareness of the wars shaped his early adult life. All Englishmen were threatened with service in the militia, and recruiting parties lurked in taverns and lodging houses in search of young men on whom the king's shilling could be pressed. The landscape bears many traces relating to the wars: the Martello towers along the coasts (pl. 119; cat. 105), the Royal Military Canal in Kent (pl. 86; cat. 66), the Column of British Liberty (seen in the *Gibside* pair; pls. 96, 97; cat. 81, 82) and the military depot at Weedon in Northamptonshire. Soaring classical columns throughout Britain commemorate the heroes of the wars: in London, Horatio Nelson and the first Duke of Wellington; in Shrewsbury, Lord Hill; and at Llanfair PG, the Marquis of Anglesey. In some churches, such as that at Alresford, Hampshire, and in the abbey at Dorchester-on-Thames, stand memorials to French prisoners of war and refugee royalists who died in captivity or exile. At Norman Cross, on the Great North Road south of Peterborough, an elegant Regency-style governor's house, a monument and many bumps in fields are evidence of a large prisoner of war camp.[18] Dartmoor, Devon, is a better-known prison built during the wars. Even during the peace that followed Wellington's victory at Waterloo in 1815, soldiers in uniform were an everyday sight, noticeable particularly when regiments moved across the country (pls. 4, 79, 86; cat. 62, 66, 104).[19] Alexander Somerville (1811–1885) described the march of the Royal Scots Greys from Brighton Camp to Birmingham. The band played at the head of the procession, its trumpets startling ex-military horses in civilian employment; mounted soldiers strove to control their prancing horses; wagons were piled high with baggage; contingents of medical staff, farriers and saddlers went along; and a straggle of women and children followed in the rear.[20] Such a convoy could overwhelm a small town with demands for food, accommodation and stabling.

Social upheavals and changes in the political structure of Britain characterized Turner's lifetime. Government was dominated by the landed classes, who made up the membership of the House of Lords and effectively controlled many seats in the House of Commons. On the surface, the composition of Parliament in 1851 may not have appeared very different from that of 1775. Nevertheless, the boundaries of the political nation were extended in the 1820s to include Dissenters and Roman Catholics, who were thereafter allowed to stand for parliament. The Reform Act of 1832, greeted with popular celebrations in most towns, deprived some blatantly corrupt parliamentary boroughs of their representation, and enfranchised places such as Birmingham and Manchester. Government authority survived a succession of extra-parliamentary challenges: the food riots of the 1790s, the agitations of the years after the Battle of Waterloo that culminated in the massacre at Peterloo, the riots of 1830 directed against the introduction of threshing machines (which took their name from the mythical Captain Swing), and the demands of the Chartist movement for the widening of the parliamentary franchise between 1838 and 1848. Turner's works indicate a subtle awareness of political issues. He well understood that Old Sarum

4 *Chatham, from Fort Pitt, Kent*, 1831, watercolour, 28.2 × 45.7 cm (11⅛ × 18 in.). Engraved 1832. Private collection

An instance of Turner describing military activity in a nation at peace. Note the soldiers on the parade ground in the top left, and the man-o'-war adapted as a prison hulk on the river. Britain is portrayed as a victorious but vigilant nation.

in Wiltshire (pl. 136; cat. 122) was the most notoriously corrupt of parliamentary boroughs, where two MPs were returned by a mere handful of venal electors. In 1783 a French visitor commented that its MPs were too embarrassed to reveal the name of the constituency they represented.[21]

Turner's travels were made possible by improvements in the roads that took place during most of his lifetime. The turnpike system, by which local trustees were made responsible for maintaining roads and financed by tolls, originated in the seventeenth century and was rapidly extended in the decades before Turner's birth. Turner drew and painted some tollhouses of the kind that survive most abundantly around such towns as Kington, Herefordshire, and Ludlow in Shropshire. He shows awareness of the fellowship that existed between slow-moving users of the roads: those who walked or rode horses, the carriers' carts (which proliferated during his lifetime) conveying country produce and passengers into market towns, gigs taking doctors to their patients and butchers to their suppliers and customers, the wagons drawn by up to eight horses lumbering to and from London, the drovers of cattle, sheep, pigs and even geese (pl. 141; cat. 119). He knew about fast-moving stagecoaches, and sketched many of them (pls. 8, 115; cat. 99, 114). Stagecoaching involved such unglamorous tasks as stabling horses overnight and washing them after their journeys, often in shallow water on river banks. Stagecoach travel was hazardous: a German minister travelled in fear of his life on the outside of a coach from Leicester to Northampton in 1782, in the company of a black Englishman who warned that he would be shaken to death.[22]

5 *Ludlow Castle*, 1798–1800, watercolour, 35.6 × 67.1 cm (14 × 26⅜ in.), University of Birmingham, The Barber Institute of Fine Arts

This composition is practically the same as *Llandilo Bridge* (pl. 25), a favourite arrangement of Turner's. Note the subtle play of light and shadow, and the rhythm of the shadows of the bridge balustrade.

Coaching inns were places of great activity, busy with posting (*i.e.* private-hire) coaches as well as advertised stage services. Coaching reached its peak in the early 1830s, when sixteen coaches a day left Birmingham for London, and there were ten departures to Liverpool, eight to Manchester and two to Bath. Some small towns became prosperous from the trade called 'thoroughfare'. The inns of Stone, with a population of only 2855 in 1831, handled fourteen coaches daily that linked London, Birmingham, Bristol, Cheltenham, the Potteries and Shrewsbury. Turner published views of the High Street in Oxford, but none reflects the bustle of the city's inns that in 1830 catered for twenty coach departures a day to London. Most of these services originated in Worcester, Gloucester, Hereford, Ross, Cheltenham, Birmingham, Shrewsbury and Holyhead. Some coaching inns remain open today, among them The George in Huntingdon, The George in Stamford (pl. 115; cat. 99) and The Lion in Shrewsbury. The last was built in the 1770s with an assembly room that was a gift to county society by a lawyer who had been agent to many landed families, and from 1780 became the hub of the services operated by the stagecoach entrepreneur Robert Lawrence (1749–1806).[23]

It was Lawrence who, in 1779–80, established coach services from Shrewsbury across North Wales to Holyhead, the port for Dublin. After the Act of Union of 1800 that united the British and Irish parliaments, demands for the improvement of roads across North Wales increased. In 1815 the Holyhead Road Commission was established, with Sir Henry Parnell (1776–1842) as its chairman and Thomas Telford (1757–1834) as its engineer.[24] The Commission provided money with which the road from London to Shrewsbury – through Stony Stratford, Dunchurch, Coventry, Birmingham and Wolverhampton – was improved by turnpike trusts. From 1819 the Commission had sole responsibility for the road westwards from Shrewsbury; by 1826 it had created the best road in Europe of its date, featuring along its course the Waterloo Bridge at Betwys-y-Coed, the pass of Nant Ffrancon, the Menai Suspension Bridge and the Stanley Embankment outside Holyhead. From 1828 the road was lined with elegantly proportioned mileposts, and most of its tollhouses followed designs by Telford.

For Turner, bridges united streetscapes and riverscapes, and represented human triumph over natural forces. Ancient stone bridges, such as the Welsh Bridge at Shrewsbury (which in 1794 was still a medieval structure supporting houses and shops; pl. 29; cat. 11), or the bridge at Llandeilo (pls. 25, 26; cat. 15), were monuments of past generations, like castles and churches. Like the triangular bridge at Crowland, however, they could also be puzzling exercises in constructional geometry; in a drawing of Monmouth of 1795, Turner contrasted the spindly wooden bridge over the River Wye with the stolid stone arches over its tributary, the River Monmow. Bridges also represented new technology. Curiously, when he visited Coalbrookdale he chose not to sketch the Iron Bridge, which had opened on New Year's Day, 1781, but found a limekiln a more interesting subject (pl. 30; cat. 21). Yet he was fascinated by the principles of the suspension bridge, making many drawings of Hammersmith Bridge and paintings of the Chain Pier at Brighton (pl. 109; cat. 75), as well as the Chain Bridge over the River Tees.

There were wooden railways in English coalfields long before Turner's birth. From 1767 crude cast-iron slabs had been used as the upper levels of wooden rails in Coalbrookdale.[25] The use of iron rails spread in the next half-century, and horse-drawn wagons plied along tracks from canal wharves at Brecon to Hereford, Hay and Kington, from Gloucester to Cheltenham, and from Stratford-upon-Avon to Moreton-in-Marsh. The Leicester and Swannington Railway, authorized in 1829, was a line incorporating iron rails and served the estate of Sir George Beaumont (1743–1827) at Coleorton. After 1800 the technology of railways developed most rapidly in Northumberland and County Durham, and that technology was applied to create the first railway linking large cities, the Liverpool and Manchester Railway, which opened in 1830. In 1831 Alexander Somerville, from a vantage point at Prescot, watched "the white steam shooting through the landscape of trees, meadows and village, and the long train, loaded with merchandise, men and women, and human enterprise rolling along under the steam", and concluded in later life that he had seen nothing to excel it: "in beauty and grandeur, the world has nothing beyond it".[26] Such sentiments put in context the way in which Turner viewed the railways in *Rain, Steam, and Speed* (London, National Gallery). In 1831 scarcely anyone could have predicted the growth of mainline railways, but in 1837 the Grand Junction Railway linked Lancashire with Birmingham. The following year trains could continue south on the London and Birmingham Railway, the terminus building of which, by Philip Hardwick (1792–1870),

6 *Lancaster, from the Aqueduct Bridge* c. 1825, watercolour, 28 × 39.4 cm (11 × 15½ in.). Engraved 1827. Port Sunlight, Lady Lever Art Gallery

Turner found ample subject-matter in the extensive waterway network of Britain, recording both its activity and, as in this case, midsummer inactivity. But the resting figures are about to be wakened suddenly by the splash from the boy falling into the canal from the barge on the left.

stands in Curzon Street, Birmingham. By 1851 six thousand route miles of standard-gauge railway linked most English towns of consequence.

Turner was attracted to the England of creaking timbers and straining ropes: the waterways network, the seas around the coasts, about a thousand miles of ancient and often unimproved river navigations, rather more than a thousand miles of rivers upon which engineers had built locks (pls. 43, 44, 57, 108; cat. 26, 42, 74), and the new navigable canals. (The first navigable canal, the Duke of Bridgwater's canal from the mines at Worsley into Manchester, had been completed in 1760.) Turner travelled by sea from London to Thanet, and sketched countless small coasting ships run up on beaches to be loaded and unloaded. He drew river barges on the Severn at Gloucester, Bridgnorth and Shrewsbury; on the Thames at Oxford and Walton; on the Medway and the Wye. He sketched waterside warehouses, cranes and hoists in Chester in 1801, and in the Midlands in 1830 (pl. 7; cat. 114), perhaps comparing the ropes and pulleys with those he observed on construction sites in London. He was impressed by the heroic structures on the narrow canal network, by the aqueducts at Chirk and Pontcysyllte on the Ellesmere Canal, and the example by John Rennie (1761–1821) that provided a viewpoint for his painting of Lancaster (pl. 6; cat. 95). Canals also represent the element of water in his paintings and sketches of the landscape around Dudley in 1830 (pl. 120; cat. 107). That area, in particular the parish of

7 *Industrial machinery in the Midlands,* 1830, pencil, 6.4 × 10.5 cm (2¹⁄₂ × 4¹⁄₄ in.), London, Tate. From the 'Birmingham and Coventry' sketchbook, TB CCXL, fol. 46

Tipton, was the home of hundreds of canal people, who transported coal to the Severn, to navigable Fenland drains, to Melton Mowbray and Oakham, to Oxford, and along the Kennet and Avon Canal. Narrow boats crewed by men, women and children from Worcestershire and Gloucestershire brought hay, as fodder for horses working in mines and ironworks, through the great tunnels under the ridge on which Dudley Castle stands. Boats from Fisher Row in Oxford carried wheat, malt and beer to satisfy the hunger and thirst of Black Country workers.[27]

The element of fire in many of Turner's views of waterways is represented by limekilns. He sketched labourers charging the tops with limestone and coal, and, a most unenviable task, removing quicklime from the arches beneath. Limekilns, continually emitting choking fumes, were a feature of the landscape wherever transport systems made it possible to bring together limestone and coal – on beaches, alongside navigable rivers or on canal wharves. The quicklime produced could be spread on fields or gardens, or used in builders' mortars, for which purpose it was largely superseded by Portland cement in the late nineteenth century.

The steam engine developed by James Watt (1736–1819) is often regarded as a symbol of the economic changes of the late eighteenth century, but running water, rather than steam, was the principal source of power for manufacturing during much of Turner's lifetime, and water-power technology was constantly improved (*e.g.* in Ludlow; pl. 5; cat. 20; and Colchester; pl. 139; cat. 121). Waterwheels were used for grinding grain, in smelting and forging iron, in making paper and cider, in sawing wood, for pumping water, in grinding bones and flints for porcelain, and (providing Turner with his raw materials) in crushing oil seeds and grinding colouring materials. Turner was fascinated by running water, and by the rugged timbers associated with milling. On the tours undertaken in his twenties he sketched many mills, including the tide mill adjacent to Carew Castle and the corn mill by the falls at Aberdulais near Neath, on the River Dulais; the latter had previously powered a copper works, and subsequently an iron forge and tin plate mill.[28] He also

CCXL — 58

8 *Passenger coach arriving in a Midlands town*, 1830, pencil, 6.4 × 10.5 cm (2½ × 4¼ in.), London, Tate. From the 'Birmingham and Coventry' sketchbook, TB CCXL, fol. 58

depicted water power in the Wye Valley and in Yorkshire, as well as weatherboarded mills charac-teristic of the area around the Medway. Turner acknowledged the significance of steam power in 1830; a sketch of this date clearly shows that he was entranced by the beams, the flywheels, the chimneys and the straining ropes of colliery winding engines near Dudley (pl. 7; cat. 107).

Windmills, like watermills, were certainly not obsolete in Turner's lifetime. Few windmills are more than three or four centuries old, and one of the most venerable in the Midlands is the elegant structure of 1632 that stands on arches at Chesterton, Warwickshire. Many were built in Turner's lifetime to satisfy the demands for food of an expanding population. One survey showed that nineteen of twenty-eight important tower mills in England were constructed between 1780 and 1830, among them that of 1821 at Wilton, alongside the Kennet and Avon Canal, and that of 1826 at Balsall, near Kenilworth.[29] Other imposing mills of that period suc-cumbed to competition from steam mills or were destroyed by the force of great winds; these included the tower 16.7 m (51 ft) high built at Newport, Shropshire, in 1796, which was reckoned to represent the most advanced thinking in wind-power technology.[30]

Windmills could be seen as structures defying the elements, but also as essential providers of food for and by local communities. While a community controlled its mills, whatever their sources of power, it could prevent the sale of local grain in distant markets, the threat of which caused many food riots. Several communal mills were established in the Midlands during the years of war with France, at Birmingham and Wolverhampton among other places. Such entrepreneurs as

9 *The Mouth of the River Humber*, *c.* 1824, watercolour, 16.5 × 24.3 cm (6½ × 9½ in.). Engraved 1826. London, Tate

Turner rarely painted clear 'portraits' of ships. Instead, acknowledging the restlessness of the sea, he made his vessels mingle with some confusion, as they might in real life.

Richard Arkwright (1732–1792) at Cromford and the ironmasters of Coalbrookdale built mills that gave them control over the local grain trade and therefore preserved social harmony.

Turner was interested in technology and in the spectacular, but did not always notice the industrial structures erected in his lifetime. He did not sketch the Iron Bridge, nor did he notice Richard Arkwright's mills at Cromford when at Matlock, nor the mills at New Lanark when he painted the Falls of Clyde. However, he did record in detail the great Cyfarthfa Ironworks at Merthyr and painted the flax mills in his watercolour *Leeds* (New Haven CT, Yale Center for British Art). He understood the impact on the landscape made by narrow canals and mainline railways. His painting of Dudley and the sketches made on his visit to the town reflect the changes in the Black Country during his lifetime. In 1775 there were large areas of heathlands, on which cottages housing nailers and other metalworkers were scattered in clusters such as that conserved at Mushroom Green. Enclosure acts made possible the expansion of collieries with steam pumping and winding engines, and the construction on private land of blast furnaces and forges with scores of puddling furnaces and steam-driven mills, while the area was intersected by narrow canals. Fire and smoke dominated the landscape by 1830. The legacies of his visit to Dudley show that Turner was certainly aware of what historians came to call the Industrial Revolution.

Like all great artists, Turner was aware of the paradoxes implicit in all that he portrayed, of the co-existence of structures evidencing long-inhabited British landscapes with innovations of his

10 *Pembroke Castle, Wales, c.* 1830, watercolour, 29.8 × 42.6 cm (11¾ × 16¾ in.). Engraved 1831. Bath, The Holburne Museum of Art

The formal similarities between this and pl. 132 reflect Turner's ability to recycle his compositional ideas, while using local incident and atmosphere to keep them fresh.

own lifetime (pl. 29; cat. 11). He observed the ways in which people made their livings in the shadows of ancient monuments, for example coasting sailing vessels being loaded or unloaded beneath Pembroke Castle (pl. 10; cat. 100), and a hunter beneath the ruins of Okehampton Castle (pl. 117; cat. 97). His views of country houses, simply through being commissioned by their owners, reflect the continuing social predominance of the landowning classes throughout his lifetime (pl. 70; cat. 46), but those of Old Sarum and Northampton show a subtle awareness of the forces of political change (pls. 135, 136; cat. 122). He sketched towns as interlocking, interdependent worlds (pls. 113, 115; cat. 98, 99). His views of Oxford depict principally the colleges (pls. 37, 38; cat. 37, 38) and, above all, the High Street, but that High Street was part of a busy world of stagecoaching. There were other worlds within the same city: the lodging houses in the other High Street in the parish of St Thomas, the boating communities of Fisher Row and Grandpont, and the carters and laundrywomen of Headington Quarry.[31]

Turner depicted the England of his times with a subtlety and an awareness of the implications of what he was doing that continually challenges our assumptions about England in the late eighteenth and early nineteenth centuries. Every artist lives through a period of change. For the historian, the glory of Turner's work is not that it provides neat and tidy views of sites of economic significance, but that it portrays tensions, of a kind prevalent in any period, between what is old and established, whether corrupt or commendable, and what is new and challenging.

CHAPTER I

"Where nature lifts her mountains to the sky"
1775 to 1802

During the first fifteen or sixteen years of his life, Turner's experience of travel in southern Britain gave him the beginning of an understanding of how landscape evolves, flows before the eye, and rolls on into the distance. Landscape wraps around the human observer and keeps on going. Joseph Mallord William Turner was born in April 1775, the child of William Turner (1745–1829), a busy and presumed successful barber in Covent Garden, London, and his wife, Mary (1738/9–1804). His father's shop was in Maiden Lane, a hundred yards from Covent Garden Piazza, and some of the boy's earliest efforts in watercolour were pinned up in the shop for sale. From an early age he was determined to be an artist. "My son, sir, is going to be a painter," the father boasted to one customer with a professional interest, the artist Thomas Stothard (1755–1834).[1]

Covent Garden Piazza was built in the Italian style surrounded by elegant arches, with the portico of Inigo Jones's St Paul's Church as its focus. The contrast between the noise and continuous activity in the light-filled market square and the dark, tightly packed buildings of Maiden Lane and nearby streets created a varied and nourishing source of imagery and atmosphere for the young Turner. The art critic John Ruskin (1819–1900), Turner's first great champion, was perhaps not far from the truth when he described the profound effect that the environment of Turner's early life had on his development as an artist:

> Dead brick walls, blank square windows, old clothes, market-womanly types of humanity – anything fishy and muddy, like Billingsgate or Hungerford Market, had great attraction for him; black barges, patched sails, and every possible condition of fog.[2]

Further down a long slope running south from Maiden Lane was the River Thames, with its constant activity and tidal flow, its wharves, mooring posts, shacks and cargo, and the comings and goings of boats. Surrounded as he was by a busy market on one side, London's river traffic

11 *Fonthill Abbey at sunset*, 1799, detail of pl. 40

on the other, and a warren of dark streets in between, Turner's boyhood was rich beyond measure. Nevertheless, it was not yet the life of the markets and the shipping that fired Turner's imagination as an artist – perhaps it was all too familiar to him – but rather the rural English landscape when he first felt the shock of seeing it for himself.

Turner's mother, a highly strung woman dismissed as 'mad', was considered incapable of bringing up her child, and in about 1785 the boy was packed off to spend months, if not two or three years, with relatives and friends in the Lower Thames Valley at Brentford, at Margate on the Kent coast, and at Sunningwell, near Oxford. In Brentford, where from the age of ten he lived with his uncle, a butcher, Turner was paid twopence a time by a local brewer, John Lees, to colour engravings illustrating *Picturesque Views of the Antiquities of England and Wales* by the antiquarian Henry Boswell.[3] Barber, butcher, brewer – men from these trades provided Turner's first income and encouragement, and it was the Britain of the tradesmen that became the wellspring for the subject-matter of his art.

Turner would most likely have made his early journeys by boat – up the river to Brentford and Abingdon (for Sunningwell) on the kind of market-boat that later appeared in paintings such as *Walton Bridges* (pl. 57; cat. 42), and past Sheerness and the Isle of Sheppey in a 'Margate hoy', a slow, wide-bellied boat used for inshore waters. When in 1791 he made his first long journey, he travelled to Bristol, presumably by scheduled stagecoach, to stay with a friend of his father, John Narraway, a leather-dresser in Broadmead. The effect of this widely spaced travelling childhood and youth was to give Turner the early experience of the slow pace of a boat or horse-drawn wagon through the undulating landscape – the Chiltern Hills, the Berkshire Downs, the Vale of the White Horse. This experience of travel might have been the norm for a pioneer family in the United States, but it was exceptional for a London tradesman's son.

John Lees's copy of Boswell's *Picturesque Views of the Antiquities of England and Wales* (pl. 12; cat. 1) is the earliest evidence for the sources of Turner's knowledge of notable British historic sites and landscapes. The main interest of this volume, in which Turner's colouring has charm but little vigour, lies in the fact that it was these and similar engravings that first revealed to him something of the range and visual richness of the antiquities of Britain. Many of the subjects coloured in the volume were depicted more than forty years later by Turner himself in his series *Picturesque Views in England and Wales*. This is not particularly surprising, given the earlier volume's wide geographical spread, but the most significant echo that the book has for us is that Turner's collection came to have practically the same title as Boswell's (see Chapter IV).[4]

Engravings were a regular source of inspiration and education for Turner. They were available everywhere, from private collections, salerooms and print shops to books and journals, and were the standard means of disseminating images in the late eighteenth century. He did not need to go to Lincoln to make the little pen, ink and wash drawing of the town from the Brayford (pl. 14; cat. 2), but instead used the composition of Samuel and Nathaniel Buck's 1743 engraving of Lincoln (pl. 15)

12 *An Antient View of St James's, Westminster Abbey, and Hall &c from the Village of Charing now Charing Cross.* From Henry Boswell's *Historical and Descriptive Accounts of Picturesque Views of the Antiquities of England and Wales,* 1786

An engraving by an unknown artist, with colouring said to have been added by Turner at the age of about eleven or twelve.

as the basis for this drawing, focusing on the left half of the image and altering the foreground. On his first visit to Bristol, in 1791, to seek patrons and landscape subjects, Turner composed the drawing *Cote House, near Bristol* (pls. 16, 17; cat. 3, 4) in the manner of fashionable engraved 'portraits' of country houses, complete with figures and animals to individualize and enliven it. Other early drawings are titled and given ruled borders as if they were coloured engravings.[5]

It was the Avon Gorge, near Bristol, that brought out Turner's first instinctive appreciation of the scale and visual drama that could be found in nature. Revealing his competence at expressing such effects in lively landscape compositions, Turner gave added value in wit and wry humour by closely observing local people and incidental detail, creating the distinct feeling that something is about to happen (pls. 13, 18; cat. 5, 6). The patched sails that Ruskin noticed in Turner's later work are there already. At the age of sixteen Turner was in business as an artist, and he chose the landscape around Bristol as the subject of a group of drawings that would be suitable both for sale to

13 *Near the Mouth of the Avon*, *c.* 1791–92, watercolour, 17.7 × 25.1 cm (7 × 9⅞ in.), Cambridge MA, Fogg Art Museum

Turner's passion for telling detail goes even as far as his describing the patched sail of the skiff scudding before the wind on the River Avon near Bristol.

14 *Lincoln*, 1780s, pencil and watercolour, 23.5 × 32.1 cm (92½ × 126⅜ in.), London, Victoria and Albert Museum

A youthful work, possibly adapted from the 1743 engraving of Lincoln by Samuel and Nathaniel Buck (pl. 15), travelling artists of an earlier generation.

15 Samuel and Nathaniel Buck, *Lincoln*, 1743, Oxford, Bodleian Library

A possible source both for the youthful view of Lincoln (pl. 14) and for Turner's 1803–04 version of the subject (pl. 44).

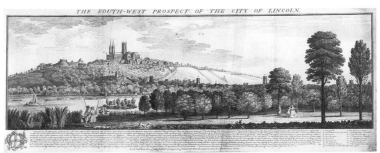

collectors and to be reproduced as engravings. Indeed, in the 'Bristol and Malmesbury' sketch-book (pl. 16; cat. 3) he lists "12 Views of the River Avon", which suggests that he was already contemplating a portfolio of watercolours, perhaps for sale as a group.[6] He was now beginning to make and to save money, and from this time on would never be poor. Before he was twenty-one, Turner had to have trustees to help him look after his wealth.[7]

Turner was accepted as a student at the Royal Academy Schools in London in December 1789, and remained enrolled until 1799. He regularly attended – at least at the beginning – classes that taught drawing from plaster casts of Classical sculpture, and at the start of his second year he graduated to the life classes, in which he learned to draw the male nude. He was also expected to go to lectures by the various professors, including the architect Thomas Sandby (1721–1798) on architecture, and the painter James Barry (1741–1806) on painting, and he was probably present in December 1790 at the last discourse by the founder President of the Royal Academy, Sir Joshua Reynolds (1723–1792). He studied with the watercolourists Thomas Malton (1748–1804) and Edward Dayes (1763–1804), and his education broadened when he was engaged to make plain drawings of buildings for the architect Thomas Hardwick (1752–1829), whom he had known during his boyhood in Brentford.[8] He found work with other architects, including William Porden (1755–1822), Joseph Bonomi (1739–1808), and perhaps also John Nash (1752–1835) (see pls. 45, 46; cat. 19), and became fully conversant with architectural terms and principles. Along with his contemporary Thomas Girtin (1775–1802), he was employed as a copyist of watercolours and engravings for the collectors Dr Thomas Monro (1759–1833) and John Henderson. As an additional short-term source of income, which gave him some inside experience of the theatre, he briefly took a part-time job in 1791 painting back-cloths for opera productions at the newly refurbished Pantheon Opera House in Oxford Street, London.[9] Among Turner's contemporaries and

16 Study for *Cote House, near Bristol*, 1791, pencil, 19.7 × 26.6 cm (7³⁄₄ × 10¹⁄₂ in.), London, Tate. From the 'Bristol and Malmesbury' sketchbook

Inscribed on the reverse "Captain Fowler Seat on Durdum [*i.e.* Durdham] Downs, near Bristol". This coloured sketch runs on to two pages of the sketchbook, and would have been drawn in pencil on the spot, and inked and coloured at home later.

17 *Cote House, near Bristol, c.* 1791, watercolour, 29.2 × 25.4 cm (11¹⁄₂ × 10 in.), Bedford, Cecil Higgins Art Gallery

The finished watercolour worked up from the study in pl. 16. During Turner's 1791 visit to Bristol he produced many drawings of houses and landscapes, which he hoped to sell locally. The owner of this house may have been John Fowler, a ship's captain and banker of Bristol, and a member of the Society of Merchant Venturers.

rivals who were also seeking recognition in the world of art, the most significant were Girtin, Charles Turner (1774–1857; no relation), who became a distinguished engraver, and the portrait painter of French extraction Jean-Jacques Masquerier (1778–1855).

Furthermore, through contacts he made among the habitués of the Royal Academy, and perhaps also among the more influential clientele of his father's barber shop, Turner took the opportunity to see Old Master paintings in collections in London and the country. Collectors whom he visited in his early career included J.J. Angerstein (1735–1823), William Beckford (1759–1844) and Sir Richard Colt Hoare (1758–1838), and the greatest living portrait painter, Sir Joshua Reynolds. Through the generosity and openness of these men, Turner saw paintings by Rembrandt, Rubens, Claude, Poussin, Jacob van Ruisdael, Jan van de Velde, Claude Vernet and many other great figures of seventeenth-century European art. He also made the effort to get to know influential figures in the art world of London – men such as the diarist Joseph Farington (1747–1821), and the painters John Hoppner (1758–1810), John Opie (1761–1807) and Henry Fuseli (1741–1825).

Turner's education as an artist thus encompassed the study of sculpture, Old Master painting, the human figure, perspective, drawing, watercolour, engraving, portraiture, architecture and stage-painting, as well as experience of the politics of the art world: he seems to have studied practically everything except miniature painting.[10] It was not long before he received his first commissions from the engraver and publisher John Walker of Rosomon Street, Finsbury, to supply landscape drawings for reproduction. Such commissions obliged Turner to travel, and paid him to do so. After his 1791 journey to Bristol he began to travel annually to different parts of Britain, and later to Europe. These journeys provided the first sources of the topographical imagery upon which he fed throughout his life.

In the 1790s Turner travelled to some of the places in Britain that he had first seen in Brentford in the album of views by Boswell, such as Malmesbury, Durham and Dover, and which came to feature in his own *Picturesque Views* of the 1820s and 1830s. Thus, from the maturity of his middle career, Turner established a practice of reaching back into his youthful experiences to recover imagery dormant both in his memory and in his sketchbooks. The 'North of England' sketchbook, used by Turner in 1797, contains a number of premonitions of later works, all waiting silently until called upon as the germ of a watercolour. Among these subjects are Kirkstall Abbey in Yorkshire, Barnard Castle in County Durham, and Stamford and Louth in Lincolnshire (pls. 112–115; cat. 98, 99).[11] Although St Agatha's Abbey, at Easby in Yorkshire, fairly rapidly became the subject of the work otherwise known as *The Abbey Pool* (pl. 20; cat. 17), Turner could not have known that it would take him as long as thirty years to bring so many of these subjects to a finished state. We can be certain, however, that in collecting information to such a depth of detail so early in his career, Turner was intentionally laying down an 'image-bank' just as a squirrel lays down nuts for the winter.

18 *Old Hot Wells House, Bristol,* 1791–92, watercolour, 27.3 × 34 cm (10¾ × 13⅜ in.), Bristol Museums & Art Gallery

This drawing was first owned by John Narraway, Turner's host in Bristol, and was probably given or sold to him by the young artist soon after it was drawn. Like pl. 13, it is a spirited rendering of a high wind in the Avon Gorge, full of incidental detail.

The Itinerant.

BIRMINGHAM.

Engraved by Storer from an Original Drawing by W. Turner.

Published Nov. 2. 1795 by I. Walker Rosomans Street.

19 James S. Storer after J.M.W. Turner, *Birmingham*, 1795, engraving, 107 × 166 cm (4¼ × 6½ in.) (image), Birmingham Museums & Art Gallery. Engraving for John Walker's *Copper-Plate Magazine*, 1795

Turner's original drawing for this is lost, but from the evidence of his many other townscapes of this period, the hard rooflines are the intervention of the engraver who lacked Turner's subtlety of line. The view is from the east of Birmingham, with St Martin's-in-the-Bullring on the left and St Philip's Church on the right.

Between 1794 and 1798 Turner produced fifteen subjects for John Walker, including views of Birmingham (pl. 19; cat. 14), Bridgenorth and Nottingham, which were published in the *Copper-Plate Magazine*. He had visited these three towns in the summer of 1794,[12] having made detailed travel plans before setting out: someone who knew the routes and the sights had written five pages of travel directions in the front of one of the sketchbooks Turner took with him.[13] Carefully writing out directions with the help of others became a characteristic of Turner's travel preparations, and similar long texts in various hands appear in later sketchbooks.[14] On the 1794 trip Turner's guide singled out Shrewsbury, Wrexham and Chester as being particularly interesting:

> Shrewsbury, a castle, Abby, two Bridges. Wrexham a stately Church. Chirk, on the left between W[rexham] and Ellesmere, on the northern bank of the river Dee. Near Chirk – Dinas Bran. Chester, a Bridge of Twelve A[postles], a Tower on the B[ridge], a Town Hall, a Cathedral, & 8 P[arish] Churches. The Walls in a square Form with walks on top, a large ancient Castle, several gates.[15]

20 *St Agatha's Abbey, Easby, Yorks (The Abbey Pool)*, 1797–1800, watercolour, 51.4 × 76.2 cm (20¼ × 30 in.), University of Manchester, The Whitworth Art Gallery

St Agatha's Abbey was a twelfth-century Premonstratensian foundation, demolished during the Reformation. The modern world does not intrude on this tranquil scene, but Turner, in painting a watercolour so large, is nevertheless challenging the status of oil painting.

21 *At Chester*, 1794, pencil, 21.5 × 27.3 cm (8½ × 10¾ in.), Cambridge MA, Fogg Art Museum

This view and pl. 22 were drawn on the same day, and reveal the neat pencil work that Turner used to convey the age and intricacy of the subject. Note the leaded windows with their diamond panes, and the way they open and shut – all clearly shown in the drawing, along with so much else.

22 *In the Main Street, Chester*, 1794, pencil, 21.5 × 27.5 cm (8½ × 10⅞ in.), Cambridge MA, Fogg Art Museum

The narrative of the shop signs is clearly of particular interest to Turner, as is the way different buildings relate to one another to make up the townscape.

23 *Wrexham, Denbighshire*, 1794,
pencil and watercolour,
23.6 × 32.4 cm (9¼ × 12¾ in.),
London, Victoria and Albert
Museum

The heart of medieval Wrexham,
with its shops and inn. A rural
visitor in a smock with baskets
of produce for sale adds the
human interest that Turner
characteristically weaves into
his urban scenes.

One particular sequence of pencil and watercolour drawings, of groups of half-timbered sixteenth- or seventeenth-century buildings that by Turner's time had become shops, show what it was that especially caught his eye on this trip. Turner sought to evoke the character of his subjects through such elements as the details of the shop signboards, which he carefully recorded, and the intricate patterns in the old and weather-worn woodwork, both of which give a strong sense of place. Thus, the watercolour *Wrexham, Denbighshire* (pl. 23; cat. 10) proclaims "COTTINGHAM & CO Cabinet Makers & Upholdsters – from LONDON – sworn APPRAISER and AUCTIONEER". To the left and right are butchers' shops. In the pencil drawings *At Chester* and *In the Main Street, Chester* (pls. 21, 22; cat. 7, 8) we see "ROBARTS" the chair-maker, with sample chairs on display, "CLARKE SHOE", "Drugs & Colours" and "DICAS Hardware Men". Although these drawings did not themselves become part of a finished work suitable for exhibition, the watercolour

Wolverhampton Green, Staffs (pl. 24; cat. 13), which Turner exhibited in 1796, is based on drawings the artist made on the 1794 journey, and it reveals how he used incidental detail in a highly complex and entertaining composition. He builds up the picture through observation not invention, and, however much the watercolour of Wolverhampton also records the irregular crush of humanity, the surrounding details in this watercolour are a faithful record of what Turner saw. Together they give a vivid idea of what it was like to be there.

Turner's energy was boundless as he discovered Britain by stagecoach or on horseback. He travelled to South Wales and the Isle of Wight in 1795, to the Midlands for the second time and the North of England in 1797, and to North Wales via Bristol in 1798. In his 1797 journey he covered more than one thousand miles in eight weeks.[16] Though he had commissions for views of country houses before he left home, these remained largely speculative journeys, with the unknown providing as much of an impetus as his expected destinations.[17]

The main turnpikes (roads on which tolls were collected) linking London with other major towns and cities were generally well-maintained and in constant use. Lesser roads, however – particularly those across country – were unpaved, and made of whatever local materials were reasonably near at hand: clay, chalk, sand or gravel, perhaps with a partial and ineffective top dressing of stone. They had to withstand whatever traffic came along, from coaches, wagons and other horse-drawn traffic, to cattle and sheep being taken dozens of miles to market. As he travelled into Wales and to the minor towns in the Midlands and the North, Turner's routes took him well off the beaten track, and he, like everybody else, had to put up with circumstances as he found them. In poor weather the roads tended to break up and become rutted and waterlogged, to the extent that holes that could engulf a horse and rider were a constant hazard. A contemporary dictionary told of roads in "that impassable county of Sussex" being "the worst in England. … Every step up to the shoulders [of a horse], full of sloughs and holes, covered with standing water".[18]

Turner's early work, whether painted for a commission, for engraving or in the hope of sale, gives little or no indication of the perils the artist endured in creating it. Rather, it reflects the fashionable manner of painting contemplative landscape in the late eighteenth century, known as the Picturesque (meaning "suitable for a picture"). Like its counterpart the Sublime, which expressed discomfort and danger, the concept of the Picturesque had been discussed extensively in literature and was well-established in current taste. At this stage of his life Turner found a ready market for his Picturesque watercolours, some of which were engraved. Inspired by the manner of the seventeenth-century French painter Claude Lorraine, and modified to reflect the peculiarities of British landscape, Picturesque views followed strict rules of composition – a tree to one side, a distant hill, a cottage, fine house or castle in the middle distance, a scattering of cows. Variety of content was the keynote, and nothing to make the heart race. The Sublime, on the other hand, rooted in the work of Salvator Rosa, Nicolas Poussin or Gaspard Dughet, depicted the 'angry' aspects of nature – shattered trees, storms and floods.

24 *Wolverhampton Green, Staffs*, exhibited RA 1796, watercolour, 31.8 × 41.9 cm (12½ × 16½ in.), Wolverhampton Art Gallery

The pace of activity in towns accelerated on fair and market days, with the arrival of itinerant traders, circus acts, travelling musicians and raree shows. This is precisely the kind of finished work that emerged from Turner's fieldwork drawings.

The leading theorist of the Picturesque was the Revd William Gilpin (1724–1804), who had developed his ideas through the study of the landscape gardens created by Richard Temple, Viscount Cobham, at Stowe in Buckinghamshire in the 1720s and 1730s.[19] Translating the changing sequences of artificial garden views into a practical way of appreciating the variety of natural landscape, Gilpin's books were read widely by connoisseurs and those artists who aspired to supply them with pictures.[20] Gilpin was, however, dully formulaic in his approach. Writing to an amateur sketcher, he advised: "Few views, at least few good views, consist of more than a foreground and two distances; all of which should be carried off with great distinctness, or the spirit of the view will be infallibly lost."[21]

25, 26 *Llandilo Bridge and Dinevor Castle*, exhibited RA 1796, watercolour, 35.6 × 50.2 cm (14 × 19¾ in.), Cardiff, National Museums and Galleries of Wales

A fine example of the masterly handling of light for which, even at this early stage in his career, Turner was becoming known. A temporary wooden bridge has replaced a stone one that was washed away in 1795.

Gilpin's *Observations on the River Wye, and Several Parts of Wales, &c Relative Chiefly to Picturesque Beauty* (1782) records a tour around many of the sites that Turner visited in 1795, and presents an attitude that was both a guide and a challenge to him. Gilpin describes the landscape of the Wye Valley as if it were already a painting of the mid-eighteenth century, and by implication suggests that this is how such landscapes should be painted:

> Every view on a river [winding like the Wye] … is composed of four grand parts: the *area*, which is the river itself; the *two side-screens*, which are the opposite banks, and mark the perspective; and the *front-screen*, which points out the winding of the river.[22]

This formality of approach was one by which Turner would not be limited. His exhibited watercolour *Llandilo Bridge and Dinevor Castle* (pls. 25, 26; cat. 15), of a site that was also on Gilpin's route, amends the Picturesque rules by making the foreground 'front-screen' a pile of shattered timber, dispensing with 'side-screens' altogether, carving the 'area' into two with a bridge that bars the way into the view, and placing the castle and distant hill against the sun so

that they practically dissolve in the light. Turner's composition breaks Gilpin's 'rules' so cleverly that one might suspect that he saw them as a challenge, and, indeed, in painting a temporary wooden structure that replaced a collapsed stone bridge, he is combining Sublime elements into a Picturesque format. A detail in *Llandilo Bridge* that indicates Turner's determination to pursue an uncompromising approach is his rendering of the two figures in the foreground. They break the Picturesque rules on staffage, which required only vague suggestions of generalized country life, since the figures are depicted wearing precisely observed local Welsh costume – blue-and-white striped wraps, and hats with a particular crown, high at the back and low at the front, and with a curly brim. Such references (pl. 26) help to establish the sense of place, a quality characteristically absent in Picturesque views, that Turner here sought to evoke.[23]

A further characteristic of these early watercolours that goes beyond what was necessary to give Picturesque pleasure is Turner's attention to the detail and texture of stone or brickwork, and to the way in which light falling on it effects its reflective quality. Such technique, for example in *Wakefield Bridge* (pl. 27; cat. 16) and *Newark-upon-Trent Castle* (pl. 28; cat. 12), was far above the standard that jobbing engravers would usually expect to see. But the care that he lavished on

27 *Wakefield Bridge*, 1797–98, watercolour, 26 × 43 cm (10¼ × 17 in.), London, British Museum

The chantry chapel on Wakefield Bridge in Yorkshire is a rare medieval survival, of special interest to eighteenth-century antiquarians. It is likely that Turner made this varied and textural watercolour not just for its own sake, but because he saw an opportunity for an engraving commission.

28 *Newark-upon-Trent Castle*,
1794–95, watercolour,
30.5 × 42.9 cm (12 × 16⅞ in.),
New Haven CT, Yale Center for
British Art

Turner shared with his
contemporaries a knowledge and
interest in Britain's history. The
slow-moving pace of everyday river
activity contrasts with massive ruins
from a distant, warlike past.

29 *Old Bridge, Shrewsbury,*
exhibited RA 1795, watercolour,
21.8 × 27.9 cm (8⅝ × 11 in.),
University of Manchester,
The Whitworth Art Gallery

By the time Turner was twenty, in
1795, his extensive travelling had
introduced him to a huge repertoire
of subjects, such as the dilapidated
Welsh Bridge, that appealed to
antiquarian taste. The new bridge
being built in the distance and
the tower of St Chad's Church
(1792) introduce ideas of change
and improvement.

these and other subjects, such as *Wolverhampton Green* (pl. 24; cat. 13) and the *Old Bridge, Shrewsbury* (pl. 29; cat. 11), changes to an approach of an entirely different kind when he presents objects in the landscape that he has clearly just stumbled upon, such as the limekiln that he came across one night and that he depicted in the informal watercolour *A Lime Kiln by Moonlight* (pl. 30; cat. 21). We might reasonably ask why this might be.

By the time Turner travelled to the North of England in 1797 he had largely completed his formal studies at the Royal Academy Schools, and was becoming a highly regarded watercolour painter. He had shown thirty-five watercolours at the Royal Academy since 1790, but only three oils. His first notice in the press, during the 1794 exhibition, commented on "the great precision in the outlines", his watercolours "well chosen and well coloured"[24] – nothing special, in other words, just another young artist who seemed to have a particularly good and fashionable technique. By the end of the 1790s, when he was also becoming known for his oils, the tone of the responses to his work had undergone a fundamental change. This was expressed in the diary of one visitor to the 1799 exhibition who noticed Turner's depth and force of tone,

30 *A Lime Kiln by Moonlight, c.* 1799,
watercolour, 16.5 × 24 cm
(6½ × 9½ in.), Coventry, Herbert
Art Gallery and Museum

Limekilns became features of the
landscape wherever transport
systems made it possible to bring
together limestone and coal. This
vividly observed scene shows the
beginnings of the industrial age
that was to transform Britain.

which I had never before conceived attainable by such untoward implements. – Turner's views are not merely ordinary transcripts of nature: he always throws some peculiar and striking *character* into the scene he represents.[25]

What had happened was that in or around the time of the 1797 North of England tour Turner set aside the formal response to subjects that is evident in the drawings of shop fronts in Wrexham and Chester. Instead he began to develop a new and a more feeling, poetic reaction to landscape, the beginnings of which are seen in the textures in *Newark*, *Wakefield Bridge*, *Llandilo Bridge* and *Lime Kiln*. It reflects Turner's developing confidence in himself and trust in his own eye, which came out of his own growing dextrous skill. But a new dimension was also revealing itself: a knowledge and love of English and Classical poetry that led Turner not only to know by heart large chunks of John Milton's *Paradise Lost* and James Thomson's *Seasons*, but also to find some deep stirrings within himself that drew him, at most by the time he was twenty-five, to write poetry of his own.

In 1798 the Royal Academy introduced a practice in its annual exhibitions that gave artists a new freedom in the way they presented their pictures. By allowing lines of verse to be published alongside individual catalogue entries, the Academy acknowledged the current understanding that painting and poetry were complementary arts. Of the five hundred artists who exhibited in 1798, however, only seventeen took advantage of the new rule. As one of the seventeen, Turner appended verses to five of his ten exhibits. This had the extra benefit of giving a special typographical prominence both to the catalogue entry and to the artist, by making the artist's name stand out on the page. In grasping the opportunity so enthusiastically, Turner revealed his own poetic interests and knowledge, and revealed that he advocated an art that united painting and poetry and gave added depth to the understanding of both.

In guiding the public at the 1798 exhibition to enjoy his oil painting *Morning amongst the Coniston Fells, Cumberland* (pl. 31; cat. 23), Turner was also guiding them to read some lines from Milton's *Paradise Lost*:

> Ye mists and exhalations that now rise
> From hill or streaming lake, dusky or gray,
> Till the sun paints your fleecy skirts with gold,
> In honour to the world's great Author, rise.[26]

It is significant that this first verse quoted by Turner carries imagery of painting, colour and atmosphere, and evokes in words the mood of the painted scene. *Morning amongst the Coniston Fells, Cumberland* is one of the most exciting and surprising of Turner's early works. Its composition allows nowhere for the eye to settle. It swings down from the central motif of sheep in a patch of

31 *Morning amongst the Coniston Fells, Cumberland*, exhibited RA 1798, oil on canvas, 122.9 × 89.9 cm (48³⁄₈ × 35¹⁄₂ in.), London, Tate

One of the most exciting and surprising of Turner's early works, this evokes the pictorial language of lines from Milton's *Paradise Lost* that were selected by Turner to accompany the painting's exhibition.

32 *The Dormitory and Transept of Fountains Abbey – Evening*, exhibited RA 1798, watercolour, 45.6 × 61 cm (18 × 24 in.), York Art Gallery

A picturesque vision of medieval ruins as dusk descends. The poetic mood was enhanced in the Royal Academy exhibition of 1798 by the quotation from James Thomson's *The Seasons* that Turner chose to accompany the work.

light to a rugged waterfall, and up to the distant sun splash and the thin clouds being blown towards the hills. Piled up on the right and left backgrounds are the lines of the distant fells, touched by veils of sunny clouds. The two small silver birch trees on the mid-left are important eye-catchers, maintaining the vertical line that runs down to the waterfall and marking the crossing point of the main vertical and horizontal lines of the composition. Following Classical rules of composition, the horizontal creates the Golden Section in the painting, which at the same time is disguised by a sublime and romantic restlessness.[27]

In his other exhibits of 1798 Turner quotes James Thomson's *The Seasons*, and chooses passages containing phrases that echo the art of painting: "rude ruin's glitter"; "the blue horizon's utmost verge"; "the kindling azure"; "in a yellow mist/ Bestriding earth". The watercolour *The Dormitory and Transept of Fountains Abbey – Evening* (pl. 32; cat. 18) takes lines from Thomson's *Seasons* that touch on the fading of the light at the end of the day, and on change and coming darkness. They have an added resonance for the subject, a ruined medieval monastery:

> All ether soft'ning sober evening takes
> Her wonted station on the middle air;
> A thousand shadows at her beck –
> In circle following circle, gathers round,
> To close the face of things.[28]

In the Royal Academy exhibition of the following year Turner quoted not only Milton and Thomson, but also the now obscure poets David Mallet and John Langhorne, demonstrating the breadth of his reading. Indeed, he seems to have acquired the thirteen-volume *Works of the British Poets* (ed. Robert Anderson, 1795) at about the time that the practice of quoting poetry alongside exhibits was first allowed at the Royal Academy.[29] Although his formal education in London, Brentford and Margate was thin, Turner was exposed in his youth and early adulthood to the theatrical and literary world of Covent Garden, and to the musical life of London through his friendship with the singer and composer John Danby (1757–1798).[30] Turner played the flute, enjoyed ballads and glees, some of which he may have first heard on the stage, and copied out extracts of music and song in early sketchbooks. In his 'Swiss Figures' sketchbook of 1803 he transcribed the ballad of the 'Friar of Orders Grey', from the 1798 Covent Garden production of *Merry Sherwood*,[31] and in the 'Swans' sketchbook he wrote out a rollicking poem about Jack the sailor and his sweetheart, Nancy.[32] Turner sucked up the popular culture of his time and place, and his life was the richer for it.

Within the sketchbooks there are also verses of Turner's own composition, over which he had evidently struggled. The reading, collecting and writing of poetry were habits that formed early in his career, and stayed with him. He never, however, found a coherent voice as a poet, despite magnificent efforts and considerable expenditure of time and trouble. His verses are generally clumsy, and there are occasions when we sense he has thrown away his pencil in frustration. But we can nevertheless hear through them echoes of his aspirations as an artist, and they offer a fresh perspective on his creativity.

One of the earliest surviving verses by Turner consists of the five lines he appended to the oil painting *Dolbadern Castle* (pl. 33; cat. 25):

> How awful is the silence of the waste,
> Where nature lifts her mountains to the sky.
> Majestic solitude, behold the tower
> Where hopeless OWEN, long imprison'd, pined
> And wrung his hands for liberty, in vain.

Shown beneath a dramatic view of this northern Welsh castle that Turner sketched on his tour of the area in 1798 is a bound captive guarded by two soldiers. 'Owen' in the verse is the thirteenth-century Welsh prince Owain Goch, who was imprisoned by his brother Llewelyn in Dolbadern Castle for twenty-three years and released after Edward I's campaigns in Wales. The history of the oppression of Wales is a subject that recurs in Turner's work of the late 1790s, and *Dolbadern Castle* is an early instance of his exploration of the theme of oppression, liberty and freedom. In exhibiting the verse with the painting, Turner reminded the public that this is a landscape of a specific history and moment, in which the sense of place is interwoven with time and incident. He is invoking a practice, which came to be a characteristic of his work, of revealing that what might appear to be a Picturesque or Sublime landscape also has its story to tell.

Turner had early aspirations to be elected an Associate of the Royal Academy, an essential stepping stone to success as an artist, and he made it his business to impress as many influential people as he could with his talent and personality. He may have been ignored when he first exhibited, in 1790, but seven or eight years later the power of his talent was unmistakable. He began to take pupils, thus increasing his income and extending his circle of acquaintances, and became particularly charming to many – "modest and sensible", as the diarist and artist Joseph Farington found him.[33] He flattered, networked and lobbied, all with the single-minded aim of becoming noticed, promoted, commissioned, and elected an Associate of the Royal Academy.

The senior artists of the Academy had not seen anybody quite like him before, and it is likely that he overdid it, becoming obnoxious and irritating to some of the grandees. Whether he knew it or not, his good friend Thomas Girtin was being promoted against him by Henry Lascelles (1767–1841), Earl of Harewood, a highly influential and wealthy patron from Yorkshire: Farington recorded that Lascelles proposed "to set up Girtin against Turner" as a candidate for an Associateship.[34] At the very time that this young upstart Turner was beginning to be noticed and

33 *Dolbadern Castle,* exhibited RA 1800, oil on canvas, 119.5 × 90.2 cm (47 × 35½ in.), London, Royal Academy of Arts

One of Turner's earliest surviving verses describes how a Welsh prince was released from imprisonment at Dolbadern by Edward I's invading army. This brooding composition, which shows Turner exploring the themes of oppression and liberty in the visual language of the Old Masters, was presented by him to the Royal Academy on his election as an Academician.

34 *Salisbury Cathedral from the Bishop's Garden*, 1797–98, pencil, pen and ink and watercolour, 51.3 × 67.8 cm, (30¼ × 21⅝ in.), Birmingham Museums & Art Gallery

Painted to be engraved, this watercolour is carefully set out to enable the engraver to translate architectural detail into line. It is enlivened by the group of labourers in the middleground, resting in the summer heat.

was ingratiating himself, the Council of the Royal Academy decided on a minimum age at which Associates could be elected, setting it at twenty-four years old.[35] He failed to be elected by four votes in 1798, when he was technically still too young to stand, but the following year achieved his aim by a wide margin. As an Associate of the Royal Academy Turner gained immediately the privilege of being able to join the Academy dining club, to meet fellow artists on equal terms and to decide himself on what pictures to show at the annual exhibitions. As part of the artistic, political and social force that the Academy represented, Turner also had the new status of the letters ARA, an added encouragement for patrons and a sign of his acceptability. From being seen by the portrait painter John Hoppner as "a timid man afraid to venture",[36] Turner had evolved into an artist who claimed he had "60 drawings now bespoke by different persons",[37] and a reputation for energy, lucidity and a startling way of looking at buildings and landscape.

Turner's youthful genius, further empowered by his physical stamina, his relentless quest for recognition and his enviable charm, led him to receive not only repeat commissions but also orders for large groups of drawings that he could take his time over. Central among the latter were the commissions from Sir Richard Colt Hoare to make watercolours of Salisbury Cathedral (pls. 34–36; cat. 32–34); from William Beckford to paint views of Fonthill Abbey, his

35 *Interior of Salisbury Cathedral, looking towards the North Transept*, 1802–05, watercolour, 66 × 50.8 cm (26 × 20 in.), Salisbury and South Wiltshire Museum

In one of the most complex of Turner's cathedral interiors, the scale is dramatically shown by the tiny figures.

vast house under construction in Wiltshire (pls. 11, 40, 41; cat. 35, 36); and from the Delegates of the Clarendon Press to provide watercolour views of Oxford and its colleges for engraving year by year as the illustrations to the *Oxford Almanack*, the calendar of university events (pls. 2, 37, 38; cat. 37–39).

The Salisbury Cathedral commission reveals the extent of the confidence that Colt Hoare had in Turner. In about 1796 he commissioned ten large watercolours of views in and around the cathedral, with a further ten smaller views of the town.[38] Colt Hoare's intention was to have the cathedral views engraved for a history of Wiltshire and, although in the event this was not achieved (nor was either series of watercolours completed), the eight large views of the cathedral that Turner finished together present a catalogue of the highly advanced manners of composition at which he was now adept.

Salisbury Cathedral from the Bishop's Garden (pl. 34; cat. 32) is a straightforward portrait of the cathedral, which is shown four-square and lit from the south-west, with a foreground articulated by resting farmworkers and a tree trunk. It reflects the manner of topographical draughtsmen of an earlier generation, such as Sandby and Malton, and gives an idea of the quality of training that Turner had received in Hardwick's architectural practice. The second Salisbury subject, *South view from the Cloisters, Salisbury Cathedral* (pl. 36; cat. 33), brings the cathedral suddenly into close-up and frames it, extraordinarily, behind a broken ogee arch. This frame-within-a-frame has the effect of focusing attention on to the building, and dramatically curtails the composition. Turner had taken bold viewpoints before – under bridges, through the ruins of abbeys – but here he also invokes the complex interiors of Giovanni Battista Piranesi (1720–1778), whose influential engravings of prisons and of Roman remains Turner saw in Colt Hoare's collection. *South view from the Cloisters* takes the viewer directly into Salisbury Cathedral's enclosed spaces, and evokes the visitor's experience of seeing the different parts of the building appearing to shift in relation to one another as he or she moves around it. In a third view, *Interior of Salisbury Cathedral, looking towards the North Transept* (pl. 35; cat. 34), the intricate Gothic spaces are articulated by shafts of light.

Perhaps because they were made for a committee of patrons rather than one collector, the ten views of Oxford and its colleges that Turner painted from about 1798 to 1804 lack the compositional bravura of the Salisbury subjects. The Oxford watercolours were for information and decoration, clear and plainly spoken, and suggest a degree of emotional detachment that Turner, as an outsider in Oxford, might have experienced. The view of *Exeter College and All Saints Church &c from the Turl* (pl. 38; cat. 37) is full of architectural detail illuminated by the afternoon sun, with the lively narratives of workmen repairing the cobbles, and dons wandering about. *Inside View of the Hall of Christ Church* (pl. 37; cat. 38) reveals the immense size of the college's dining hall, and reflects in the carefully painted detail of the portraits (Hans Holbein's sixteenth-century portrait of Henry VIII is easily distinguished) the long history of the college. The view of *Oxford from the South Side of*

36 *South view from the Cloisters, Salisbury Cathedral, c.* 1802, watercolour, 68 × 49.6 cm (26¾ × 19½ in.), London, Victoria and Albert Museum

In this dramatic composition Turner brilliantly conveys the sensation of walking through the cloisters and pausing to wonder at the height of the spire. The boy playing on the stone slabs, with his basket and hoop nearby, adds scale and incident. To give highlights to the upper windows Turner has made a series of very fine vertical scratches.

37 *Inside View of the Hall of Christ Church*, 1803–04, pencil, watercolour and scratching out, 32.9 × 44.8 cm (13 × 17⅝ in.), Oxford, Ashmolean Museum. Engraved for the 1807 *Oxford Almanack*

The central portrait of Henry VIII conveys the historic authority of one of Britain's oldest academic institutions. The sparkling light is enhanced by the extensive scratching out of the pigment by the artist's fingernail.

38 *Exeter College and All Saints Church
&c from the Turl*, 1803–04, pencil
and watercolour, 32.1 × 45 cm
(12⅝ × 17¾ in.), Oxford,
Ashmolean Museum. Engraved
for the 1806 *Oxford Almanack*

Turner's quiet views of Oxford
show the city as a haven for
scholarly study, but do not reflect
the reality of the town's rapidly
growing number of inns and daily
coach departures for London
and elsewhere.

Heddington Hill (pl. 2; cat. 39) is a vivid allusion to Turner's childhood experience of travelling around the edge of Oxford to stay with his uncle at Sunningwell in the late 1780s, when he painted another distant view of the city from below Boar's Hill.[39] The wall running down the hill makes a purposeful divide in the picture between town and country, and the post-and-rail fence and the harrows in the foreground suggest the effects of the Enclosure Acts on the British landscape in the late eighteenth century.

The Salisbury and Oxford series were on the stocks in Turner's studio across the same years; and it is likely that as his days progressed he would put a Salisbury view aside to pick up an Oxford one, or *vice versa*. This manner of working on a number of subjects at the same time developed early in Turner's career, and, such was the pressure on him to maintain his productivity as an artist, became standard practice for him in both watercolour and oil.

Ever experimenting, Turner went on a trip to the beech woods at Knockholt in Kent in October of 1799 to paint in the open air.[40] Among the small, fresh works that he produced there is a study in

39 *A beech wood, Knockholt, Kent,* 1799, oil on paper, 16.5 × 24.1 cm (6½ × 9½ in.), Cambridge MA, Fogg Art Museum

This swiftly made oil painting reveals Turner's growing interest in the effects of light and shade in an anonymous landscape, at a time when his main employment was the making of Picturesque watercolours for collectors and the engraving trade.

40 *Fonthill Abbey at sunset*, 1799, pencil and watercolour, 46.8 × 33.1 cm (18⅜ × 13 in.), London, Tate

This work was left unfinished, but it does give an idea of how the interior 'glow' often apparent in the artist's watercolours (*e.g.* pls. 102, 107) is accomplished through the use of warm-toned underpainting.

oil on paper of the mysterious light inside a wood on an autumn day (pl. 39; cat. 22). Quite unlike anything Turner had painted before, it reveals the extent to which he pushed at the boundaries of his art. Informal, and lacking any sort of 'style' or rhetoric, it shows the young man who would spend a lifetime exploring the nature of light here examining the subdued illumination of a forest. At Fonthill Abbey, where Turner had worked in the summer of the same year, he drew studies of the building and its surroundings, which he later developed into a series of distant views for William Beckford (pls. 11, 40, 41; cat. 35, 36). In a number of unfinished watercolours of Fonthill, Turner flooded the paper with colour to build up the various forms in the picture and to create a warm underpainting that would glow through the final work (pl. 40). This building up of formal elements was a practice that Turner pursued until the end of his life, most visibly in his watercolour 'beginnings' and in later oil paintings of Venetian subjects.[41] The Knockholt and Fonthill views, painted within months of each other, demonstrate the range of Turner's experimentation in his art, and show his active determination to use the landscape subjects as his laboratory.

41 *Fonthill, from a stone quarry*, 1800, pencil, watercolour and bodycolour, 29.8 × 44.2 cm (11¾ × 17⅜ in.), Leeds City Art Gallery

The extraordinary scale of William Beckford's Fonthill Abbey intrigued Turner and his contemporaries. He depicted it from all directions soaring above the surrounding countryside.

42 *Dunstanborough Castle, c.* 1798, oil on canvas, 47 × 69 cm (18½ × 27⅛ in.), Dunedin Public Art Gallery, New Zealand

Lively brushwork captures the chill wind and turbulence that threatens to submerge the small boat. The jagged outlines of the castle echo the foreground rocks, and both evoke the impenetrable remoteness of Britain's northern coastline.

The Knockholt and Fonthill studies reveal Turner to be surprising and delighting himself as the pigment unrolled under his brush. With works such as his Picturesque watercolours painted to commission and for sale (pls. 17, 18, 24, 32; cat. 4, 5, 13, 18), these pictures represent the two poles of Turner's youthful production. On one side he is experimenting privately, with the nature of his experiment perhaps obscured by the lack of finish; and on the other he is conforming willingly to current fashion and showing off his talents publicly. Two other pictures reveal more of these twin concerns and how they were woven into his art. *Dunstanborough Castle* (pl. 42; cat. 24) describes the powerful motion of a stormy sea, with the ruins of the castle beyond evoking the transience of human activity. Inspired by the paintings of Richard Wilson (1714–1782), Turner is also expressing here a personal experience of the cold, bleak northern coast that he visited in 1797: this is a glimpse of reality dressed up as an essay in the Sublime. The large commissioned watercolour *Lincoln from the Brayford* (pls. 43, 44; cat. 26) is presented, on the other hand, as a genuine product of a Midlands tour. So in part it may have been, as Turner went to Lincoln in 1794;

43, 44 *Lincoln from the Brayford,*
1803–04, watercolour, bodycolour
and scraping out, 66 × 102 cm
(26 × 40⅛ in.), Lincoln,
Usher Gallery

This watercolour is huge by
contemporary standards, and reflects
the extent of Turner's ambition in
watercolour. With the foreground
boat-building, it combines ideas
of continuity and of transience.
The spires on the cathedral's west
towers were removed in 1807.

but comparison with the Buck engraving of Lincoln and Turner's own youthful version of the
same work (pls. 14, 15; cat. 2) reveals not only that it has the same general composition as
the print, but also that the cast of the shadows on the cathedral as painted by Turner are practically identical to those in the Bucks' work. This clearly indicates that while his own studies were
his main source of imagery, Turner continued to use engravings as reminders when they gave
him the information he needed.

Other works, such as the large presentation watercolour *Hafod* (pls. 45, 46; cat. 19), reveal
another ability, that of combining formal architectural drawing with atmospheric Sublime landscape.[42] This watercolour reveals that Turner was perfectly prepared to use the profound experience of landscape form and mood that he had gained on his travels to enhance a workaday drawing
that may have been commissioned by an architect to impress a client. *Hafod* (and there are many
other architectural presentation drawings from Turner's early career)[43] is an example of the work
that developed directly from his early association with Thomas Hardwick and other architects.

45, 46 *Hafod, c.* 1798, watercolour, 61 × 91.5 cm (24 × 36 in.), Port Sunlight, Lady Lever Art Gallery

This scheme, possibly by John Nash, for Hafod near Aberystwyth was never built, despite Turner's beguiling vision of it. The pale building in the gothic style is enhanced by Turner's magnificent mountain setting.

The study and drawing of architecture gave Turner great pleasure, and the experience he gained through his early architectural training remained with him throughout his life. It was expressed both in his paintings (for example pls. 113, 115; cat. 98, 99), and in his skill in practical construction when he built (and later rebuilt) his private gallery, and designed his neat house, Sandycombe Lodge in Twickenham, in the 1810s. Very few of Turner's exhibited or engraved landscapes do not include buildings, and it was through his representation of architecture in the landscape that Turner expressed the long historical process of the building of Britain. He developed a profound knowledge of architectural form and language, derived from his reading of architectural treatises. One of his early poems shows that he had studied Sir Henry Wotton's *The Elements of Architecture*, first published in 1624 and available in reprinted eighteenth-century editions. Though getting the author's name wrong, he turns Wotton's anthropomorphic descriptions of the orders of architecture into jaunty verse. Where Wotton writes of the Tuscan column as "resembling some sturdy well-limbed labourer", Turner versifies:

> Sir William Wootton often said
> Tuscan was like the Labourer made
> Ioniac with her scrowl-like fan
> The meretricious courtezan

Corinthian looked mature and chaste
Not like the Corinth maid in haste.

Then he repeats himself, reworking the lines in his sketchbook, and continues:

Misplaced mouldings much abused
At Gateway corners thus we find
That carriage wheels its surface grind
Or placed beneath some dirty wall
Supports the drunken cobbler's stall.[44]

47 *Edinburgh from St Anthony's Chapel*, 1801, pencil, 26.3 × 41.3 cm (10³⁄₈ × 16¹⁄₈ in.), Cambridge MA, Fogg Art Museum

This penetrating drawing of the Old Town of Edinburgh shows how well rooted Scottish subjects must have been in Turner's experience when, twenty years later, he came to make a long series of pictures of Scotland as part of a business relationship with Sir Walter Scott.

At the turn of the nineteenth century Turner was living at a hectic pace – producing oils and watercolours in the autumn, winter and spring for exhibition at the Academy in April and May; travelling about the country in the summer and early autumn; politicking to be elected into the

Academy. On top of all this he was trying to manage his love life, being heavily involved by 1799 with Sarah Danby, the widow of his musician friend John Danby. They had a daughter, Evelina, in 1800 or 1801, and appear to have lived together in a loosely organized way at this time. Turner's was not a neat life. His single-mindedness to pursue a career as an artist did not make for tranquil domesticity, and it may not have crossed his mind to marry Sarah. But the relationship continued for ten or more years, and the couple had a second daughter, Georgiana, in 1811 or 1812. Theirs must have been a stormy relationship, and an anguished, self-justificatory expression of their life together is felt in Turner's poetry:

> Love is like the raging Ocean
> [Wind?] that sway, its troubled motion
> Woman's temper ever bubbling
> Man the early bark which sailing
> In the unblest treacherous Sea[45]

49 *Loch Awe*, 1801, pencil, 34 × 48 cm (13⅜ × 18⅞ in.), London, Tate

One of the group of large pencil studies Turner made in Scotland in 1801, and a direct source for the watercolour *Kilchern Castle* (pl. 50).

Turner's life was changing in other ways at this time. His father appears to have given up his barber's practice in about 1800 and became Turner's studio assistant: he continued in this role until his death in 1829. Turner's mother was tidied away in 1799 to the grim surroundings first of St Luke's Hospital, then of Bethlem Hospital for the Insane, in London, where she seems to have been quietly forgotten by her husband and son. She died in 1804.[46] With or without Sarah, Turner improved his way of life by moving in 1799 from a back room in his father's house in Maiden Lane to new airy premises in fashionable Harley Street, in the Portland Estates north of Oxford Street, which he rented in his own right.

This move signalled not only a change in status for Turner, but also clearer light, fresher air and proximity to wealthy patrons. The change of scene had a marked effect on Turner's out-look and his approach to his subjects. Those paintings in oil and watercolour that he made in Maiden Lane have a formality and tightness that may be attributed to lack of space and light in which to work. In his *Self-Portrait* (pl. 1), for example, one of the finest and most mature and accomplished of his oil paintings from the period, the stark top-lighting and heavily shadowed eyes and neckerchief suggest that the work was painted in a small room. A further cramped quality in some of the early oils suggests he was unable to step back and consider them from a reasonable distance.

50 *Kilchern Castle, with the Cruchan Ben Mountains, Scotland: Noon*, exhibited RA 1802, watercolour, 53.3 × 72.2 cm (21 × 28⅜ in.), Plymouth City Museums and Art Gallery

The long title spells out precisely the subject of this picture, and the time of day it represents. But it is likely to be an imaginary construct, because rainbows in Britain at noon are rare. For Turner and his contemporaries mountains were a source of wonderment and were beginning to raise geological questions about the earth's formation.

This all changed with the paintings he made when he returned from his tour of Scotland in 1801. Although he carried out at least one commission there, and made many lyrical sketches of Edinburgh and other places (pls. 47, 48; cat. 28, 29), the most significant product of that trip was the series of about sixty large drawings of Scottish landscapes, the group that Ruskin termed 'The Scottish Pencils', (pl. 49; cat. 27). These drawings, with their subtle shades of pencil that show the shifting quality of the light, became rich sources of imagery for Turner over the next twenty or thirty years. Judging by their generally dog-eared condition when they were found after Turner's death, he consulted them and turned them over regularly. One great work that grew out of these drawings, *Kilchern Castle, with the Cruchan Ben Mountains, Scotland: Noon* (pl. 50; cat. 30), has a scale, majesty and optimism that suggests that it can have been made only in a large, light-filled room such as those of the houses in Harley Street.

CHAPTER II

"All that my powers hold"
1802 to 1814

Turner rose from being an Associate of the Royal Academy to Royal Academician when he won a vacancy in the Academy election of February 1802. From signing his paintings *William Turner* or just *W Turner*, as he had at the lower left of the watercolours *Old Bridge, Shrewsbury* (pl. 29; cat. 11) and *Ludlow Castle* (pl. 5; cat. 20), he began to mark his work with the grand-style *J.M.W. Turner RA*, as in *Windsor Castle from the Thames* (pl. 56; cat. 41). As a Royal Academician Turner was now a full member of the senior body of artists in England, with the social status and prestige that went with it.

As an indication of why Academicians had elected him to their number, Turner's first exhibits at the Academy in April and May 1802 surveyed the wide range of his abilities and manners as a painter. Whether or not this was intentional we do not know, but it remains the case. His supreme talent for painting the sea, in which he revealed his understanding of seventeenth-century Dutch painting, was represented by *Fishermen upon a Lee Shore, in Squally Weather* (Kenwood, Iveagh Bequest) and the imposing *Ships Bearing up for Anchorage* ('The Egremont Seapiece'; on loan to London, National Gallery). The latter was bought by the Earl of Egremont (1751–1837), who became one of Turner's most significant patrons. Turner's manner of handling biblical and historical drama, in which he evoked the work of Poussin, was represented by *The Fifth Plague of Egypt* (Indianapolis Museum of Art); another oil painting, *Jason* (London, Tate), takes a medievalizing angle on the ancient myth of Jason's search for the Golden Fleece. An enormous watercolour, *The Fall of the Clyde, Lanarkshire: Noon. – Vide Akenside's Hymn to the Naiads* (pls. 51, 52; cat. 31), has the style and presence of an oil painting for exhibition, peopled with nymphs straight out of the Academy life class. In referring to Mark Akenside's poem *Hymn to the Naiads* in the title, Turner reminded his audience of this influential mid-eighteenth-century poet's praise of the Naiads. In ancient Greek belief these minor river deities made breezes blow, nourished vegetable growth and kept navigable rivers flowing: thus in early nineteenth-century Britain they could be read as a poetic metaphor for the maintenance of commerce and the national economy, and with support of the navy.[1] The three other watercolours in the 1802 exhibition depicted subjects that Turner had seen on his 1801 Scottish tour, including *Kilchern Castle, with the Cruchan Ben Mountains, Scotland: Noon* (pl. 50; cat. 30).

51 *The Fall of the Clyde, Lanarkshire: Noon. – Vide Akenside's Hymn to the Naiads*, 1802, detail of pl. 52

73

Taking all these paintings together as samples of his talents, there was little, except perhaps a wide landscape based on the style of Claude, missing from his portfolio of outstanding picture-making.

A grand painting in the manner of Claude was to appear in the following year's Royal Academy exhibition, after Turner had taken the opportunity given by the short-lived pause in the war with France – the Peace of Amiens – to travel to France, Switzerland and briefly into northern Italy in September 1802. This painting, *The Festival upon the Opening of the Vintage of Macon* (pl. 53; cat. 40), one of Turner's greatest early landscapes, is important not only because it shows a panorama in the style of Claude in which the view extends for perhaps fifty or sixty miles into the distance, but because the subject is actually a view in England. What we see masquerading as the valley of the River Saône in Burgundy is the bend in the River Thames as seen from Richmond Hill in Surrey. The view from Richmond Hill was famous in literature and art, having been exalted by James Thomson in 'Summer' from his poem *The Seasons* as "this glorious view/ Calmly magnificent", and painted in the eighteenth century by many artists including Leonard Knyff (1650–1721) and Richard Wilson. Further, it was the view that Sir Joshua Reynolds chose as the outlook from The Wick, the house built for him in the 1770s.

Proving beyond doubt by exhibiting the painting that he was as fine an artist as Claude, Turner also plainly expressed his view that the landscape of Britain was as worthy a subject for

53 *The Festival upon the Opening of the Vintage of Macon*, exhibited RA 1803, oil on canvas, 146 × 237.5 cm (57½ × 93½ in.), Sheffield Galleries and Museums Trust

Turner passed through Macon, in Burgundy, in September 1802, the month of the grape harvest. Although this ambitious early painting is nominally of a French subject in the style of Claude, it depicts the view of the Thames from Richmond Hill. Turner challenged the prevalent view that the landscape of Britain was not as worthy a subject for high art as that of France or Italy.

painting as the Roman Campagna or the plains of Flanders. The landscape of Turner's own country simply did not feature in the canon of European art in the eighteenth century. When paying his moving tribute to Thomas Gainsborough (1727–1788) in his fourteenth discourse to Royal Academy students in 1788, Reynolds challenged this prejudice and affirmed that "I take more interest in, and am more captivated with the powerful impression of nature, which Gainsborough exhibited in his portraits and in his landscapes," adding:

> I am well aware how much I lay myself open to the censure and ridicule of the academ-
> ical professors of other nations, in preferring the humble attempts of Gainsborough
> to the works of those regular graduates in the great historical style.[2]

The Festival upon the Opening of the Vintage of Macon was bought by Charles Percy (1749–1823), first Lord Yarborough, after a dispute over pricing with Sir John Leicester (1762–1827).[3] Although it may have been shown again at Turner's own gallery in 1804, the painting disappeared otherwise from public view and was never engraved. Although it was not universally praised, some influential contemporary critics found the work breathtaking and saw its Claudian connections immediately. John Opie considered it to be "very fine – perhaps the finest work in the room";[4] the *British Press* newspaper said it was "without comparison; the first landscape of the kind that has been executed since the time of Claude Lorrain … [Turner] has even surpassed that master in the richness and forms of some parts of his picture."[5] As far as is known, nobody publicly noted its connection with the Richmond Hill view, though this may be because the link was so obvious as to require no comment.[6]

For Turner the significance of this masquerade lay in the fact that the view he painted was so famous, so very much an 'English' view and indeed the symbol of poetic England. It was also a view that he returned to again and again, notably in two large oils, *Thomson's Aeolian Harp* (exh. 1809; Manchester Art Gallery) and *England: Richmond Hill, on the Prince Regent's Birthday* (pl. 106; cat. 73), and in the watercolour *Richmond Terrace, Surrey* 1836; (pl. 128; cat. 109).[7] In the case of *England: Richmond Hill* Turner goes so far as to name the view as the epitome of England, and use it as the setting for a public appearance of the Prince Regent. (This will be discussed fully in Chapter III.)

When Turner was elected an Academician, the Royal Academy was going through a stormy period in which the 'Court' faction, consisting of artists who supported strong royal influence over the Academy's affairs, was pitted against the 'Academicals', who wanted greater control of the Council by the membership.[8] Turner became an active 'Academical' immediately, and, as the rules dictated that new Academicians should sit on the Council, he was pitched into the heart of the controversy. Meetings during the first few weeks of Turner's membership are characterized by minutes being written and then struck out by order at the following meeting;[9] Turner being voted into the chair;[10] the president being absent through illness;[11] a walk out of members;[12] and "surprise and abhorrence" expressed at a news report that the president had seriously transgressed by exhibiting in 1803 a painting that he had already shown at the Academy in 1776.[13] Turner seconded the motion that the president's picture be rejected.[14]

Controversy was not new to the Royal Academy, but it was becoming clear that the Academy had created more trouble for itself by electing as a member an artist who was headstrong, opinionated and eager to be active. Sir Francis Bourgeois (1756–1811) called Turner "a little reptile"[15] after one stormy Council meeting, which led Turner to make a knee-jerk response and resulted in a bout of tit for tat name-calling. As Joseph Farington, previously such a support, expressed: "his manners, so presumptive and arrogant, were spoken of with great disgust".[16] Matters came to a head when Turner caused a scene in the meeting of 11 May 1804 and walked out, not to return until 1806. This may have been a calculated outburst, because at the same time Turner was altering his house in Harley Street and building a gallery of his own. Such a move could be read as a purposeful snub to the Academy, but it also gave him an escape route, which if necessary he could offer to other artists in the event of the Royal Academy collapsing through internal strife.

54 *Landscape with Richmond Bridge*, 1805, pencil, 17.1 × 26.4 cm (6¾ × 10⅜ in.), London, Tate. From the 'Hesperides I' sketchbook, TB XCIII, fol. 35a.

A leaf from one of the sketchbooks Turner used during the summer of 1805, which he spent on and around the River Thames.

Turner had found a new talent: one for finding the heart of a controversy and making enemies. Some of the influential people who had supported and encouraged him when he was coming up, including Sir George Beaumont and Lord Lascelles, were now set against him. Others, such as Sir John Leicester and Lord Yarborough, handled him with care because he had already played one off against the other over the pricing of *The Festival upon the Opening of the Vintage of Macon*. Nevertheless, Turner retained a complementary talent for making friends. Among those who supported him at this period were the Yorkshire landowner and radical politician Walter Fawkes (1769–1825), and two great landowners from Sussex, the Earl of Egremont, of Petworth, and the MP John Fuller (1757–1834), of Rosehill, near Lewes. What is evident from the lasting effect of these and other friendships and enmities, and from his work and pattern of travel as a whole, is that Turner's Britain is not any handful of local areas but the whole extent of the island itself, taking in England, Wales and, as far as was possible for him, Scotland. Through his need and desire to travel so widely, and, as shall be discussed later, to know the history, to observe the life, and to understand the climate and geography of Britain, Turner was the first British artist to express the integrity of the nation.

After busting out of the Academy Turner spent the summers of 1804 and 1805 travelling up and down the lower River Thames, painting on the banks or from a small boat at and around Brentford, Isleworth and Walton, and further up river at Windsor, Sonning and Caversham. Painting in the open air, as he had done some five years earlier at Knockholt (pl. 39; cat. 22), he worked in watercolour in his sketchbooks and in oil on small panels. The damp freshness in the

studies, particularly those in the 'Hesperides I' sketchbook (pls. 54, 58; cat. 53), is characteristic of this reflective period when he ceased to be bombastic, and perhaps also ceased to try too hard to impress. Evolving out of the fluid sketches that Turner painted from his boat, such as *The Thames near Walton Bridges* (pl. 55; cat. 47), were paintings that he showed at his own gallery only, and not at the Royal Academy. Including *Windsor Castle from the Thames* (pl. 56; cat. 41) and *Walton Bridges* (pl. 57; cat. 42), these scenes are as much conundrums in their own way as was *The Festival upon the Opening of the Vintage of Macon* two or three years earlier.

Though they are scenes of England in title and subject-matter, these paintings are far removed from the prevailing Picturesque manner. *Windsor Castle from the Thames* is Poussin's Rome transported to the lower Thames, with the solid central frieze of trees and the castle's bulk lowering on the same horizontal, quite in the manner of the great French master. Even the gathered foreground sheep, the punting boatman and the piling clouds have Poussinesque roots. In *Walton Bridges* the complex architecture of the two bridges that span the Thames and the surrounding muddy flood plain gives the work a rippling background energy that offsets the evening calm of the foreground. The style of this painting is rooted in the work of the Dutch artist Aelbert Cuyp, but the cows standing around in the water and the verticals of masts and sails make it a work that creates its own rules. Under the disguise of randomness and with the apparently accidental placing of wandering cows, Turner has created a tightly gridded composition that pleases the eye without

55 *The Thames near Walton Bridges*, *c.* 1806–07, oil on mahogany veneer, 37.1 × 73.7 cm (14⅝ × 29 in.), London, Tate

In this freshly atmospheric study, painted quickly from a boat in the middle of the river, Turner reaches the same level of immediacy with oil paint that he achieved on the riverbank with watercolour (see pl. 58). The Walton bridges are visible in the distance (see also pl. 57).

56 *Windsor Castle from the Thames*, 1805, oil on canvas, 91 × 122 cm (35⅞ × 48 in.), London, Tate, on loan to Petworth House, Sussex

Although this is a classical composition in the manner of Poussin, the river traffic is well observed and thoroughly contemporary. The shepherdesses, sheep and straining boatmen introduce an Arcadian element.

easily revealing why this should be. The main horizontal bands are clear, but the verticals dividing the work into four equal sections are more subtle. From left to right these are the main arch of the first bridge, which runs down through the shoulders of the cow; the slim mast at the centre; and the raised sail to the right. These are countered by a pair of low crossing diagonals that meet at the base of the central mast. By disguising the classical rules of his art so successfully, this renegade Royal Academician has himself defined what is so revolutionary about his art in this apparently placid period of his career.

In this period Turner rented riverside houses, first at Sion Ferry, Isleworth (1804–06), and then at The Mall, Chiswick, and he may also have had his family around him. He started to write some of his more concentrated bursts of poetry beside the river, and continued with his

other favourite occupation on the riverbank, fishing. He resumed exhibiting at the Royal Academy in 1806. The most constructive result of Turner's country sojourn for his art in the longer term was that beside the Thames he reflected deeply on Shakespeare and Greek and Roman literature and history, and came to see the England that lay around him as a new classical Arcadia: paradise here and now. Many of the pages in the 'Hesperides I' sketchbook (pls. 54, 58; cat. 53) evoke this new found calm. It is likely that at this stage Turner renewed his old friendship with the Revd Henry Scott Trimmer (1775–1859), whom he had first met as a boy in Brentford. This friendship was to last for the rest of Turner's life. Trimmer was now rector of Heston, about half a mile north-west of Sion Ferry, and, having been a Classics scholar at Merton College, Oxford, was well placed to chew over aspects of Classical literature with his

57 *Walton Bridges*, 1806, oil on canvas, 92.7 × 123.8 cm (36½ × 48¾ in.), Oxford, Ashmolean Museum

The double bridge at Walton-on-Thames was built in 1783 to the design of the architect James Paine. Turner's limpid treatment of light and atmosphere gives this English view the authority of an Old Master painting.

58 *Kew Bridge and Palace*, 1805, watercolour, 17.1 × 26.4 cm (6¾ × 10⅜ in.), London, Tate. From the 'Hesperides I' sketchbook, TB XCIII, fol. 38a

friend. Though impossible now to test,[17] the coincidence of the two classicists, Trimmer and Turner, at the riverbank should have been enough to spark ideas for paintings to last Turner a life-time. In the 'Studies for Pictures, Isleworth' sketchbook (1805) Turner lists subjects from Homer and Virgil as possible for future pictures.[18]

An event that disturbed the reflective atmosphere of life along the river was the destruction in 1807 of the villa at Twickenham owned until his death by the poet Alexander Pope (1688–1744). It was torn down by a new owner, Lady Howe, and the weeping willow that Pope himself had planted, said to be a shoot from the first willow to arrive in Britain, was felled. The demolition of the house offended many lovers of literature who had made pilgrimages to it, and defiled the sense of place that the poetry of both Pope and Thomson had created at the Thames riverside.[19] It was the Classical inheritance of the poetry of Pope and Thomson, and Turner's own lifelong experience of the river, that enthralled Turner about the landscape of the Thames. The destruc-tion of this inheritance fuelled his anger at the demolition of the house.

To express the full richness of allusion and metaphor in the destruction of the villa, Turner painted *Pope's Villa at Twickenham* (pl. 59; cat. 43), which he exhibited at his own gallery in 1808. The roofless shell of the house is far in the background, but the mood of sadness and melancholy is clear enough. A group of old rustics sitting on the trunk of a felled willow tree gesture theatri-cally at the ruin; beside them is an empty picture frame and the capital of a Corinthian column that they seem to be discussing blankly; nearby is a pair of country lovers; and to the far right are

some sheep and day-to-day riverside activity. Pope's poetry evokes the life of the river, and the whole also has the air of Shakespeare – scenes in *As You Like It* or *A Midsummer Night's Dream* come to mind. Turner seems here to be suggesting that, despite the destruction of an integral part of the poetic life of Britain, it is only rustics, with their dull and incomplete understanding of the meaning of art, who seem to know or care.[20] Meanwhile, the cycle of life goes on. Pope's was not the only fine house along the Thames to vanish during the period, as the engraver John Landseer (1769–1852) pointed out, but its destruction did have the deepest resonance:

59 *Pope's Villa at Twickenham*, 1808, oil on canvas, 91.5 × 120.6 cm (36 × 47⅜ in.), Sudeley Castle, Gloucestershire

In this enigmatic work Turner draws attention to the demolition of the house of the poet Alexander Pope, an event that damaged Britain's literary heritage and scandalized Turner and his contemporaries.

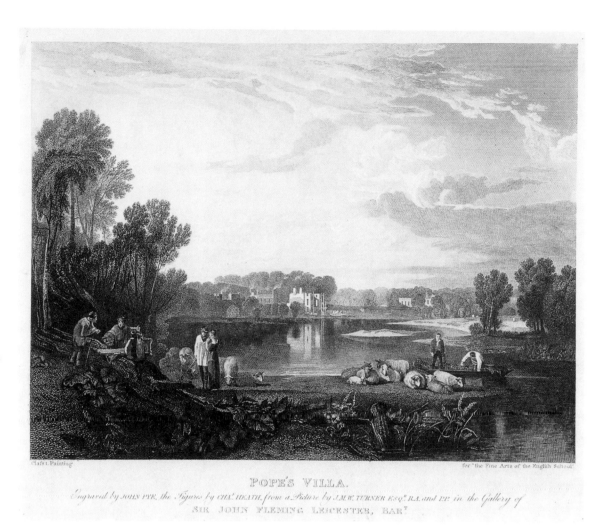

60 John Pye and Charles Heath after J.M.W. Turner, *Pope's Villa*, 1811, engraving, 17.5 × 22.9 cm (6⅞ × 9 in.), Birmingham Museums & Art Gallery. Engraving after *Pope's Villa at Twickenham* (pl. 59), 1811

The detail and delicacy of the effects in this engraving demonstrated to Turner just what the best engravers could achieve, and gave him a particular confidence in the skills of Pye and Heath.

At least it should mitigate our regret, that the pencil of Turner has rescued the Villa of Pope from the oblivion in which other mansions which have from time to time adorned the borders of the Thames, have been suffered to sink.[21]

What is significant is not so much that Turner should choose to paint the demolition of Pope's house, but that he should conceal it within a formal evening landscape in the Classical mould, and exhibit it in his gallery. What Turner is doing in this work is transferring the symbolism of ruins from their accepted, distanced place in the Roman Forum or in a Classical landscape painting by Claude or Poussin into the here and now of the Twickenham landscape of his own day. Within the language of the medium, that is a considerable shock. Turner made a habit of concealing the full meaning of pictures, hiding a controversial message within a placid setting. We have seen a purposeful sleight of hand in his concealing of an English landscape within

The Festival upon the Opening of the Vintage of Macon, and in this book there are further examples of details that should be examined and considered in order to reveal their full meanings (for example pls. 137–39; cat. 120, 121, 123).

Pope's Villa at Twickenham was bought from Turner's gallery in 1808 by Sir John Leicester, and was engraved in 1811 by John Pye (1782–1874), with Charles Heath (1785–1848) working on the figures (pl. 60; cat. 68). Using a very wide variety of sensitive and considered strokes, dots and nicks in the copper plate, with none of the mechanical carelessness of the many commercial engravers who had handled Turner's work, Pye gave the engraved landscape a luminosity that delighted Turner. He exclaimed: "This will do! you can see the lights; had I known that there was a man who could do that, I would have had it done before."[22] The making of the engraving appears to have fuelled Turner's fury at the demolition of the house, for he wrote and rewrote many lines of poetry, some of which he might have hoped would be quoted in the margin of the print:

> Dear Sister Isis 'tis thy Thames that calls
> See desolation hovers o'er those walls
> The scattered timbers on my margin lays
> Where glimmering Evening's ray yet lingering plays
> There British Maro sung by Science long endear'd
> And to an admiring Country once rever'd
> Now to destruction doom'd thy peacefull grott
> Pope's willow bending to the earth forgot
> Save one weak scion by my fostering care
> Nursed into life … wild fell destruction there
> On the lone Bank … to mark the spot with pride
> dip the long branches in the rippling tide
> And sister stream the tender plant to rear
> On Twickenham's shore Pope's memory yet to hear.[23]

When, in the poem, Turner refers to "British Maro", he is specifically comparing Pope with the great Latin poet Virgil (Vergilius Maro); and when he creates in his Thames-side subjects an Arcadia on a slow-flowing British river, he is attempting to render the landscape feeling of Pope, Thomson and Virgil in paint. Turner goes even further in his poem to identify himself with Pope by switching clumsily to the first person: when he writes of "one weak scion by my fostering care" he is bringing himself into the poetic picture, and may also be referring back to Pope's planting of the willow shoot. The whole affair had outraged Turner's sense of propriety and the rightness of things, offending the memory of a great man, and allowing fashion to dictate the nature of progress – "capricious fashion's chain", as Turner described it in one of the drafts of his poem.[24]

61 J.M.W. Turner, or possibly Thomas Lupton, *Stonehenge*, c. 1824, mezzotint, 19.2 × 26.2 cm (7½ × 10¼ in.) (image), Boston, Museum of Fine Arts

In the *Liber Studiorum* series Turner published prints of his oil paintings both to broaden his audience and to protect himself from copyists. In doing so he enabled the creation of superbly atmospheric works of art such as this, which gave familiar subjects a fresh approach.

In 1809 a writer in the *Repository of Arts* declared that two paintings of Tabley House (pls. 71, 72; cat. 44, 45) "touched by his magic pencil have assumed a highly poetical character. It is on occasions like this that the superiority of this man's mind displays itself."[25] These words are an indication that it was becoming understood that Turner gave more than just an image in his art: that there was an inclusivity to his pictures, and an awareness of a wider poetic world, to which contemporary painters might aspire but few could match. Throughout his work we see how Turner understands the relationship between person and place, whether it be the gentle rustics whose lives and works are themselves woven into the fabric of the Thames landscape, or the great characters of history and literature. Pope and Thomson are his exemplars in the context of the Thames-side landscape, and we shall see later how Charles I, Oliver Cromwell, Horatio Nelson and the Duke of Wellington (as well as the man-o'-war the *Temeraire*) play their own parts through Turner's brush in his grand parade of British history.

The early 1800s were the years in which Turner, in his early thirties, consolidated his reputation as an artist of the first rank. Well aware that his work had resonance and value beyond the walls of the Academy, his patrons' houses or his own gallery, he began in about 1806 to make and commission engravings of his past and current work. Taking inspiration from Claude's own

62 *Steeton Manor House, near Farnley*, *c.* 1815–18, gouache and watercolour, 10.5 × 16.2 cm (4¹⁄₈ × 6³⁄₈ in.), New Haven CT, Yale Center for British Art

This rural idyll, with its fruitpickers and laundrymaids, depicts the former home of Sir Thomas Fairfax, a seventeenth-century forebear of Walter Fawkes, whose commanding role in the Parliamentarian army during the English Civil War was one of the inspirations behind Turner's *Fairfaxiana* (see pls. 143–47).

engraved record of his compositions, the *Liber Veritatis*, Turner instituted his *Liber Studiorum* ('Book of Studies'), in which his compositions were recorded in etching and mezzotint.[26] What might have begun as a primitive self-help exercise in copyright protection developed over twelve years into a pocket-sized guide to the master's work, divided into thematic sections (pl. 61; cat. 72).[27] Turner's first collaborator on this venture was Charles Turner, with whom he had worked on the engraving of the oil painting *The Shipwreck* (exhibited and engraved in 1805; London, Tate). From the beginning the plan was to issue groups of five prints for sale every few months, and this gave the painter his first experience of the risky business of multi-plate print selling to subscribers. The choice of subjects – from pastoral groups freshly worked out in pen and ink to epic subjects from oils and watercolours exhibited at the Academy – revealed that Turner's intention was to make all aspects of his work available as prints, and foreshadowed the purposes of his print series yet to come.

63 John Varley, *Portrait of Walter Fawkes*, *c.* 1820, pencil, London, Victoria and Albert Museum

A Yorkshire politician, landowner and collector, Walter Fawkes was one of Turner's staunchest friends.

The man whose friendship with Turner was deeper and more rewarding than any other, and who introduced the world of national politics to him, was Walter Fawkes (pl. 63). The two men first met in the early 1800s, a few years after Fawkes had inherited Farnley Hall and its 15,000-acre estate near Otley in Yorkshire. From his youth Fawkes had been a passionate democrat and he stood twice for election to Parliament in the Whig interest: once in 1796, when he was defeated by his neighbour the Tory Henry Lascelles, and again in 1806, when he was elected MP for York. His radical credentials, and his unswerving support of the radical MP Sir Francis Burdett

64 *Caley Hall, c.* 1818, watercolour and bodycolour, 30.2 × 42.7 cm (11⅞ × 16¾ in.), Edinburgh, National Galleries of Scotland
Turner evokes all aspects of life on the Farnley estate in a series of fifty watercolours made for Walter Fawkes. Here, a hunting party is returning to Caley Hall, the home of John Raistrick, Fawkes's steward. The gardening tools and beeskeps to the left indicate the pleasures and duties of rural life.

(1770–1844), caused many to be wary of him. Writing in 1815, the botanist Charles Lyell (1767–1849) said that there was much to admire at Fawkes's "magnificent seat" and "nothing to regret but his being a furious *Burdettite*!!"[28] He and Turner sat together regularly at the annual dinner to celebrate Royal Academy exhibitions,[29] and that and other indications marked Turner out as also having radical tendencies.

Fawkes was rich, generous and eager to collect art by living artists for his house, which had a spacious new south wing waiting to be hung with pictures. He ordered thirty of the Alpine watercolours that Turner painted after his 1802 tour, and as their friendship developed he bought fifty-one watercolours painted after Turner's 1817 journey down the Rhine and commissioned dozens of views of Wharfedale, of life on the Farnley estate, and of exteriors and interiors of the hall itself. He also came to own five of Turner's most important oil paintings, including *Portrait of the Victory, in Three Positions* (exh. ?1806; New Haven CT, Yale Center for

British Art), and *Dort, or Dordrecht, the Dort Packet-Boat from Rotterdam Becalmed* (1818; New Haven CT, Yale Center for British Art).

The Wharfedale subjects, of which there are six in this book (pls. 62, 64–68; cat. 54–59), range from the broad view of *Bolton Abbey, Yorkshire* (pl. 68; cat. 54), to the delicate scale of *Steeton Manor House, near Farnley* (pl. 62; cat. 55). In the latter, a small and intense picture, everyday domestic incidents become moments of universal significance: the light of the setting sun is reflected in the windows of the manor; a woman hangs up washing to dry; others pick apples. In its tiny scale it is quite unlike anything else Turner had painted before he embarked on his long series of vignettes of the 1820s and 1830s. *Caley Hall* (pl. 64; cat. 56) is an entrancing image in gouache of men and dogs returning from a hunt carrying a deer, with intimate details of beeskeps,

65 *Huntsmen in a Wood*, 1820s, pen and sepia ink and wash, 19.4 × 26.3 cm (7⅝ × 10⅜ in.), London, British Museum

This lively pen and ink study may represent a hunt at Farnley. It was purchased by the British Museum in 1861 and, outside the Turner Bequest, was one of the first Turner drawings to enter a public collection.

66 *Lake Tiny, with Alm's Cliff in the distance*, c. 1818, watercolour and bodycolour, 33 × 43.9 cm (13 × 17¼ in.), Hereford Museum and Art Gallery

A view from Thornberry Hill on the Farnley estate. Alm's Cliff is in the distance on the left, with the Wharfe valley on the right.

67 *Farnley Hall from above Otley*, c. 1815, watercolour, 28 × 39.8 cm (11 × 15⅝ in.), Amsterdam, Rijksmuseum

This view reveals the wide extent of the moorland in which Farnley Hall is sited. The house is just visible in the distance, with the River Wharfe in the middleground. The prominent pine trees and boulders in the foreground invite comparison with Turner's Swiss views, as if the artist were referring to the Swiss watercolours that he had already sold to Walter Fawkes.

garden implements and summer flowers evoking the homeliness of Farnley estate life. An exquisite sepia drawing, *Huntsmen in a Wood* (pl. 65; cat. 58), depicts an earlier moment in a hunt, with men and animals in hot pursuit of the quarry. The detail and feeling in Turner's drawings in and around Farnley evoke not only his happiness in being part of the family environment that Walter Fawkes created around himself, but also reflect the freedom that Turner felt in Fawkes's company. According to Ruskin, Turner's emotions overcame him when in later life he recalled Wharfedale, the memory of which "he never could revisit without tears; nay, which for all the latter part of his life, he never could speak of, but his voice faltered."[30]

Turner was also a regular visitor to Fawkes's London house, 45 Grosvenor Place, on the edge of Hyde Park. There Fawkes organized two exhibitions for his friend, the first in 1819 comprising over sixty of the Turner watercolours in his collection – including pls. 68, 95; cat. 54, 80 – and paintings by other artists such as Joshua Cristall and John Glover. Animated crowds were attracted to this exhibition, the crush being graphically described in the *Literary Gazette*:

68 *Bolton Abbey, Yorkshire*, 1809, watercolour, 27.8 × 39.5 cm (11 × 15 ½ in.), London, British Museum

The full signature "JMW Turner RA PP" (*i.e.* Professor of Perspective) suggests that Turner was thoroughly satisfied with this limpid evening view in Wharfedale. It is a celebration of the marriage of Britain's natural beauty with her historic past.

… the ebb of one ocean was opposed by the flow of another, which came pounding
into the hall and up the stairs … . The scene that then presented itself was certainly
far from decorum – "Quite a noonday rout", as a lady remarked. We … remained
jammed in the landing-place for at least half an hour, during which we saw rouge
melted, teeth dropped, feathers broken, bonnets crushed, flounces torn, humps
pulled off … . Indeed if Mr F. was in future to close his doors against the public, it is
only what they have deserved.[31]

When there was space to do so, Turner himself patrolled the room "like a victorious Roman
General", as one visitor observed.[32]

Turner's watercolour *London, from the windows of 45 Grosvenor Place* (pl. 69; cat. 60) suggests that
the artist had time on his hands when staying with Fawkes in Grosvenor Place. Turner's own
house was not far away in Harley Street, but he may have been Fawkes's guest late in 1820, when
his own house was uninhabitable owing to construction work.[33] This atmospheric view from

Fawkes's house, faintly echoing the composition of the engraving of London that Turner had coloured as a boy in Boswell's *Picturesque Views of the Antiquities of England and Wales* (pl. 12; cat. 1), shows Buckingham House in the middle distance, with St Paul's Cathedral beyond, and Westminster Abbey and St Margaret's, Westminster, to the right. Buckingham House was remodelled by John Nash in 1825, indicating that the drawing was made some time earlier.

Though displayed to the invited London public in 1819, Turner's drawings and watercolours for Fawkes had been shown off regularly to visitors to Farnley, and had an impact far beyond Turner's or Fawkes's expectations. One Farnley visitor, Anna Maria Crompton, reported to her son William Rookes Crompton that

> Mr Cope … saw Mr Turner's drawings at Farnley, which he is so frantic about, that upon his little daughter's being born a few days after he has called her Turner, which has no little amused Mr Fawkes.[34]

In this extraordinarily productive period of Turner's life, in which his fame as an artist reached so far that an admirer's baby daughter was burdened with his name, he carried out a series of paintings of the houses and estates of some of the most influential men in England. Sir John Leicester commissioned him to paint two views of his Cheshire house, Tabley, and Lord Lonsdale to paint Lowther Castle, near Penrith in Cumbria (pls. 73–75; cat. 50–52). Portraits of Cockermouth Castle, Cumbria (exh. 1810; Petworth) and Petworth House in Sussex were commissioned by the Earl of Egremont. Some other paintings may have been speculative, such as *Cassiobury Park: Reaping* (c. 1809; London, Tate), which may have been intended for the Earl of Essex; yet others, such as *Linlithgow Palace, Scotland* (exh. 1810; Liverpool, Walker Art Gallery), were painted for collectors whose connection with the property was indirect.

The subject of celebration in these paintings is certainly property and landscape, and of Britain as a European power, but it is also the celebration of the *status quo* of the English landed families, their roots, riches and influence, something to which Turner could not yet have expected any end. The naturalism of this sequence of paintings is apparent in the examples in this book, the two Tabley House pictures (pls. 71, 72; cat. 44, 45) and *Petworth, Sussex, the Seat of the Earl of Egremont: Dewy Morning* (pl. 70; cat. 46), where effects of wind or its absence, of morning light, of dryness and dewiness, of specific times of day are integrated subtly into the day-to-day activities of the place depicted, and signalled in the titles.

Painted to hang together, that is as 'pendants', the two paintings of Tabley, *Tabley, the Seat of Sir J.F. Leicester, Bart.: Windy Day* (pl. 71; cat. 44) and *Tabley, Cheshire, the Seat of Sir J.F. Leicester, Bart.: Calm Morning* (pl. 72; cat. 45), show contrasting times of day and weather effects. Each reflects the influence of a seventeenth-century Dutch painter: *Windy Day* is rooted in the manner of Ruisdael and *Calm Morning* in that of Cuyp. The differing moods, the one active, the other passive,

70 *Petworth, Sussex, the Seat of the Earl of Egremont: Dewy Morning,* exhibited RA 1810, oil on canvas, 91.4 × 120.6 cm (36 × 47½ in.), London, Tate, on loan to Petworth House, Sussex

The title of this work is encyclopaedic, in the manner of early nineteenth-century paintings of property, indicating place, ownership, time of day and weather conditions.

are self-evident, but particularly subtle is the way in which Turner has shown how a very small shift of viewpoint in a landscape can produce a disproportionately significant change in composition. The house, as distant in these paintings as is the ruin in *Pope's Villa*, hops from the right-hand side of the water tower in one painting, to the left of it in the other. Having spent so much of his life travelling, Turner would have many times enjoyed the way landscape features appear to shift in relation to one another from the perspective of a moving vehicle. By introducing this effect into the paintings Turner adds a twist of visual pleasure that is entirely characteristic of him, but that is only noticeable when they are hung together.[35]

In *Petworth, Sussex ... Dewy Morning* the house also hovers in the background, with the golden sunrise casting the fishermen into shadow. Like the Tabley pictures, *Calm Morning* and *Windy Day*,

71 *Tabley, the Seat of Sir J.F. Leicester, Bart.: Windy Day*, exhibited RA 1809, oil on canvas, 91.5 × 120.6 cm (36 × 47½ in.), University of Manchester, Tabley House Collection

The stiff wind that has suddenly set the becalmed boats into motion links this painting with its pendant, pl. 72. Together, they are a celebration of Britain's varied and changeable climate, which produces such a range of pictorial natural effects.

72 *Tabley, Cheshire, the Seat of Sir J.F. Leicester, Bart.: Calm Morning,* exhibited RA 1809, oil on canvas, 91.5 × 116.8 cm (36 × 46 in.), London, Tate, on loan to Petworth House, Sussex

While it's pair, pl. 71, is composed in horizontal bands leading one deep into the picture, this work has a calming set of verticals that carry the eye across the composition in the manner of Aelbert Cuyp.

its title contains a deliberate indication of a particular time of day and weather. Turner's landscapes are never static – a carriage or boat may be on the move in one, some figures may be shouting or dancing in another, the light shifting in all of them – and what the artist is evoking with these and other devices is the passage of time. In *Petworth, Sussex … Dewy Morning* the time change is subtle and slow, but distinctly present. Evoking the movement of time from dawn to day, the light creeps in from the left directly in front of the house and etches the window frames in shadow. It flows over the hill on the left, lighting the valley bottom as it does so, and most dramatically lights the upper section of the boathouse on the bank. The clothes of the fishermen in the left-hand boat are touched by light, while those on the right are not. Contrasts and oppositions of this kind flicker meaningfully around the picture, in which Turner is presenting a solemn moment of transition.

73 *Lowther Castle*, 1809, pencil,
22 × 35.3 cm (8⁵⁄₈ × 13⁷⁄₈ in.),
Oxford, Ashmolean Museum

74 *Distant view of Lowther Castle*,
1809, pencil, 21.3 × 35.7 cm
(8³⁄₈ × 14 in.), Oxford, Ashmolean
Museum

75 *Distant view of Lowther Castle*, 1809, pencil and watercolour, 22.5 × 35.4 cm (8⅞ × 14 in.), Oxford, Ashmolean Museum

A working study, like pls. 73 and 74, in which Turner gathers topographical and tonal information for a pair of oil paintings commissioned by Lord Lonsdale.

So subtle is his treatment that as we follow the rolling light around the canvas we may suspect that on looking again at the glowing sky it has, in fact, got brighter.

Complete though these paintings are, there is closely observed pencilwork in the *Lowther Castle* studies (pls. 73–75; cat. 50–52) that is of an intensity that does not reach the oils. This sequence of preliminary drawings for Turner's paintings of Lowther Castle reveal the precision with which the artist approached the subject, sitting with his pencil and sketchbook on a gate or stile intently observing the landscape and placement of the building within it. We can share the thrill of his encounter with something as humble and ordinary as the thistle, the pencilled lines of which Turner articulated with watercolour, perhaps when he got back to his room that same evening. While Turner's ability to draw and paint with the precision and care of a recording angel remained with him well into his old age, the focus of his intensity as an artist did not remain static. When a critic saw *Linlithgow Palace, Scotland* in Manchester in 1829, nineteen years after it had been first exhibited, he wrote: "Ah, Turner, Turner! Why will you not paint thus now? Why will you not leave gamboge, maguilp and quackery, and return to nature?"[36]

In addition to purchasing the leasehold of his house in Harley Street and later another house nearby in Queen Anne Street West, Turner had built himself a small country lodge, Sandycombe Lodge in Twickenham, and owned property in Wapping, Barkingside, Great Missenden and perhaps also latterly in eastern Kent. He may have bought other properties in London for investment and income, as an alternative to keeping his money in government securities.[37] At a time when banks were unstable, Turner did not have a bank account.[38] A pencil sketch on a double-page spread in the 'River and Margate' sketchbook (1806–08), inscribed "Court Leet", shows a group of figures at a rural hearing, and was almost certainly drawn during one of the many court appearances Turner seems to have made to secure his rights and income as a landlord (pl. 76).[39] The inscriptions beside the figures include "Clerk of the Court", "Chairman Jury", "… of Rent", "Villain", "Lawyers … session", indicating Turner's close attention to court business, and also perhaps that he was forming an idea that might serve as the basis for a genre painting in the manner of *The Country Blacksmith* (exh. 1807; London, Tate), *The Unpaid Bill* (exh. 1808; Christies sale, 27 November 2002, lot 5) or *The Garreteer's Petition* (exh. 1809; London, Tate). There is much evidence that Turner was careful, if not close, with his property and money throughout his life. Many sketchbooks – used for personal notes, as well as for sketches – have banknote numbers listed for security; others list money he was owed or was claiming, and yet others money that he had lent.

Growing deeper into the fabric of the Royal Academy, Turner was elected Professor of Perspective in 1807, a post he held for thirty years. His words to his students were lucid, rousing and inclusive, and showed them how aware he was of the hard lifelong task for which they were preparing. In an early draft of one of his first lectures Turner praised and encouraged his students with a call to their patriotic spirit:

76 *Group of figures at a Court Leet*, 1806–08, pencil, 11.5 × 19 cm (4½ × 7½ in.), London, Tate. From the 'River and Margate' sketchbook, TB XCIX, fols. 48-47a.

A rapid study from life, revealing that Turner attended court sessions. He was highly litigious over property matters, and this may be a hearing in which he took part.

To you young gentlemen must the nation look for the further advance of our profession and in our toil at the steep ascent we have made … the pursuit of all that is meritorious to fix irrevocably the triple standard of the art in the British Empire.[40]

The extensive poetry in Turner's 'Perspective' sketchbook, in use in around 1809 when he was first beginning to think about his lectures at the Academy, contains lines that reflect his profound love of Britain, expressed with fierce but fashionable anti-French sentiments:

And now the ensigns broad displayed
Britannia glory waved arrayed
In Crimson grounds the moral Crown
Of Commerce fair resplendant shone
The cross and Union sympathise
And wide oer all thy banner flies
Of fam'd St George of sanguine hue
Whose trenchant sword the dragon slew
Waved oer the field of maiden white
Thy crimson cross appear more bright
The humbled pride of Gallic chance
The boasted triple flag of France.[41]

In 1811 Turner was invited by the engravers William Cooke (1778–1855) and his brother George Cooke (1781–1834) to take part in creating a set of engravings of scenes in southern England; the plan was to issue them in sixteen parts, one part every two months. The work was completed in 1826 and published in two volumes as *Picturesque Views on the Southern Coast of England*. Although thirteen other artists contributed images, Turner was the celebrity whose name was required to ensure the project's commercial success.[42] The *Southern Coast* commission came at exactly the right time for Turner, and it presented him with some reasonably well-funded and achievable opportunities that were in tune with the pattern of his creativity. In contrast to his private *Liber Studiorum* venture Turner was not expected to take on a financial risk. The Cookes initially asked Turner to provide twenty-four watercolours for £7. 10s. each, raised to 10 guineas in 1824. Although his relationship with the Cookes came to grief some years later, it was in high hopes and spirits that Turner set off in mid-July 1811 on his first tour of the West of England.

He left London with a passionate feeling for the history and purpose of Britain high in his mind. Before he set off he had written much, if not all, of a sixty-four-verse poem that described at a rapid and fulsome pace what Britain had achieved, who its great heroes were and in which direction it might be headed as a nation. It opens with what is essentially a prayer:

To that kind Providence that guides our step
Fain would I offer all that my powers hold
And hope to be successful in my weak attempt
To please. The difficulty great but when nought
Attempted nothing can be wrought
Trials thankfull for the mental powers givn
Whether innate or the gift of Heaven
Perception reason's actions close ally
Thoughts that in the mind embedded lie …

                                 … power

A steady current nor with headlong force
Leaving fair nature's bosom in its course
But like the Thames majestic broad and deep
Meandring greatness behold the yon
On each circling sweep.[43]

If the last few lines refer, as they might, to Turner's view of how he should conduct himself as an artist – "like the Thames majestic broad and deep" – he is also presenting himself as having a role in the making of a new perception of Britain. Passing from yet another allusion to Alexander Pope and his demolished house, Turner describes how "the stimulus act from Runny mead" (*i.e.* the signing of the Magna Carta at Runnymede in 1215) spurred Britons on to maintain their liberty and freedom, and to travel the world bringing peace: "The parched tracks of Memphis arid sands/ And planted laurel wreath in hostile lands". As 'history', the poem, and with it Turner's outlook, may be partial and partisan, but it was written by a great patriot in the hope of arousing patriotic feeling at a time when Britain was at war with France, and had no certainty of ultimate victory. The poem rolls on with some jaunty couplets and wordplay; although Turner's poetic sources are usually quite clear – Shakespeare, Milton, Pope, Thomson and Gray all sing in ragged concert here – his enthusiasm for epitomizing Britain in verse is heartfelt and infectious. Its rhythms and cadences suggest that the poetry should best be heard declaimed through a megaphone. In choosing a few examples of his phrases, we can discover different characteristics of Turner. Here, the knowing topographer:

Hill after hill incessant cheats the eye
While each the intermediate space deny[44]

Here, the practised sailor with a real knowledge of local conditions:

77 *Falmouth Harbour, Cornwall,*
c. 1812–13, watercolour,
15.2 × 22.9 cm (6 × 9 in.).
Engraved 1816. Port Sunlight,
Lady Lever Art Gallery

The carousing sailors on shore leave
make an appropriate counterpoint
to the ships at anchor in the
harbour. Painted during the last
years of the Napoleonic Wars, the
peacefulness of the scene reflects
the dominance of Britain's naval
power at this time.

Whoever lucklessly are driven
From Portland seeks an eastern haven
Must luff against the south west gale
and strike for Poole alone the tortured sail
For Wight again their safe return denys
The needles brave the force of Southern skies.[45]

Here, the observer of industry:

… summer skies
Permit the Quarry to give up its prize
The tinkling hammer and the driving bore
Detaching fragments from the massy store

Then squared or rough in a shallow yawl

The wadding workmen by mere strength do hawl.[46]

Here, the Classical scholar:

Thus Regulus whom every torture did await

Denyd himself admittance at the gate

Because of captive to proud Carthage power

But his firm soul would not the Romans lower

Not wife or children dear or self could hold

A Moments parley – love made him bold

Love of his country for not aught beside

He loved but for that love he died.[47]

In a final burst he campaigns for a monument to Horatio Nelson, following the example of John Opie, who had presented such a proposal before he died:[48]

Such that most een follow Nelson …

Would pleasing view his Cenotaph arise

On some bold promontary where the western main …

A Sea mark emulating reverd and ever known

My nation gratitudes [in] monumental stone.[49]

Turner had high hopes for his poetry and had already published extracts as epigraphs to exhibited paintings. For this long untitled poem, however, he had particularly great ambitions and offered it to the Cooke brothers as the text to be published alongside the *Southern Coast* engravings. It was summarily rejected,[50] but the intellectual effort that Turner generated to write it speaks clearly of its importance as an indication of the depth and richness of his engagement with British history. The hand that wrote the poems is the same hand that painted the pictures, and that reason alone should be sufficient for us to take Turner's verse seriously: how 'good' or 'bad' it is as poetry is irrelevant. These verses are the text for Turner's evolved purpose as an artist, for his mission to express the collective identity of Britain, and are a sign that he had at last defined what his life's work was to be.

The first set of nine images published by the Cookes in January 1814 comprised views by Turner of St Michael's Mount, Poole, Corfe Castle, Weymouth, Lulworth Cove, Lyme Regis, Teignmouth, Dartmouth and Land's End. Although most of these are views in Dorset, they do not represent a tour in any rational geographical order, but reflect those subjects that first quickened

78 George Cooke after J.M.W. Turner, *Land's End, Cornwall*, 1814, engraving, 14 × 22 cm (5¹⁄₂ × 8⁵⁄₈ in.), Birmingham Museums & Art Gallery. Engraving after a lost original for *Picturesque Views on the Southern Coast of England*

The importance of this fine engraving is greatly enhanced by the fact that is represents the only record of the lost original. That was described in 1822 as being 'truly Miltonic'.

79 *Plymouth, with Mount Batten*, *c*. 1814, watercolour, 14.6 × 23.5 cm (5³⁄₄ × 9¹⁄₄ in.). Engraved 1817. London, Victoria and Albert Museum

Even during the peace that followed Wellington's victory at Waterloo in 1815, soldiers and sailors in uniform were an everyday sight. Here, the fleet safely in dock and the resting soldier, marine and country women evoke the calm of a nation at peace.

Turner's interest. With the exception of *Corfe Castle* (Harvard, Fogg Art Museum), all of the first set are views of the sea from the land (pl. 78; cat. 69): Turner places the viewer within the security of the nation, looking out to the vast and unpredictable sea. This firm stance on land is evident in the majority of the *Southern Coast* subjects, and has a potency that is immediately apparent and inclusive: these are Britons'-eye-views observing the nation's mercantile and naval entrances from within, and hence from a position of belonging. By contrast, the title of the main commercial rival of the Cooke brothers' project – *A Voyage Around Great Britain*, the set of eight volumes, published from 1814 to 1825, of aquatints by William Daniell ARA (1749–1840) with accompanying text by Richard Ayton – suggests a wholly different attitude and point of view.[51] Daniell's commission took him by ship clockwise around the coast, starting and finishing at Land's End in Cornwall. Although Daniell made excursions inland, his 308 aquatints are made from drawings done after innumerable landings from the sea, and take a long look at Britain from the outside, as an invader would.

In his *Southern Coast* verse Turner is not uncritical of Britain, but suggests quite frankly that those wanting more sun should go to India, otherwise:

80 *Boscastle, Cornwall, c.* 1824, watercolour, 14.1 × 23 cm (5 1/2 × 9 in.). Engraved 1825. Oxford, Ashmolean Museum

Tiny groups of figures struggle to control the passage of a damaged trading vessel through the dangerously narrow entrance to Boscastle harbour. By contrasting the huge rocks with the fragile vessel in shifting light and stormy weather, Turner vividly describes the constant tension between man and the forces of nature.

81 *Bow and Arrow Castle, Island of Portland, c.* 1815, watercolour, 15.2 × 23 cm (6 × 9 in.). Engraved 1817. University of Liverpool Art Collections

The rugged coastline is echoed in the outlines of the eleventh-century castle. Beneath it the quarry swarms with activity as workmen prepare stone for building in a country at peace.

Plant but the ground with seed instead of Gold
Urge all our barren tracts by Agriculture skill
And Britain Britain British canvass fill
Alone and unsupported prove her strength.
By means her own to meet the direful length
Of continental hatred called blockade
When every power and every port is laid
Under the proscriptive term themselves have made.[52]

With the paintings to be engraved Turner is fully at home with his material. Although both *Falmouth Harbour, Cornwall* (pl. 77; cat. 61) and *Plymouth, with Mount Batten* (pl. 79; cat. 62) were painted before the final Allied victory at Waterloo in 1815, Turner shows a nation at peace with itself in these two watercolours of quiet harbours with distant ships at anchor. In both, the foreground figures of resting sailors, soldiers and harvesters beneath tranquil but atmospheric skies suggest that a long struggle is nearly over. *Bow and Arrow Castle, Island of Portland* (pl. 81; cat. 63)

depicts rather more than just the quarrying, "the tinkling hammer and the driving bore", that Turner described in his long untitled poem. In this complex picture the lines of natural forms – rock clefts, fallen cliffs and the distant Portland Bill – are echoed in those of the man-made castle, the wall running below it and the curve of the masons' sled in the foreground. Although there are no more than a dozen figures in the picture, it appears to be swarming with activity, with workmen preparing huge stones and slabs for the peacetime reconstruction of Britain.

The activity is yet more urgent in *Boscastle, Cornwall* (pl. 80; cat. 67). Here the enemy is the weather, and the task is to control the passage of a damaged trading vessel through the dangerously narrow entrance to Boscastle Harbour on the north coast of Cornwall. The technique shown of allowing the vessel to inch forwards under the guidance of men on the cliff edge was specific to Boscastle, where it developed over centuries of trading. Though bright in colour and with industrious activity, *St Mawes, Cornwall* (pl. 82; cat. 65) has a mood with darker undertones. The glistening piles of pilchards are being shovelled not for storage and sale as food, but to be dumped on the fields as manure.[53] As Sam Smiles has shown, St Mawes lost its traditional market

82 *St Mawes, Cornwall, c.* 1822, watercolour and scraping out, 14.1 × 21.7 cm (9½ × 8½ in.). Engraved 1824. New Haven CT, Yale Center for British Art

In contrast with his townscapes, to which he gives a romantic and atmospheric glow, Turner never tried to beautify his human figures but portrayed them as ordinary people, shaped by their work.

83 *Rye, Sussex, c.* 1823, watercolour, 14.5 × 22.7 cm (5¾ × 9 in.). Engraved 1824. Cardiff, National Museums and Galleries of Wales

Rye, in the distance, is shown to be much higher than in actuality, an example of Turner amending geographical reality to make his composition just that bit more dramatic. Beside the Royal Military Road, the workmen, now overwhelmed by the tide, have been building a temporary wooden dam.

84 Edward Goodall after J.M.W. Turner, *Rye, Sussex,* 1824, engraving, 14.8 × 23.3 cm (5⅞ × 9⅛ in.), Birmingham Museums & Art Gallery. Engraving after pl. 83 for *Picturesque Views on the Southern Coast of England*

The engraving increases the contrast between dark and light and sharpens the drama of the watercolour, at the same time clarifying some of Turner's detail.

85 George Cooke after J.M.W. Turner, *Hythe, Kent*, 1824, engraving, 15.1 × 23.2 cm (6 × 9⅛ in.), Birmingham Museums & Art Gallery. Engraving after pl. 86 for *Picturesque Views on the Southern Coast of England*

By his comments on an early proof of this engraving, Turner encouraged George Cooke to greater efforts: "I want flickering lights on [the Marsh] up to the sea."

for the fish – the Roman Catholic France, Spain and Ireland – during the Napoleonic Wars, but mindless as fish are of international politics, huge shoals continued to appear on the southern Cornish coast in late summer every year. The consequent depressed price of the fish brought poverty to the area in the midst of natural abundance. However, it is unlikely that by the time Turner painted the subject, about ten or eleven years after he had visited St Mawes, he gave a moment's thought to past economic conditions. Beyond the abundance of fish there is no other reference in the picture that touches on economic depression, and the most striking feature is the shining blue-green of the pilchards that fill the foreground and lie along the waves' edge and the distant sea wall.

A sudden storm is the setting of *Rye, Sussex* (pl. 83; cat. 64), and a mood bordering on panic is evident as the sea crashes on to the Royal Military Road running between Winchelsea and Rye. This is a much more actively gestural painting than *St Mawes*, with the lines of the rearing waves being echoed by those of the shattered timbers and gesticulating figures, and is a masterly example of Turner's orchestration of mood in landscape. Everything is 'rushing' in this work: the storm, the sea, the people, the dramatic diagonal of the road, the figure with upraised arms. All these elements play a part in heightening the tension. Though they differ in pace and tonality, *Rye, Sussex* is comparable with *Lancaster Sands* (pl. 116; cat. 96) in the way in which it depicts both the weather and the immediate and instinctive human response to it.

86 *Hythe, Kent, c.* 1823, watercolour,
14 × 22.9 cm (5 ½ × 9 in.).
Engraved 1824. London,
Guildhall Art Gallery

Britain's coastline bore many
traces relating to war – here we
see the sizeable barracks at Hythe.
Regiments moving across country
with their wagons, medical staff,
farriers and saddlers, together with
a straggle of women and children,
could overwhelm a small town.

Turner offered trenchant comments on the margins of proofs to the engravers of his work.
They reveal eloquently the lengths to which he would go to ensure that his watercolour and the
engraving of it were in harmony, and that neither was subordinate to the other. To George
Cooke, who engraved *Hythe, Kent* (pls. 85, 86; cat. 66, 71), he wrote:

> First I shall say in general *very good*, secondly the Figures and Barracks excellent; but
> I think you have cut up the Bank called Shorne Cliff too much with the graver by
> Lines [here a diagram] which are equal in strength and width and length, that give
> a coarseness to the quality, and do not look like my touches or give work-like look to
> the good part over which they are put – the Marsh is all swamp. I want flickering
> lights on it up to the sea, and altho' I have darkened the sea in parts you must not
> consider it to want strength, but that the whole Marsh and Sea down to the canal
> before the Barracks is too dark and not clear. Get it into one tone, flat, by dots or
> some means, and let the sea and water only appear different by their present lines.[54]

Turner's attachment to Devon, so evident in his *Southern Coast* watercolours, was confirmed when he returned to the county in the late summer of 1813.[55] On this visit he renewed friendships made in 1811, and painted a series of oil studies in the open air, directly in front of the subject (pls. 87, 88; cat. 48, 49). These works have a breadth of approach that distinguishes them from the constructed narratives of the *Southern Coast* watercolours, on which Turner, at home in London, was by now working one by one. Through the 1813 oil sketches he expressed another side of his nature, reconnecting with a more immediate and personal response to landscape which had already become evident in the Knockholt and Thames-side oil studies of 1789–99 and 1806–07 (pls. 39, 56; cat. 22, 41). These two threads, the impulsive and the ruminative, ran through Turner in counterpoint, and we see them emerging and re-emerging throughout his life.

87 *The Plym Estuary looking North*, 1813, oil on prepared paper, 15.5 × 25.7 cm (6⅛ × 10⅛ in.), London, Tate

On his second visit to Devon, in 1813, Turner painted in oils in the open air using a paintbox assembled for him by a friend. The studies on this trip are of a more informal nature than those made in and after 1811 for *Southern Coast*.

88 *The Plym Estuary from Boringdon Park*,
1813, oil on prepared paper,
24.5 × 30.5 cm (9⅝ × 12 in.), London,
Tate

This extensive vista is one of the sources
for Turner's oil *Crossing the Brook* (1815;
London, Tate) and prefigures his watercolours of the Roman Campagna of
1819–20. The eye is attracted forward by
the slight indications of haymakers and
their piles of coats in the foreground.

CHAPTER III

"The soil is British and so should be the harvest"
1815 to 1830

Looking out of a window in Richmond, Yorkshire, at the end of July 1816, Turner wrote to his friend James Holworthy (1781–1841): "Weather miserably wet; I shall be web-footed like a drake … but I must proceed northwards".[1] This was no usual complaint against the British weather, but a heartfelt response to what was becoming the wettest and coldest summer in living memory. The extreme weather was caused by the quantities of dust and ash thrown into the atmosphere by the eruption of the Tambora volcano, in what is now Indonesia, in 1815. It led to 90,000 deaths in the region around the volcano, a disastrous harvest in Britain, and for Turner – in Yorkshire to find subjects to illustrate a *General History of the County of York* – extreme inconvenience, delay and foul travelling conditions.

Turner had been offered 3000 guineas (£3150 – equivalent today to between £120,000 and £150,000) to produce 120 new watercolours of Yorkshire subjects, to be engraved under the commercial leadership of the publisher Thomas Longman. They were intended to illustrate an ambitious new history of that county conceived by the antiquarian the Revd Thomas Dunham Whitaker (1759–1821). The fee offered,[2] which was triple that of the initial fee paid by the Cookes for Turner's *Southern Coast* watercolours, was unprecedented for any British artist. It reflected both the value that such a shrewd publisher as Longman believed that Turner would bring to the project, and Longman's optimistic financial outlook in the year after the end of the Napoleonic Wars. The contract with Longman sent Turner northwards initially in high spirits, despite the rain. He went first to Farnley, where he made his base, then west to Whalley and Browsholme in Lancashire, and north-east to Askrigg, Richmond and Barnard Castle.[3] He proceeded on a 130-mile loop westwards over the moors to Appleby-in-Westmorland, Kendal and the Lake District, across Lancaster Sands to Lancaster and back via Skipton to Farnley.

On the first part of the journey into Lancashire Turner travelled with Walter Fawkes and his family, the women and children in a coach, Fawkes and Turner riding behind on horseback. After nine days in the rain, they parted at Malham.[4] Being under contract to Longman did not,

89 *Lancaster Sands, c.* 1818, detail of pl. 95

113

however, mean that Turner's obligations to the Cooke brothers for the *Southern Coast* series had ceased. His life was just becoming more complicated, and with Yorkshire on his mind he was still being pursued at a distance by Cooke to produce watercolours of southern subjects. A parcel from Cooke caught up with Turner at Farnley. It was there, one of the few places outside his London studio where he could actually paint in peace, that Turner seems to have commented on and amended a proof of an engraving, and finished a watercolour of Devon. Writing from Farnley to William Cooke, Turner remonstrated, "I really do think you must, notwithstanding you have waited, still give me some praise for sending you a drawing by the same parcel and so *soon*."[5]

The studies he made in the sketchbooks he took with him to Yorkshire are modest pencil notations of landscape form, and do not in themselves give much of a flavour of the extraordinarily rich effects that Turner invested in the coming watercolours.[6] In this respect the sketches are comparable not with the atmospheric and free watercolour studies in the sketchbooks for the 1798 and 1801 Welsh and Scottish tours, but with the workmanlike information-gathering of the 1794 Midlands drawings and of the sketches made on his visits to the Low Countries in 1817 and Italy in 1819. Thus Turner altered his manner of sketching to suit his varied purposes.

While Turner's pencil studies of the landscape through which he passed were drawn as rapidly as time and weather allowed, the watercolours were produced over subsequent years, at home in tranquility. In the comparative calm of the studio Turner appears to have remembered, as is evident in the watercolours, that the sun came out rather more than it actually did on his journey. This suggests first that Turner was not dealing in these works with momentary, literal 'impressions'; secondly, that he wanted to communicate his understanding that change in landscape is immeasurably slow, and that although the landscape may be washed by rain or obscured by cloud, it is not materially altered by them; and thirdly, that, being mindful that the weather in 1816 was exceptional, he attempted as best he could to represent the normal conditions of Yorkshire weather. The role of the works, as engravings, was after all to reflect the form and essence of the North of England as it had been for centuries; it was not to be a diary of 1816. This leads to a fourth observation: that memory, like change in landscape, is long, slow and selective. The order in which the invariably undated watercolours were made is not known for certain: although the order in which the engravings were published may be a guide, this measure is unreliable, especially since some engravers may have taken longer over their work than others.

It is clear through looking carefully at the watercolours from the 1816 tour that they are concerned with universals in nature and the place of people in the natural scheme. There is an insistent 'hugeness' about them that belies their small scale. The examples here have been chosen to reflect some of the variety of approaches and meanings that Turner brought to his subjects. *Junction of the Greta and the Tees at Rokeby* (pl. 90; cat. 77) is a complex composition with a succession of three focal points across the picture plane: from left to right the wooded crag, the glimpse through the trees towards Rokeby Hall and the long, distant view up the River Tees. The River

90 *Junction of the Greta and the Tees at Rokeby*, c. 1816, watercolour, 29 × 41.4 cm (11⅜ × 16¼ in.). Engraved 1819. Oxford, Ashmolean Museum

In 1816 Turner was offered the huge sum of 3000 guineas to produce 120 new watercolours of Yorkshire subjects to be engraved. While depicting specific places, they also prompt the viewer to consider the universal truths of nature and the place of people in the natural scheme.

Greta, running across the foreground to the confluence with the Tees, is not depicted in the spate that it would have been in the summer of 1816. The central vista to the house is framed through an 'eye' of trees and shrubs, and, in its dappled effect of light, is a picture-within-a-picture, a miniature view encircled by the two rivers. Though nowhere near as expansive, and always remaining a modest image of privacy and enclosure, *Junction of the Greta and the Tees at Rokeby* does bear some comparison with *England: Richmond Hill* (pl. 106; cat. 73). In both there is a river on a right-hand curve, an enclosed vista (in *England: Richmond Hill* this is on the extreme right) and on the left an 'eye-catcher' that returns the viewer's attention to the centre. Turner used these compositional elements throughout his mature career, and in their variety they demonstrate how firmly constructed and how carefully thought out his pictures are; further variations on these features can be seen, for example, in *Huntsmen in a Wood* (pl. 65; cat. 58), in the two versions of *Okehampton Castle* (pls. 100, 117; cat. 84, 97), and *Blenheim House and Park, Oxfordshire* (pl. 138; cat. 123).

91 *Crook of Lune*, 1816, pencil, 12.5 × 20.3 cm (4⅞ × 8 in.), London, Tate. From the 'Yorkshire 4' sketchbook, TB CXLVII, fol. 35a.

An on-the-spot sketch. Comparison with pl. 92 shows that the Crook is much lower in reality, and the river is barely visible on the right. Thus, Turner altered the geography for pictorial effect.

This leads us to consider the intellectual side of Turner, and how he transmuted his initial ruminations on his subjects into constructed works of art. The pencil study of the Crook of Lune, a dramatic bend in the River Lune near Lancaster, was made on the spot and simply maps out the view, with annotations. It is an exercise of skill, and is not of itself art (pl. 91).[7] In the finished watercolour, *Crook of Lune, looking towards Hornby Castle* (pl. 92; cat. 78), the depth of the landscape is foreshortened to compress the view of the central spit of land encircled by the river; the hillside to the left rises up in response; and a meandering segment of dry-stone wall runs up the back of the encircled area to the extent that the whole thing takes on the character of a serpent. Though based on the actual view, this is a constructed work of art in which Turner heaved and tugged the forms of the landscape into shapes that reflect the character of the place, if not so much its actual appearance: it is a portrait, not a map.

Turner used many visual tricks to help the viewer to read the image. Sitting discreetly in the central far distance is Hornby Castle. Though it is practically invisible, its presence is signalled from the left by the distant curve of the river; from the right by the line of the further plain; from above by the neat meeting of the descending lines of two hills; and from below by a group of cows, a slab of rock and a man holding a pickaxe. Tied in by such subtle horizontal and vertical indicators, Hornby Castle thus becomes the focus of the painting. Dancing around the whole composition are the curves of the river, set off by the plume of smoke and bent trees on the left, and the shifting shadows to the right and left of centre. In reading the picture in this way we are

witnessing a master at work, orchestrating the eternal landscape form to make it look more like the real landscape than it had ever been, or is ever likely to be.

Simmer Lake, near Askrigg (pl. 93; cat. 79) has quite different associations. The composition is simple, centralized and presented in bands that give prominence to the huge foreground boulder, the Carlow Stone, on the shore of Semer Water in Wensleydale. A local legend tells that the Devil dropped the rock when he failed to throw it across the lake and left his claw marks on it. Eric Shanes suggests very convincingly that Turner silently recounted the story in his picture by giving the black cow sitting to the right of the rock a distinctly devilish pose, and by peppering the foreground with a procession of horned shapes – the milkmaid's hat, left; the prongs of the mooring post and the pitchfork, right; and the cows' horns throughout. Also, he has shown the Devil's supposed claw-marks on the rock itself.[8] Legends of this kind, set here in a peerless sun-dappled landscape, recur with other historical and social references as the fabric underlying Turner's

93 (above) *Simmer Lake, near Askrigg,* *c.* 1817, watercolour, 28.7 × 41.2 cm (11¼ × 16¼ in.). Engraved 1822. London, British Museum

According to legend, the Devil dropped the huge foreground boulder and left his claw-marks on it. Turner depicts the Devil's supposed marks on the rock, and has given the black cow to the right a distinctly devilish pose.

94 (left) Henry le Keux after J.M.W. Turner, *Simmer Lake, near Askrigg,* 1822, engraving, 19 × 26.7 cm (7½ × 10½ in.), Birmingham Museums & Art Gallery. Engraving after pl. 93 for *History of Richmondshire*

95 *Lancaster Sands, c.* 1818, watercolour, 28 × 36.6 cm (11 × 14⅜ in.), Birmingham Museums & Art Gallery

This is one of Turner's most clearly autobiographical watercolours. He made the journey across Lancaster Sands in 1816, during the worst summer in living memory. The driver flogs the horses as the tide begins to lap around the coach wheels. Sprigs of laurel, or 'brobs', mark out a safe route ahead.

watercolours for engraving. By trying to decode the associated narrative, however lightly it may be alluded to, we are able to experience to a far greater degree the richness of Turner's art.

Out of the 120 subjects planned initially for the *General History of the County of York*, Turner painted only about twenty. Eighteen of these had been engraved by the time the project petered out at the end of the decade for lack of the anticipated finance and subscribers. Longman had already curtailed his geographical ambition and retitled the first few issues of prints, published from 1818, as *The History of Richmondshire*, 'Richmondshire' being part of the North Riding of Yorkshire. When Whitaker died in 1821 the contract lapsed. One of the casualties, a work painted but never engraved, was *Lancaster Sands* (pls. 89, 95; cat. 80). Here Turner painted the weather in something approaching its prevailing character of 1816 – cold, wet, windy and very dangerous – as a coach and other travellers hurry against the incoming tide to cross the ten miles of sands from Kent's Bank on the Cartmel Peninsula to Hest Bank, near

Lancaster. For those travelling from Ulverston to Lancaster this was the second of two stretches of sands, and was one of the most dangerous water-crossings in mainland Britain. Travellers had only about six hours to get across the sands, which were made more treacherous by the likelihood of quicksands and disorientating fogs. The urgency and danger are explicit in Turner's watercolour, as is the careful detail of the laurel sprigs, or 'brobs', laid out by guides after each tide to mark the safest route.[9]

The year after Turner's long, wet journey into the North of England, he left Britain for the first time since 1802. Crossing the Channel in August 1817,[10] he travelled to Ostend, and went on to make a rapid tour of the Low Countries (Bruges, Ghent, Brussels, Waterloo, Liège, Aix, Antwerp, Amsterdam, Rotterdam, The Hague and Dordrecht) with an expedition down the Rhine from Cologne to Mainz. By the middle of September he had sailed home from Rotterdam to Harwich. Forays into Europe such as this became characteristic of Turner's travels, and over the next three decades he undertook many journeys into the Alps and to Italy, Germany, Austria and Denmark, as well as eight trips to northern France, where he explored the river systems. Boxing the compass, Turner travelled south as far as Naples, east to Vienna, north to

96 *Gibside, Co. Durham (SW View)*, 1817–18, watercolour, 26.5 × 44 cm (10½ × 17⅜ in.). Engraved 1819. Barnard Castle, County Durham, The Bowes Museum

Turner has incorporated two works by the Neo-classical architect James Paine into this view – the 140-foot (43-metre) high Column of British Liberty (right) and the Gibside chapel (left). Turner prompts us to consider that a British landscape is at its most impressive when its elements are unified, just as the British nation depends on collective action to retain its liberty.

97 *Gibside, Co. Durham (N View)*, 1817–18, watercolour and gum arabic, 27.5 × 45 cm (10⅞ × 17¾ in.). Barnard Castle, County Durham, The Bowes Museum

In this view we look back at the landscape in pl. 96. The Classical female figure in that work is here replaced by traditional British features – the lad and his dog, the weir, the cows, the mill.

Copenhagen and west to Brittany. As well as providing him with dozens of sketchbooks full of information about European landscape, architecture and people, foreign travel also gave Turner a new perspective on his own country. This is seen, for example, in his treatment of *The Festival upon the Opening of the Vintage of Macon* (pl. 53; cat. 40) and *Raby Castle* (see below; pl. 98), and in the strong Italianate light in *Lancaster, from the Aqueduct Bridge* (pl. 6; cat. 95).

Turner travelled north from Harwich in September 1817 to carry out work that may have been arranged before he left England. He went first to County Durham, where he made studies of Raby Castle for William Vane, Earl of Darlington, and then was spirited away from Raby by the Earl of Strathmore to draw his two county houses – Gibside, near Gateshead, and Hylton Castle, near Sunderland – and their surrounding landscapes.[11] Strathmore's intervention seems to have been unexpected, as Turner had planned to visit one of his friends, the painter and architectural writer Henry Gally Knight (1786–1846), at Langold, near Worksop, on the way home. With some exasperation Turner asked James Holworthy to call on Knight in London and explain: "I had written a letter to say I could be with him at Langold from the 23rd to the 29th October, but Lord Strathmore called at Raby and took me away to the north."[12]

It was not the embrace of the aristocracy that drew Turner from his planned route home, since he was indifferent to grandeur and preferred the company of friends. But what did turn his head was exposure for his art, and the money that that brought. Both Darlington and Strathmore were subscribers to another ambitious engraving project of the period, a two-volume *History and Antiquities of the County Palatine of Durham*, undertaken by the antiquarian Robert Surtees (1779–1834). Unlike Whitaker's *History of Richmondshire*, this was funded by its subscribers, and was not a commercial venture in which the artists carried some of the financial risk. The first volume appeared in 1816, and the second, with engravings after Turner's views of Gibside, Hylton and Raby, in 1820.

The images of the County Durham landscape that Turner began soon after returning to London in the last few weeks of 1817 mark the point at which his art reached the peak of its maturity. In the oil painting *Raby Castle, the Seat of the Earl of Darlington* (pl. 98) and the watercolours *Gibside, Co. Durham (SW View)* (pl. 96; cat. 81) and *Gibside, Co. Durham (N View)* (pl. 97; cat. 82) we have three paintings that rank high among the artist's masterpieces. There is a vastness to each image in which the artist, without rhetoric or falsehood, gives a breathtaking account of geographical extent. This does not flatter the patron by suggesting that all that is depicted is in the keeping of Darlington or Strathmore; on the contrary it reminds the viewer of the exuberance and generosity of nature, and the hugeness of nature beyond human ownership. A further characteristic of Turner's instinctive understanding of landscape form is the way in which he marshalls all the parts that make up a view and binds them together. In so doing he suggests that a landscape view is at its most powerful and impressive when hill, forest, plain and sky are unified, just as a nation depends on collective and concerted action to retain its liberty. In one of his first lectures as Professor of Perspective at the Royal Academy Turner linked landscape painting with the concept of nationhood. Of the Italian landscape sources of Salvator Rosa, Poussin and Claude, he wrote:

> They have provided what they saw to be practicable in their atmosphere, and we should prove what is so in ours. An endless variety is on our side and opens a new field of novelty, if we use the deep instructing tool of Salvator, the higher style of Poussin or the milder [?] solar of Claude, the soil is British and so should be the harvest.[13]

The Column of British Liberty, designed in the 1750s by James Paine for the then owner of Gibside, Sir George Bowes, is the eye-catcher in the two *Gibside* watercolours, being placed prominently each work. A symbol of liberty is thus shown surrounded by hundreds of square miles of British landscape, and by the serpentine line of the River Derwent. There is a poetic reciprocity between the two works – the foreground of one forms the distant view of the other – and there is a yet further balance in the understated touch of humanity in each. In the view from

98 *Raby Castle, the Seat of the Earl of Darlington*, exhibited 1818, oil on canvas, 119 × 180.6 cm (46⅞ × 71⅛ in.), Baltimore, The Walters Art Museum

One of Turner's finest panoramic landscapes, in which the variation of light and shade gently takes the eye into the distance. Here, Turner proclaims not only that he himself is equal to the Old Masters, but that the landscape of Britain can stand comparison with any in Europe.

the south-west (pl. 96) a woman in a Classical, toga-like garment carries an urn on her head – a touch of ancient Rome – while in the view from the north a typical British lad and his black-and-white dog peer over a cliff edge. There can be no doubt that such staffage was considered and deliberate – a figure straight out of an Old Master, that is, a 'southern' European painting, in the view from the south-west, and a northern boy in that from the north. Thus Turner takes us yet further into the idea of liberty, the central columnar feature of a landscape that takes two paintings to encompass it, by also demonstrating that liberty reaches from the ancient world of Rome right through to the Britain of his day.

The great oil painting *Raby Castle, the Seat of the Earl of Darlington* (pl. 98) reveals Turner at his most breathtaking, a landscape of vast extent, in which the undulating square miles before and beyond are as active in the composition as the centrally placed house. With its majestic balance of cloud, light and rolling countryside, this work is as near to seascape as landscape ever gets. The castle stands still, but the light plays around it; the wind – as the distant smoke indicates –

blows from the left past it; and the fox hunt (the earl was a passionate huntsman) runs from the right in front of it. *Raby Castle* is perhaps the greatest Rubens that Rubens never painted; and with this picture we witness Turner proclaiming once again not only that he himself is the equal of the Old Masters, but that the landscape of Britain can stand comparison with any country across the sea. The fact that he had just travelled across Holland and Flanders, and had seen Rubens's paintings in Antwerp,[14] is a certain pointer to the way in which Turner chose to treat Raby Castle. Nevertheless, the painting was widely disliked at its first exhibition, at the Royal Academy, and Turner was put under pressure to alter the foreground chase and paint out the fox kill, which he did. One critic wrote that Turner's abilities in landscape "are more successfully employed in the poetical department of that province, than in the representation of local and individual scenery."[15] This critic may have identified the heart of the problem of Turner's equivocal public reception: fifteen years earlier, in *The Festival upon the Opening of the Vintage of Macon*, Turner had given universality and a foreign disguise to a local English view, of the Thames from Richmond Hill; in 1818, however, he presented universality once again, but this time he named his subject.

During the late 1810s and 1820s Turner was heavily committed to publishing projects, which variously overlapped with one another, elided or failed. Although the watercolours he produced for such ventures together form the finest and most integrated suite of images of any nation by a single artist before or since, the contracts he entered into with engravers brought him frustration and exhaustion. "No holiday ever for me," he sighed, on being upbraided by Cooke for delays one Sunday at Sandycombe.[16] Turner may have both shocked and enchanted with his exhibits at the Academy, but entering the mucky world of print publishing was another thing altogether. Like everybody else he was bound by the market, dependent on many different people putting their money into the projects and keeping it there, and also dependent on the security of investments. Dealing with print publishers was not the same as a one-to-one relationship with a patron. Nevertheless, he persisted in producing watercolours for engraving, and it is worth trying to discover why he did not just rest on his fame and sell pictures to patrons.

The answer is complex. First, it was a long-established practice with Turner; he had been working for print publishers since he had started his career as an artist, and he knew and valued the trade. Secondly, as is evident in the purpose of his *Liber Studiorum*, he believed that with reproduction of paintings as prints came security of image, personal recognition and a form of copyright protection for which William Hogarth had fought more than eighty years previously. Thirdly, it meant income – though from his own experience of trying to sell *Liber Studiorum* prints he knew how uncertain that could be. But a fourth, and perhaps much more potent reason, is that he knew and loved Britain, and was a tireless advocate of its art, literature and history. The landscape watercolours for engraving were thus at the heart of his purpose.

From his early engravings for the *Copper-Plate Magazine* to the images of Scotland for the writings of Sir Walter Scott (1771–1832) and the *Picturesque Views in England and Wales*, the series of

99 *Dartmouth Castle, on the River Dart*, 1822, pencil and watercolour, 15.9 × 22.4 cm (6¼ × 8⅞ in.). Engraved 1824. London, Tate

Turner keeps the eye and mind roving around his pictures. Here a sailor waves farewell as a ship sets sail into hazy sunlight, a scene reminiscent more of a European landscape – to which the ship, perhaps, is bound.

100 *Okehampton Castle, on the River Okement*, c. 1824, pencil, watercolour and bodycolour, 16.3 × 23 cm (6⅜ × 9 in.). Engraved 1825. London, Tate

Turner sought constantly to make 'rhymes' in his compositions. Here the twin forms of the ruined castle rhyme with the two trees and the fork of the foreground log.

over four hundred engraved images of Turner's work embodies a collective, kaleidoscopic image of Britain. Made across a turbulent span of the nation's history, they show clearly, and with pertinent historical and social reference, just what it was that Britain looked like, from the sea-girt castles of Scotland (pl. 107; cat. 89) to the naval ports of the South of England (pl. 130; cat. 101), and from Snowdonia in Wales to Great Yarmouth on the east coast. There is incidental detail packed with meaning (as discussed in Chapter V), and yet further detail indicative only of the depth and clarity of Turner's passing observation, the sharpness of his eye, and his sense of the appropriate. Turner depicts fishermen at work on sea and shore (pl. 10; cat. 100); quarry and quarrymen (pl. 81; cat. 63); coach and coachman (pl. 115; cat. 99); cow and milkmaid (pls. 93, 122; cat. 79, 102); canal, barge and bargee (pl. 6; cat. 95); tinker, tailor, soldier, sailor. Very rarely, if ever, are the tradespeople separated from their trades.

But even so Turner did not attempt to create a documentary history, recording and commenting on the state of the nation, as did the agricultural reformer Arthur Young (1741–1820) and the radical journalist William Cobbett (1762–1835). There are huge gaps in his ken: steamboats but no steam railway; pastures but barely a sign of the effects of the Enclosure Acts (but see pl. 2; cat. 39); poor working people, but no poverty. Though he painted their houses and estates, and enjoyed their hospitality and generosity, the aristocracy, the landed gentry or the professional classes themselves are practically invisible in his work. When they do appear, they are usually figures of fun or satire – a prime example is the man with the gun in *Blenheim House and Park, Oxfordshire* (pl. 138; cat. 123); another is the comic figure of the parson sloping off to the right in *Stamford, Lincolnshire* (pl. 115; cat. 99). There is also just a hint of gentle mockery in the studies of fellow guests at Petworth. Only Walter Fawkes and his family are spared this sly wit, as scenes of hunting and shooting in and around Farnley reveal (pl. 64; cat. 56).

Turner's images of his nation were made to be engraved so that they should be seen by Britons in Britain – a single engraving here, framed on a parlour wall, or a small group there, bound in an album. Some were intended to stand alone, others to accompany text, the latter most notably in the illustrated volumes of the works of Sir Walter Scott (pls. 105, 107; cat. 89, 90). Together they create a comprehensive image of nationhood, what Britain is about and what it meant to live there. As an indication of the geographical extent of Turner's work, no place in England and Wales is more than about forty miles from the subject of an engraved landscape; and in Scotland, south of the Great Glen, this rises only to about sixty miles (see map).

No sooner had Turner finished his modest contribution to the *History of Durham* than he agreed, in July 1820, to contribute to a volume of engravings of London scenes that William Cooke was proposing to publish, with Augustus Wall Callcott (1779–1844) and William Westall (1781–1850) among the other artists.[17] In 1820, therefore, Turner had perhaps seven separate contracts or understandings with print publishers, of greater or lesser binding, further or less advanced, running at the same time.[18] Some projects, such as *Picturesque Views on the Southern Coast of*

Map of Turner's engraved views of Britain.

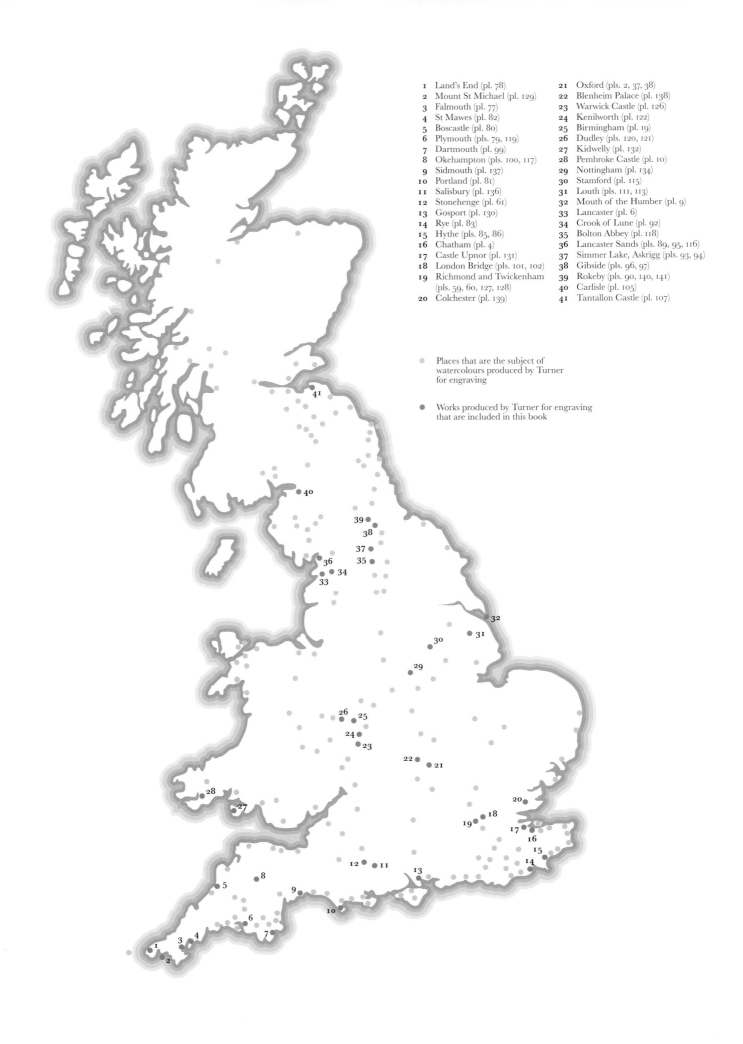

1 Land's End (pl. 78)
2 Mount St Michael (pl. 129)
3 Falmouth (pl. 77)
4 St Mawes (pl. 82)
5 Boscastle (pl. 80)
6 Plymouth (pls. 79, 119)
7 Dartmouth (pl. 99)
8 Okehampton (pls. 100, 117)
9 Sidmouth (pl. 137)
10 Portland (pl. 81)
11 Salisbury (pl. 136)
12 Stonehenge (pl. 61)
13 Gosport (pl. 130)
14 Rye (pl. 83)
15 Hythe (pls. 85, 86)
16 Chatham (pl. 4)
17 Castle Upnor (pl. 131)
18 London Bridge (pls. 101, 102)
19 Richmond and Twickenham
   (pls. 59, 60, 127, 128)
20 Colchester (pl. 139)

21 Oxford (pls. 2, 37, 38)
22 Blenheim Palace (pl. 138)
23 Warwick Castle (pl. 126)
24 Kenilworth (pl. 122)
25 Birmingham (pl. 19)
26 Dudley (pls. 120, 121)
27 Kidwelly (pl. 132)
28 Pembroke Castle (pl. 10)
29 Nottingham (pl. 134)
30 Stamford (pl. 115)
31 Louth (pls. 111, 113)
32 Mouth of the Humber (pl. 9)
33 Lancaster (pl. 6)
34 Crook of Lune (pl. 92)
35 Bolton Abbey (pl. 118)
36 Lancaster Sands (pls. 89, 95, 116)
37 Simmer Lake, Askrigg (pls. 93, 94)
38 Gibside (pls. 96, 97)
39 Rokeby (pls. 90, 140, 141)
40 Carlisle (pl. 105)
41 Tantallon Castle (pl. 107)

• Places that are the subject of
  watercolours produced by Turner
  for engraving

• Works produced by Turner for engraving
  that are included in this book

101 Edward Goodall after J.M.W. Turner, *Old London Bridge and Vicinity*, 1828, engraving, 17.5 × 26.5 cm (6⅞ × 10⅜ in.), Birmingham Museums & Art Gallery. Engraving after pl. 102 for *Views in London and its Environs*

This engraving is a retrospective view of old London. When it was published, the medieval bridge was already being replaced by John Rennie's five-arched structure.

England, were successful commercial undertakings; others, such as the *Rivers of Devon* and the *General History of the County of York*, began with high hopes but ended with a whimper when they failed to appear, or were radically scaled down in the light of commercial and production realities.

The Cooke brothers' volume, entitled *Views in London and its Environs*, was a case of hope triumphing over experience.[19] The artists were engaged; an engraver, Edward Goodall (1795–1870), contracted; and terms agreed for the production of fifteen plates over six years. It was not until 1824 that the project was announced publicly. Then a rival publication with a teasingly similar title, *Picturesque Views in London and its Environs*, was announced the same year by the publishers Hurst & Robinson, with engravings by Charles Heath. Turner finished his first watercolour for the Cookes, *Old London Bridge and Vicinity*, also known as *The Port of London*, in 1824 (pl. 102; cat. 86) and soon after delivered three others, *The Tower of London* (private collection, USA), *View of London from Greenwich* (pl. 104; cat. 87) and *The Custom House* (untraced). No engravings for the Cookes were completed until the print of *The Custom House* appeared in 1827, and that of *Old London Bridge and Vicinity* in the following year. Neither of Turner's other two watercolours was engraved. All four of these works have an intense graphic complexity, incorporating architectural details, ships, rigging, figures, chimneys, smoke, atmosphere and the general bustle of London. Knowing the engraving trade as he did, Turner painted these subjects in a manner that would challenge, entertain and enthrall the engraver, and provide endless fascination for the viewer.

102 *Old London Bridge and Vicinity*, also known as *The Port of London*, 1824, watercolour, 29.2 × 44.5 cm (11½ × 17½ in.). Engraved 1828. London, Victoria and Albert Museum

Despite the central position of the medieval London Bridge, it is the river itself that is the focus of activity in this work. Note the eloquent incidental detail – the chain, hooks and balance in the foreground and the barge lowering its sail to pass under the bridge. The bridge was demolished in 1832.

View of London from Greenwich (pl. 104; cat. 87), with its anecdotal and introductory air, might have been intended as a frontispiece. The full extent of London's mercantile and maritime activity is laid out before the viewer from the heights above Greenwich. In the foreground are references to London's history – a map is inscribed "LONDON 1526", a rolled plan labelled "ST PAUL'S cathedral Sir C Wren" – that reinforce the purpose of the watercolour as a celebration of London through three centuries of development, exploration and commerce. Elsewhere in the image there are two hemispheres, one marked "NORTH POLE" and the other "NEW WORLD", a "Grand plan to reclaim land", a "PLAN for [improving?] LONDON" and, on the easel beneath the 1526 map, another marked "LONDON 1825", the last presumably dating the watercolour.

Turner gave the work an overall jocular mood of pantomime – an excited old man on crutches, another man gesticulating and another looking through a telescope – but underpinning it is his intensive study, evident in his many sketchbooks, of the way London looked at the time, and of the meaning of what he saw. Drawings such as *St Paul's from the Thames* (pl. 103; cat. 88), which may be

103 *St Paul's from the Thames*, ?1820s, pencil, 12.8 × 20.8 cm (5 × 8¼ in.), Cambridge MA, Fogg Art Museum

A sparkling drawing that so clearly reveals Turner's excitement at the constant activity on the Thames in London. The dome of St Paul's is dominant in the background, as in pls. 69 and 104.

a study for *The Custom House* and is a detached page from a sketchbook, are typical examples of Turner training his keen eye on the city of his birth, and together they provide a foundation of factual observation from which considered compositions for engraving could emerge.

The engraving of such subjects was a long drawn-out, laborious process, exacerbated by artists' unpredictable timekeeping and temperament, by precarious financial support, and by overstretched publishers. The Cooke brothers were still bringing out plates for *Southern Coast* when they took up the *London Environs* project, and in 1822, long before the first of the *London* plates appeared, they launched another scheme with Turner and with William Collins RA (1788–1847), to be called *The Rivers of England*. A celebration of the watery landscape of Britain, this series travelled from such inland subjects as the River Aire at Kirkstall Abbey, near Leeds, and the River Okement at Okehampton Castle, Devon (pl. 100; cat. 84), to the mouths of the River Humber off Spurn Head (pl. 9; cat. 85) and of the River Dart at Dartmouth (pl. 99; cat. 83). Turner loaned the watercolours to the Cookes for 8 guineas each, rather than sell them, and they were engraved, unusually, in mezzotint on durable steel plates. The plates were made by a new process that resulted from research into the making of printing plates for banknotes; thus contemporary scientific and industrial research fed rapidly into improvements in the materials available to artists.[20] The engravings were made in the same small size as those of the *Southern Coast*, and, as the Cooke brothers wrote in the introductory notes to the first set of three subjects, published in 1823: "*The Rivers of England* will form a companion presenting a series of picturesque

104 *View of London from Greenwich*, 1825, watercolour, 21.3 × 28.4 cm (8⅜ × 11⅛ in.), New York, Metropolitan Museum of Art

This is Turner's celebration of the huge growth of London as the world capital of trade, exploration and invention in the three hundred years that followed the reign of Elizabeth I. The dome of St Paul's Cathedral dominates the horizon.

delineations of the *Interior* of the Country, while the [*Southern Coast of England*] displays the most prominent features of its shores." This indicates a remarkable community of purpose between Turner and his publishers, who shared an ambition to present Britain from all geographical angles, as a place with many parts, characteristics and facets.

The commercial production of prints in the 1820s was of a rate and to an artistic standard that were both unprecedented. One particular factor among many that Turner brought to this new commerce in engraved views was the extent to which he integrated the actual presence of the human figure, or its implied presence in industry, trade and building, into the landscape. Collectively, these are thus not just topographical views but a social history. However, in choosing to work with engravers Turner had to relinquish the total control of artistic process that he enjoyed as an exhibiting painter: other temperaments and timetables were involved, and there were few timetables so tight or temperaments so difficult as William Cooke's when in contract with Turner. After a sixteen-year-long fractured and irritable relationship, the men fell out finally in 1827 when Cooke proposed a second *Southern Coast* series, offering Turner 12½ guineas for each watercolour.[21] Turner, however, also wanted the extra money for some *Southern Coast* water-colours he had already delivered. Cooke's offer was much less than he had now come to expect,

105 *Carlisle, c.* 1832, watercolour with scratching out, 8.3 × 14.2 cm (3¼ × 5⅝ in.). Engraved in 1834 for *Scott's Poetical Works*. New Haven CT, Yale Center for British Art

Within a tiny compass, Turner evokes atmosphere, a large distant crowd and a wide landscape in this image of Carlisle, the border town that features greatly in Sir Walter Scott's poetry. The bridge is the focal point of the composition, and by continuing the line of the rainbow into the bridge Turner suggests a harmony between man and nature.

and furthermore he demanded twenty-five early proofs of each plate. This was too much for Cooke. The two men exchanged angry letters and were seen to quarrel in public. The idea of the sequel to *Southern Coast* was dropped, and they did not work together again.

One of many aspects of his life that makes Turner stand out from his contemporaries is the fact that he did not specialize. Artists in general could not escape the gradual tendency in the early nineteenth century towards the separation of professions in British society. Engravers tended to stick to engraving, while both oil painters and watercolourists began to regard their arts as requiring a lifetime's commitment in order to build up a solid commercial following. While he had no choice but to leave the engraving of his watercolours to specialists, Turner was exceptional among artists in the 1810s and 1820s in being able to move in his studio practice with apparent ease, perhaps even from day to day, from large-scale oil painting to pocket-sized watercolour. Being both a showman and committed to refining popular understanding of the shape and purpose of Britain, he might be working on an enormous canvas such as *England: Richmond Hill, on the Prince Regent's Birthday* (pl. 106; cat. 73) one day, and on a series of landscape watercolours for engraving on another. These two sides of his practice reflect at least two of the different facets of patronage that supported Turner professionally and financially. The engraved watercolours kept his art on view all around the country, while his oil paintings, shown first in the exposed public forum of the Royal Academy, maintained his reputation as an artist of unrivalled powers, kept his name in the newspapers, and brought him increased esteem and grand fees from the collectors who purchased them.

106 *England: Richmond Hill, on the Prince Regent's Birthday*, exhibited RA 1819, oil on canvas, 180 × 334.5 cm (70⅞ × 131⅝ in.), London, Tate

The viewer takes the place of the Prince Regent as he arrives at this majestic panoramic landscape. The wide sweep of the Thames as seen from Richmond Hill epitomized Turner's patriotic feelings for the nation. Though hidden behind trees, the site of Turner's Twickenham home, Sandycombe Lodge, is in the dead centre of the canvas.

Turner was well used to aristocratic patronage, but the one source of esteem and income that he had never received by the time he set off on a six-month tour of Italy in 1819 was from royalty. It has been reasonably suggested that in exhibiting *England: Richmond Hill, on the Prince Regent's Birthday* at the Royal Academy in 1819 Turner was making a deliberate pitch for evidence of royal approval. If that was the case, his attempt was subtle and dignified.[22] Although the name of the Prince Regent appears in the title, he does not appear to be placed centre stage in the work. He seems to be absent, until one gradually notices that there is a particular stir in the central foreground, as the three young women turn to look towards the viewer. This ripple of excitement through the painting leads to an awareness in figures further from the centre that something significant is happening. Turner may be alluding to a press report that the prince rode up Richmond Hill in August 1818, two days before his actual birthday, when he makes the viewer the cause of the excitement.[23] He gives the viewer the role of the arriving Prince Regent, and so whenever we look at this painting, we are indeed playing the prince.

This theatrical treatment, in which the Prince Regent is the star actor offstage, is a characteristic of Turner's work that reaches a peak of subtlety and wit in this painting. The artist's interest in and experience of theatre, and his enjoyment in seeing plays, have already been mentioned, and throughout his work there are instances of theatricality being employed to make a picture –

107 *Tantallon Castle*, 1821, watercolour, 17.5 × 25.4 cm (6⅞ × 10 in.). Engraved in 1822 for Sir Walter Scott's *Provincial Antiquities of Scotland*. Manchester Art Gallery

The human interest, with people putting themselves in danger among the rocks, adds greatly to the drama of this powerful scene. Scott wrote of Tantallon: "Here was square keep, there turret high, / Or pinnacle that sought the sky."

one example is *Pope's Villa at Twickenham* (pl. 59; cat. 43). But in *England: Richmond Hill* Turner extends these allusions: first, the Prince Regent was born in August, but his official birthday was 23 April, St George's Day, the national day of England, and also both Turner's and Shakespeare's birthday. Secondly, the use of Richmond Hill as the subject introduces layers of meaning that were particularly personal to Turner, and have been discussed in Chapter II. Finally, Turner brought himself into the picture not by introducing a self-portrait but by constructing the work in such a way that his country house, Sandycombe Lodge in Twickenham, is out of sight among the distant trees at the horizontal dead centre of the canvas. *England: Richmond Hill, on the Prince Regent's Birthday* was the largest painting Turner had exhibited to date, and in showing it in the few months before he left on his 1819–20 journey to Italy he highlighted his position as the leading artist of Britain. And, of course, when he was standing in front of the canvas, painting the work, Turner was himself the prince.

It was three years later, and after some intervention by others, that Turner won the royal commission that he appears to have desired so greatly.[24] Nevertheless, when he returned from Italy in February 1820 he could look forward to appreciation from both old and new friends and patrons. The 1819–20 journey was a watershed not only because of his experiences of the Italian landscape, and of the warmth and strength of southern European light that gave him a fresh perspective on Britain, but also because it marked a significant shift in the pattern of his

108 *Chichester Canal, c. 1828,* oil on canvas, 65.4 × 134.6 cm (25¾ × 53 in.), London, Tate

The Earl of Egremont's support for the construction of the Chichester Canal ended in financial disaster. Here the sun sets on the canal, which is empty of traffic apart from a single, stationary collier and a rowing boat.

patronage. The old landed gentry and aristocrats, such as Richard Payne Knight, Sir John Leicester, Lord Yarborough, and the Earls of Darlington and Strathmore, had all bought their last Turners well before the artist left for Italy. When he returned to Britain, the old patrons and friends who remained most actively loyal were his two longest-standing supporters, Walter Fawkes and Lord Egremont. To replace the aristocrats and gentry Turner found a new group of patrons among the industrialists and tradesmen, for example the horse-dealer Robert Vernon (1774–1849), the clothing manufacturer John Sheepshanks (1787–1863), the whale oil merchant Elhanan Bicknell (1788–1861), the coachmaker B.G. Windus (1790–1867) and others, including Joseph Gillott (1799–1872) of Birmingham and Henry McConnel (1801–1871) of Manchester. These men, and their fathers and grandfathers, had come up through society as Turner himself had done. With Britain changing so radically, Turner was now painting, for large fees, for the same kinds of people who had once provided his subject-matter.

Walter Fawkes died in 1825; of the old guard only Lord Egremont continued his patronage of Turner, and, until his death in 1837, even exceeded the depth of his generosity in the years before 1819. Turner did not return to Farnley after Walter Fawkes's death; the place of that house in his social calendar, if not his memory and emotions, was taken by Petworth, Lord Egremont's house, which he began to visit regularly from 1827. It was an easy-going place: Turner, his friends and fellow artists were welcome to stay for as long as they liked, and many took full, even excessive, advantage of Lord Egremont's hospitality.[25] Turner repaid this debt through the dozens of spirited

gouache and watercolour studies that he made of all aspects of life in the house, and of the landscape that surrounded it.[26] Although only two of these works on paper entered the Petworth House collection,[27] in about 1827–28 Egremont added to his already substantial collection of Turner oil paintings (pls. 56, 70, 72; cat. 41, 45, 46) by commissioning four long, narrow works to be installed in panels beneath the dynastic portraits in the dining-room, known as the Carved Room (pls. 108–110; cat. 74–76). As became apparent when they were returned after many years to their original positions in 2002, the paintings were set relatively low on the wall so that they would be at the eye level of the diners seated with their backs to the windows.

Before he began painting these canvases Turner made six sample studies from which the earl could choose.[28] After a period of experiment, those ultimately selected for the Carved Room were *Chichester Canal* (pl. 108; cat. 74) and *Petworth Park*, which were hung to the left of the central fireplace, and *The Chain Pier, Brighton* (pl. 109; cat. 75) and *The lake in Petworth Park*, to the right. All are views to the west with dramatic sunsets, and the theatricality of the arrangment was enhanced by the fact that the dining-room was in particular use on summer evenings – thus sunsets could be enjoyed both by those opposite the west-facing windows, and by those with their backs to them.

The choice of subjects available to Egremont (although there might have been others under discussion that did not reach the sample study stage) included, in addition to the Petworth scenes, two paintings of contemporary innovations that he had helped to finance. The earl was a major

109 *The Chain Pier, Brighton, c.* 1828, oil on canvas, 71.1 × 136.5 cm (28 × 53¾ in.), London, Tate

Intrigued by the principle of the suspension bridge, Turner made drawings of the Chain Pier at Brighton, and of the suspension bridges at Hammersmith and Freiburg. Built in 1823 and 335 m (1100 ft) long, the Chain Pier gave deep-water mooring to steamships from London and Dieppe. It was blown down in 1896.

110 *A Ship Aground*, c. 1828,
oil on canvas, 70 × 136 cm
(27½ × 53½ in.), London, Tate
Although this is one of the bleakest
of Turner's paintings of sailing
ships in trouble, the artist gives
the suggestion of hope in the busy
activity of trying to secure the
stranded ship before nightfall.

shareholder in the plan to link London and the south coast with a series of navigable waterways, the final section of which, the Chichester Canal, opened in 1822. The venture was a financial disaster (Egremont pulled out in 1826), which Turner emphasized eloquently by depicting an idle collier on a canal otherwise empty except for a man in a rowing boat. The Chain Pier at Brighton, in which Egremont had also invested, was, on the other hand, a social, commercial and structural success. Effectively a suspension bridge leading out to sea, it enabled ships to land and board passengers at any state of the tide. From the early 1820s holiday-makers and other travellers began to come to Brighton in their thousands by steamboat from London and south coast ports, relying on timetables that could now be produced with some chance of accuracy. As well as being the route for a bracing and enjoyable walk out to sea, the Chain Pier was in itself an economic necessity for Brighton before the railways established the landward link to London in 1841.

A painting that reached a more finished state than the sample studies, and was temporarily installed in the panelling, was *A Ship Aground* (pl. 110; cat. 76).[29] This melancholy subject may have had a personal association for the earl that he chose to forget. The location is unclear: the pier on the left is not the Chain Pier at Brighton, though it may conceivably be at Margate. If that is the case, the sun in the picture is setting (Margate is on a north-facing coast), and the painting would have accorded with the theme of sunsets in the dining-room. For whatever reason, *A Ship Aground* was ejected from the dining-room and returned to the artist.

CHAPTER IV

"A most splendid work from Turner the Academician"
1825 to 1838

The engraver Charles Heath, who had first worked with Turner in 1811 on the figures in the engraving of *Pope's Villa* (pl. 60; cat. 68), made an agreement with the artist early in 1825 to collaborate with him in the production of a new series of engravings of 120 English and Welsh scenes. Heath proposed that he buy Turner's watercolours for this series for 30 guineas each, and, when each engraving was complete, that he would sell its original at a profit. Turner, whose mission to express the collective identity of Britain was fully in tune with Heath's entrepreneurial vision, was to be the sole contributor. The series carried the title *England and Wales* on publication of the first parts from 1827, and was given (not necessarily in consultation with the artist) the longer and now more familiar title *Picturesque Views in England and Wales* only when bound into volumes in 1838.

"I have just begun a most splendid work from Turner the Academician", Heath wrote to the banker and collector Dawson Turner (1775–1858) when he and J.M.W. Turner had reached their agreement.[1] Beginning the project with high hopes, Heath went on to say that he had already received four watercolours from Turner, "and they are the finest things I ever saw". An additional remark reflects the buoyancy of the art market in early 1825: "The Art of Engraving never flourished as it now does – there is so much doing that every Engraver is full." This optimism was short-lived, for in December 1825 a financial crash in Britain resulted in bankruptcies and bank closures throughout the country. The main backer of Heath's scheme, the publishers Hurst & Robinson, went bankrupt the following month, and Heath had to find new backers.

The *England and Wales* series was just one expression of a popular and developing trend in the recording of landscape in Britain: in the eighteenth century Samuel and Nathaniel Buck had published over four hundred engravings of towns and antiquities throughout the England and Wales. Their works, *Buck's Antiquities*, were published for the first time as a complete set in three volumes in 1774. William Daniell's eight-volume *Voyage Around Great Britain* (1814–25) has been discussed above (see Chapter II), while John Buckler (1770–1851) and his son John Chessell

111 *Louth, Lincolnshire, c.* 1828, detail of pl. 113

112 *Louth*, 1797, pencil, 20.9 × 27 cm (8¼ × 10⅝ in.), London, Tate. From the 'North of England' sketchbook, TB XXXIV, fol. 80.

The source for pl. 113, drawn about thirty years earlier, has the air of a stage set awaiting the actors. Note the many changes of detail and emphasis in the watercolour, for example the second and third houses in from the left, which are invented and give weight to that side of the composition.

Buckler (1793–1894), both nearer to Turner's age, were also travelling extensively and producing watercolours of architecture to be engraved. The doyen of them all was the engraver-publisher John Britton (1771–1857). Turner and Heath's new series was, however, distinctive in that it attempted to be a comprehensive account of the appearance of the nation for the generation after the Napoleonic Wars. It sought nothing less than to depict the whole of England and Wales from the inside – not just a county or region, such as Sussex, Richmondshire or the southern coast, or specific geographical or urban features, such as rivers or ports. In the letterpress to the third set of four engravings of the series, published in 1827, Heath wrote a passage that summarizes the project's mission, and echoes the aims that Turner had been pursuing since the beginning of his career:

> There is no topic on which a Briton may exult more proudly than the scenery of his native isle. If, in particular points of natural grandeur, other countries can outvie GREAT BRITAIN, she presents a union of the agreeable with the grand and imposing, of the confirmed works and triumphs of art, with the magnificence of nature, no where to be found. … While, therefore, great and deserved encouragement has been

113 *Louth, Lincolnshire, c.* 1828, watercolour, 28.5 × 42 cm (11¼ × 16½ in.). Engraved 1829. London, British Museum

Thirty years after painting *Wolverhampton* (pl. 24), Turner retains his fascination for country market places and the crowds they attract. Now, however, his emphasis has moved on to sunlight and its effect on architecture, space and narrative. There is a divide between the male world of the horse fair and the mob-capped women clustered around the market stalls.

given of late to various series of Views illustrating the Scenery of the Continent, the proprietor of the work here announced, Mr CHARLES HEATH, has been induced to suppose that similar illustrations of British Scenery would be acceptable to the public.[2]

Heath stressed in this advertisement that "nothing of this kind has recently been attempted on a general scale". The particular characteristic of British scenery, he added, is its variety, and his intention was to reveal the nature of this "union of the agreeable with the grand and imposing". Turner was the one artist who could demonstrate with sufficient depth the integration of land, people, custom and building in Britain. Variety, whether natural, geographical, urban or social, is thus the common theme of the subjects that artist and publisher chose to depict in *England and Wales*, and is the vibrant linking thread that gives the collection its richness.

114 *Stamford*, 1797, pencil, 20.9 × 27 cm (8¼ × 10⅝ in.), London, Tate. From the 'North of England' sketchbook, TB XXXIV, fol. 86

This drawing is the source for pl. 115.

By the late 1820s Turner had travelled so widely in England and Wales that he already had almost all he needed in his sketchbooks to begin, and in some cases to complete, what was required of him by Heath. The watercolour of *Louth, Lincolnshire* (pl. 113; cat. 98), for example, is based on a study in the 'North of England' sketchbook of 1797 (pl. 112),[3] and that of *Stamford, Lincolnshire* (pl. 115; cat. 99) on another in the same sketchbook (pl. 114).[4] *Lancaster, from the Aqueduct Bridge* (pl. 6; cat. 95) derives from a drawing made on Turner's rain-sodden 1816 tour of Yorkshire and Lancashire.[5] When preparing his watercolour of Stoneyhurst, Lancashire, he may even have torn a 1799 drawing of it out of a sketchbook to place by him as he worked: the page was found loose, with watercolour splashes on the back.[6] Such a project as *England and Wales* revealed the artistic and commercial value of the dozens of sketchbooks that Turner had filled during his career.

Interested though he was in experiment, Turner refused, against Heath's wishes and prevailing commercial sense, to allow his images to be engraved on the new type of steel plates, as had been used for the *Rivers of England*. The use of such hard-wearing plates would have allowed more prints to be produced, but by insisting on copper plates Turner encouraged the engravers to create softer and more atmospheric impressions. The continuation of *England and Wales* was, however, a severe financial burden to Heath, since by the late 1820s the market had become

115 *Stamford, Lincolnshire, c.*1828, watercolour, bodycolour and scratching out, 29.3 × 42 cm (11½ × 16½ in.). Engraved 1830. Lincoln, Usher Gallery

A sudden storm soaks the ground and washes the sky in this watercolour, while umbrellas (there are eight) and overcoats continue the story of this day's weather. In the 1820s a number of towns like Stamford became elegant places of transit and resort, and a smartly dressed family is shown arriving by stagecoach.

flooded with steel-plate-engraved landscape subjects of highly variable quality, and prints of Turner's scenes failed to sell as well as expected. Heath attempted to stimulate further sales by organizing an exhibition of forty-one of the completed watercolours (whether engraved yet or not) at the Egyptian House, Piccadilly, London, in June and July 1829. The exhibited works included *Salisbury, from Old Sarum* (pl. 136; cat. 122), *Lancaster Sands* (pl. 116; cat. 96), *Okehampton, Devonshire* (pl. 117; cat. 97), *Louth, Lincolnshire* (pl. 113; cat. 98), *Plymouth Cove, Devonshire* (pl. 119; cat. 105), *Colchester, Essex* (pl. 139; cat. 121) and *Stamford, Lincolnshire* (pl. 115; cat. 99).[7] Heath organized further exhibitions in London at the Freemasons' Tavern (1831) and at the galleries of the picture dealers Moon, Boys & Graves in Pall Mall (1833).

Six works from the 1829 Egyptian House exhibition, including *Colchester*, were shown in September of that year at the Birmingham Society of Arts in the inaugural exhibition of their grand new porticoed building in New Street, designed by Thomas Rickman and Henry

Hutchinson (demolished 1913). This was the first time that Turner's work had been seen publicly in Birmingham and also the first time that he had shown more than two works at once outside London.[8] It was also an early instance of collaboration in art exhibitions, the works of a celebrated artist fresh from a London exhibition arriving in a regional town to help celebrate the opening of a new gallery.

The 1829 Birmingham Society of Arts exhibition, which attracted as many as eighty-six artists resident in London – including the President of the Royal Academy, Sir Thomas Lawrence, and twenty-three other Royal Academicians – was enthusiastically received. According to the local newspaper *Aris's Gazette* it met with "crowded attendance and unqualified expressions of delight".[9] On Turner's work itself *Aris's Gazette* showed some caution, introducing readers gently to this controversial giant by invoking the informed opinion of other artists:

116 *Lancaster Sands*, *c.* 1826, watercolour, 27.8 × 40.4 cm (11 × 15⅞ in.). Engraved 1828. London, British Museum

Turner depicts an assortment of tired but relieved travellers who have nearly completed the dangerous journey across the sands to Lancaster begun in pl. 95. The tide is coming in across Morecambe Bay in the distance, and in the foreground an itinerant wheelwright and his family struggle on while a pair of dogs snap at the seagulls.

117 *Okehampton, Devonshire, c.* 1826, watercolour, 28.5 × 41.1 cm (11¼ × 16⅛ in.). Engraved 1828. Melbourne, National Gallery of Victoria

As in pl. 100, Turner's sense of compositional 'rhyme' is revealed in the two parts of the ruined castle, the gap in the ring of trees on the mound, and the gap in the trees on the left.

The six drawings by Turner afford an instance of great talent not exactly intelligible to the unpractised eye.[10] Yet artists give them that high applause they richly merit, and those who doubt their excellence may turn from the Entrance to 'Fowey Harbour', no. 356, and Mr Turner's other drawings, to the engravings from them, in the Room for Engravings and Sculpture. They will thus learn what material for fine pictures the slightest or most eccentric sketches of men of genius afford, and they will likewise appreciate duly the great merits of the engraver.[11]

A significant point here is that the Birmingham journalist guides his readers immediately to the engravings after Turner's work. This tells us a number of things: that the engravings were being sold in Birmingham at the earliest opportunity, thus extending their reach and influence; that the local press was anxious for Birmingham to be seen as welcoming art from London however

sophisticated it may be; and that engravings were rightly considered to be helpful as aids to the understanding of an art that was perceived to be 'difficult'. It follows, Birmingham being a centre of the engravers' trade, that engravings were considered in themselves to be works of art, and not reproductions. An anonymous letter, written to the *Birmingham Journal* in December 1829, reflects the depth of appreciation that Turner found in Birmingham (see Appendix I, p. 196).

This letter is highly perceptive, and reveals its author to be well read in contemporary art and science theory. Like James Skene (1775–1864), the prescient author of the article on 'Painting' in the *Edinburgh Encyclopedia* (1830),[12] the Birmingham author introduces the language of science to help define what is new and challenging in Turner's art:

> The speculative astronomers tell us that there may be stars, whose light, travelling at the rate of millions of miles in a minute, has not yet reached our globe; we see

118 *Bolton Abbey, Yorkshire, c.* 1825, watercolour, 28 × 39.4 cm (11 × 15 ½ in.). Engraved 1827. Port Sunlight, Lady Lever Art Gallery

Turner, an enthusiastic fisherman, brings a touch of autobiography to this calm and sun-filled scene. Despite the title, the ancient abbey is the least important feature of the composition.

119 *Plymouth Cove, Devonshire,*
c. 1829, watercolour, 28 × 41.2 cm
(11 × 16¼ in.). Engraved 1832.
London, Victoria and Albert
Museum
Although war with France had
ended more than a decade before
Turner painted this work, the
prominent Martello tower and
the scale of the naval fleet shows
an island nation in readiness to
defend its shores.

them not, but they may be seen hereafter. So I could fancy that Turner has *anticipated* nature – that he has forcibly 'seized the forelock of time' …

This carries understanding of Turner into new territory, making note of the artist's use of metaphor to exaggerate reality in order to seek a further truth or insight that may be more real than the actual thing depicted:

If a bright spot would effectually relieve a dark mass, he introduces a figure illuminated on the side the farthest from the source of light. … His bold and skilful use of *reflected* lights permits him to introduce these reliefs when they touch the very verge of the possible; … he gives – shall I say it – in the emanation of his genius, something more valuable, *in that instance*, than truth itself.

120 (above) *Dudley, Worcestershire*, *c*. 1833, watercolour, 28.8 × 43 cm (11⅜ × 17 in.). Birmingham Museums & Art Gallery

121 (left) Robert Wallis after J.M.W Turner, *Dudley, Worcestershire*, engraving, 1835, 16.2 × 23.8 cm (11⅜ × 17 in.). Port Sunlight, Lady Lever Art Gallery

Dudley Castle and its medieval church are lit by the dying daylight, as fire from the new world of industrial manufacture floods the foreground. These works reveal how the Midlands of Britain were turning into a 'region of Vulcans'.

122 *Kenilworth Castle, Warwickshire,*
c. 1830, watercolour and
bodycolour, 29.2 × 45.4 cm
(11½ × 17⅞ in.). Engraved 1832.
Fine Arts Museums of San
Francisco, Achenbach Foundation
for Graphic Arts

This richly chromatic picture was
painted from studies made on
Turner's 1830 tour to the Midlands.
The artist contrasts ruined castles
with living people to evoke the long
passage of time and the transience
of human life.

It is likely that there was a specific connection, as yet undiscovered, between the exhibition
at the Birmingham Society of Arts and Turner's decision to travel in 1830 to the Midlands. There
he visited Birmingham, Dudley, Coventry, Kenilworth and Warwick (pls. 7, 8, 120, 122–26;
cat. 102, 103, 107, 113–15) to gather fresh material specifically for *England and Wales*. The drawback
for Turner in his relying too heavily on his sketchbooks, some of which were more than thirty
years old, was that in creating works for engraving he could not depict any recent changes that
had occurred in the landscape, and particularly in the towns. Some of the most profound changes
in the landscape of Britain were taking place in the industrial Midlands, and if he was to continue
to be reliable as an observer of the nation he had to see them for himself.

On his 1830 Midlands journey Turner saw the ferocious industrial landscape of Dudley, which
he distilled into the watercolour *Dudley, Worcestershire* (pl. 120; cat. 107), and it is also likely that he
paused outside Warwick, on the road to Kenilworth, to take note of the view of the tower of
St Mary's Church from Hill Wootton (pl. 125; cat. 115).[13] The 'Kenilworth' sketchbook (pl. 123;
cat. 113) reveals the route taken by Turner – through Oxford, past Blenheim Palace, near

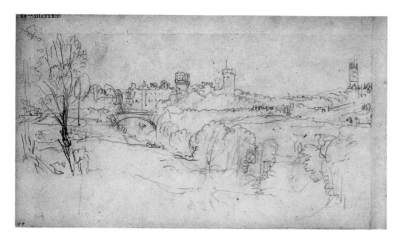

123 *View of Warwick*, 1830, pencil, 11.4 × 18.9 cm (4½ × 7½ in.), London, Tate. From the 'Kenilworth' sketchbook, TB CCXXXVIII, fol. 40

An assured and fluent sketch of Warwick Castle, Avon Bridge and St Mary's Church seen from what is now St Nicholas Park.

124 *View of Birmingham*, 1830, pencil, 6.4 × 10.5 cm (2½ × 4⅛ in.), London, Tate. From the 'Birmingham and Coventry' sketchbook, TB CCXL, fol. 49

By this time Birmingham was a teeming metropolis of over 140,000 inhabitants. This rapid sketch evokes the profound changes Birmingham had undergone since 1794.

Woodstock (pl. 138; cat. 123), and then to Leicester, Ashby-de-la-Zouch, Kenilworth (pl. 122; cat. 102), Warwick (pl. 126; cat. 103), Lichfield, Tamworth and Dudley. In the sketchbook are characteristic, rapidly produced pencil sketches, among them a remarkable series of drawings of Warwick that includes a view of the castle from the Avon Bridge and panoramic views of the skyline from what are now Priory and St Nicholas parks (pl. 123; cat. 113). The breadth of the drawings in the 'Kenilworth' sketchbook is mirrored by the intensity of Turner's tiny drawings in the 'Birmingham and Coventry' sketchbook (pl. 124; cat. 114), a notebook small enough to fit into the palm of his hand. The detail in these studies is spare, but there is an intensity of expression in the drawings of the church spires and towers of the two towns, and of the dirty and heavy industrial equipment lying about.

Heath had begun the *England and Wales* project by planning to issue a set of four engravings three times a year. This pace was maintained for the first dozen issues, but as the money supply faltered and production became delayed, so the issues appeared at more widely spaced intervals. By 1836 Heath had decided to complete the series when only ninety-six prints had been

125 *St Mary's Church, Warwick, from below Hill Wootton*, formerly known as *Gloucester Cathedral*, ?1830, watercolour, 23 × 30 cm (9 × 11¾ in.), London, Tate

This simple but evocative composition of a church tower against a glowing sunset sky is a quintessential image of a nation proud of its history and independence.

126 *Warwick Castle, Warwickshire*, *c.* 1830, watercolour, 29.7 × 45.1 cm (11⅝ × 17¾ in.). Engraved 1832. University of Manchester, The Whitworth Art Gallery

Introducing a theme of repair and renewal, Turner contrasts the repairing of the late eighteenth-century Avon Bridge with the ruins of the medieval town bridge in the middle distance. The tower of St Mary's (see pls. 123, 125) is seen on the right.

127 James T. Willmore after J.M.W. Turner, *Richmond Terrace, Surrey*, 1838, engraving, 16.3 × 25 cm (6⅜ × 9⅞ in.), Birmingham Museums & Art Gallery. Engraving after pl. 128 for *England and Wales*

made. It is clear that, although Turner's insistence on high standards may have itself caused delays, his production of watercolours kept just – but not too far – ahead of that of Heath and his engravers. Relatively few of the watercolours were not ultimately engraved, and of those one, *Northampton, Northamptonshire* (pl. 135), of a Midlands town that Turner had visited in 1830, had overtly political content, and Heath may have deliberately avoided publishing it (see Chapter V).

As the project progressed it became more complex, and the number of people involved increased – by 1833 twenty different engravers had been involved in making the plates for *England and Wales*. Complicating matters further, Heath had started a sumptuous new publication, *The Keepsake*, for which Turner provided seventeen watercolours between 1828 and 1837. The two men collaborated further in producing series of engravings from watercolours made on Turner's tours in France along the rivers Loire and Seine, which appeared as *Turner's Annual Tours* (1833–35).[14] Such a multiplicity of projects with publishers and engravers had been characteristic of Turner's work in the early 1820s; now, in addition to his work with Heath, Turner was also painting small-scale vignettes for reproduction by commercial book publishers such as John Murray, Edward Moxon and Robert Cadell (pls. 105, 107; cat. 89, 90).[15] Furthermore, in the 1830s he worked intensively on oil paintings for exhibition and sale, and all these projects had to be accommodated both in his mind and in his schedule of work. When he was arranging to leave Italy after his tour of

128 *Richmond Terrace, Surrey,* 1836, watercolour, 28 × 43.5 cm (11 × 17⅛ in.). Engraved 1838. Liverpool, Walker Art Gallery

This extensive vista had a particular resonance for Turner and was one he painted many times in his career (see also pls. 53, 106). The fore-ground figures welcome the viewer into the scene, and reflect Turner's lifelong practice of creating landscapes that are inhabited, articulated and used by people.

1828–29 he urged Heath not to send any more *England and Wales* proofs to him in Rome to correct "without very urgent cause or so that it can be in Rome by Xmas day or the end of Dec^r".[16]

Turner gave everything to his art, to the extent that he lacked patience with others whom he considered less dedicated than he, or who had other priorities. The Birmingham-born engraver James Willmore (1800–1863), who cut eight plates for *England and Wales*, including *Tamworth Castle, Staffordshire* and *Richmond Terrace, Surrey* (pl. 127; cat. 112), had long discussions with Turner, who, "with many most cordial grunts … gave him an hour's lecture, difficult to understand, on the art of engraving".[17] Turner urged Willmore "by all means to sacrifice everything to [your] art", adding, after visiting Willmore at home with his family, "I hate married men, they never make any sacrifice to the Arts, but are always thinking of their duty to their wives and families, or some rubbish of that sort."[18]

Heath's motive in launching other projects while *England and Wales* was continuing was not so much out of artistic endeavour, but rather a desperate effort to prevent financial disaster. He

paid each engraver £100 (about £5000 today) to engrave a plate, sometimes two years' work, and the sluggish sales caused serious problems of liquidity. Also, Turner had negotiated a deal in which he took the first thirty proofs from each plate, thus limiting the number of fresh prints available before the plates wore out. The exhibitions of Turner's watercolours in London and Birmingham had helped to promote the sale of prints, but not in the quantities necessary for financial survival, and in 1835 Heath sold off the rights, and some stock of *England and Wales* prints, to Thomas Longman in order to pay for what turned out to be the final twenty or so engraved subjects. Longman bought these final engravings in 1838, and had all ninety-six bound into a set of two volumes, entitled *Picturesque Views in England and Wales*. They, too, failed to sell, and Longman offered everything – bound and loose prints and the copper plates – to the dealer H.G. Bohn for £3000. As Bohn would only pay £2800, Longman sent them for auction, where, at the rostrum, Turner himself made a dramatic intervention.[19] He offered £3000 on the spot,

129 *Mount St Michael, Cornwall*, 1836, watercolour, 30.5 × 43.9 cm (12 × 17¼ in.). Engraved 1838. University of Liverpool Art Collections

This and pl. 128 were among the last of Turner's *England and Wales* subjects to be engraved. The dramatic castle framed by threatening skies provides a backdrop to the families salvaging wood from a wreck. Turner impresses on us the fortitude of an island nation that must continually face challenges from the sea.

130 *Gosport, the Entrance to Portsmouth Harbour, Hampshire, c. 1829,* watercolour, 29.2 × 43.2 cm (11½ × 17 in.). Engraved 1831. Portsmouth City Museums

The helmsman, who is not looking where he is going, has put his skiff on a collision-course with the larger vessel, adding sudden drama to an everyday harbour narrative. This comic touch counterpoints the serious business of the naval ships in Portsmouth Harbour.

and took everything away. In a conversation recorded with some added dramatic aplomb by the journalist Alaric Watts, Turner reserved a parting shot for Bohn:

> So, sir, you were going to buy my "England and Wales", to sell cheap, I suppose – make umbrella prints of them, eh? – but I have taken care of that. No more of my plates will be worn to shadows.

Bohn protested that all he wanted was the prints. "Oh, very well", said Turner,

> I don't want the stock. I only want to keep the coppers out of your clutches. So if you like to buy the stock, come and breakfast with me tomorrow, and we will see if we can deal.[20]

When Bohn went to Turner's house the next morning, he offered £2500 for the prints alone, as the copper plates and copyright had been valued at £500. But Turner dismissed the offer contemptuously: "Pooh, I must have my £3000 and keep my coppers; else good morning to you." Bohn left empty-handed.

Turner's *England and Wales* watercolours were painted when his powers as an artist were at their peak. In the same period he was also painting some of his greatest masterpieces in oils: when he began the series he was exhibiting such glowing canvases as *Cologne, the Arrival of a Packet Boat. Evening* (exh. 1826; New York, Frick Collection), and when it was ending in 1838 he was developing his idea of painting the last voyage of the obsolete man-o'-war the *Temeraire* (pl. 151; cat. 118). All the *England and Wales* watercolours were painted after his first visit to Italy, in 1819–20, and the later ones after his second visit, in 1828–29. Thus they were made with the knowledge and experience of Italian light, and some, such as *Lancaster, from the Aqueduct Bridge* (pl. 6; cat. 95) and *Warwick Castle, Warwickshire* (pl. 126; cat. 103), were enriched by it. The

131 *Castle Upnor, Kent, c.* 1831, watercolour, 28.6 × 43.5 cm (11¼ × 17⅛ in.). Engraved 1833. University of Manchester, The Whitworth Art Gallery

Turner makes a quiet allusion to British history here. The barricade of ships across the River Medway refers to the defeat of an invading Dutch fleet by the British Navy and the Castle Upnor garrison in 1667.

132 *Kidwelly Castle, South Wales,*
1835, watercolour, 28.9 × 44.5 cm
(11 ³⁄₈ × 17 ¹⁄₂ in.). Engraved 1837.
Preston, Harris Museum and
Art Gallery

Turner shows an awareness of the
fellowship that existed between
the slow-moving users of the road:
people on foot or horseback, drovers
of livestock, and lumbering carriers'
carts and wagons.

atmospheric and marine effects that Turner created in such watercolours as *Pembroke Castle, Wales* (pl. 10; cat. 100) and *Kidwelly Castle, South Wales* (pl. 132; cat. 108) were unparalleled challenges for engravers. In the engraving of *Dudley, Worcestershire* (pl. 121; cat. 111) the engraver, Robert Wallis, succeeded in reproducing such effects almost perfectly. The best of the *England and Wales* engravings are triumphs of early nineteenth-century printmaking; they are not simply attempting to be reproductions of watercolours, but, as the correspondent to Birmingham's *Aris's Gazette* had instinctively appreciated, works of art in their own right.

CHAPTER V

The Morning Star of Liberty

We can learn little or nothing from written documents about Turner's considered attitude, if he had one, to political reform in Britain in the 1820s and early 1830s. The momentous movement for reform and social change had developed in the late eighteenth century, and reached its climax in the widespread demonstrations that preceded the passing in Parliament of the Third Reform Bill in 1832. Turner had the vote, for he was a property owner, but we have no knowledge of how, or if, he used it.

The evidence of his pictures, however, suggests that although Turner thought deeply about the need for reform of Parliament, his understanding of it was idealistic. Guided through the confusing waters of politics by Walter Fawkes, Turner fostered a heartfelt understanding of the benefits of individual freedom, which he expressed through pictorial allusion and metaphor. His idea of 'liberty' was broader than the struggle for a wider franchise, and incorporated other freedoms – of religious worship, freedom from oppression, and freedom of speech. Despite the passionate advocacy for reform that Fawkes must have rehearsed for him, it is unlikely that Turner ever sought to consider how to organize the machinery of argument and popular support required to achieve it, still less become an activist himself. But although he might not go on a demonstration to express political discontent, he would go to his easel.

Turner had come from a lowly background, and, although his genius brought him riches and took him to some of the grandest houses in the land, he never pretended that he was anything other than a barber's son. His origins gave him a personal context for his championing of the idea of liberty, which also flourished through his reading of and reflection on the history and literature of the Classical world and of Britain. He celebrated modern Greek independence in *The Temple of Jupiter Panellenius Restored* (exh. 1816; New York, private collection) and its companion painting, *View of the Temple of Jupiter Panellenius, in the Island of Ægina, with the Greek National Dance of the Romaika* (exh. 1816; Alnwick Castle, Duke of Northumberland), and in many other works painted for exhibition he explored the rise and fall of empire – Carthage, Rome and Venice are among his exemplars. Turner further depicted the struggle against oppression in British history through such subjects as *Dolbadern Castle* (pl. 33 ; cat. 25). When he protested against the infringement of

133 *The Fighting 'Temeraire', tugged to her Last Berth to be broken up, 1838,* 1839, detail of pl. 151

religious freedom – for example by allowing a politically charged rubric to be engraved on three or four presentation proofs beneath his image of *The Birthplace of John Wycliffe, near Rokeby* (pl. 140; cat. 125; see Appendix II, p. 196) – he did so in what appears to be a burst of indignation.

In his early career Turner had left understated topical, even political, messages in his pictures – one example among many is his warning of dangers to Britain from the French navy in 1804 in *Boats carrying out Anchors and Cables to Dutch men o'War, 1665* (exh. 1804; Washington, DC, Corcoran Gallery).[1] This reminder that the Dutch had rebuilt their navy in 1665 and returned to harry the British navy was expressed so subtly that nobody commenting on the 1804 Royal Academy exhibition seemed to have noticed it, nor noticed the contemporary parallel with growing French naval power. He re-echoed the theme of British supremacy over Holland in the watercolour *Castle Upnor, Kent* (pl. 131; cat. 106). The watercolours that Turner made for engraving in the 1820s and 1830s, however, are clearer and richer sources of political and historical allusion. On the mast of the central boat in *Nottingham, Nottinghamshire* (pl. 134; cat. 124) he painted the Greek flag, a symbol

134 *Nottingham, Nottinghamshire*, 1832, watercolour, 30.5 × 46.3 cm (12 × 18¼ in.). Engraved 1833. City of Nottingham Museums and Galleries. From the *England and Wales* series

The double rainbow and the passing storm reflect the national mood of optimism felt after the passage of the Reform Act in June 1832. A Greek flag flies from the central boat, a symbol of that nation's successful struggle for independence.

135 *Northampton, Northamptonshire,* 1830–31, watercolour, 29.5 × 43.9 cm (11⅝ × 17⅛ in.), private collection, on loan to the Indiana University Art Museum

Turner depicts the chairing of Lord Althorp, who was re-elected in December 1830, unopposed, as Whig member of parliament for Northampton. Althorp's party supported reform, and Turner leaves no doubt in this watercolour that his own political sympathies lie with the reform movement.

of that nation's successful struggle for independence that ran parallel to the struggle for parliamentary reform in Britain.[2] The Greek flag sets up a series of further allusions to liberty in this picture for the *England and Wales* series. Specifically, Nottingham Castle, seen on the left, was itself a symbol of oppression and the fight for liberty through the legend of Robin Hood, dramatized by Sir Walter Scott in his novel *Ivanhoe* (1819); furthermore, Nottinghamshire was the home county of Lord Byron (1788–1824), the champion of liberty for Greece and one of Turner's literary heroes.

The clearest instance of Turner's sympathy for the reform movement is evident in his watercolour *Northampton, Northamptonshire* (pl. 135), in which he does no less than paint a political demonstration. Such an overtly political image contrasts strongly with the overall theme of occasional and subtle historical and social allusion in the imagery of the *England and Wales* series, and it may be for that reason that the watercolour was never engraved. The show of political excitement in the picture was the local expression of a great victory for the pro-reform Whigs through the re-election in December 1830 of Lord Althorp as MP for Northamptonshire.[3] The banners

that the crowds wave reflect their, and by inference the artist's, feelings on the current political ferment: "REFORM", "NO BRIBERY" and "The Purity of Elections is the Triumph of LAW" are among the slogans depicted. The presence on the extreme left of a woman wearing Greek costume makes another point about liberty, while that of the figure in the tricorn hat, slumped in a wing chair, may symbolize the 'tired' old order.

In the foreground of *Salisbury, from Old Sarum* (pl. 136; cat. 122), another *England and Wales* subject, is depicted one of the most notorious 'rotten boroughs' in Britain: an ancient mound of earth uninhabited since the Middle Ages that traditionally elected two MPs. Turner shows it populated largely by sheep, who outnumber the shepherd and his family by about twenty to one, and emphasizes its emptiness by comparison with the majesty and implied order of Salisbury Cathedral in the distance. The light falling on Salisbury, also known as New Sarum, is in stark contrast to the shadowed form of Old Sarum; and in showing the shepherd and his family preparing to shelter from the approaching storm, Turner may be reflecting on impending political turmoil.

136 *Salisbury, from Old Sarum, c.* 1828, watercolour, 27.2 × 39.5 cm (10¾ × 15½ in.). Engraved 1830. Salisbury and South Wiltshire Museum. From the *England and Wales* series

In the foreground children huddle under a shawl as a heavy shower approaches. What appears to be a peaceful rural scene provides a context for Turner's comment on 'rotten boroughs'. Old Sarum was a notoriously corrupt parliamentary borough, and a central issue in the campaign for parliamentary reform.

137 *Sidmouth, Devon*, 1825–27, watercolour, 18.4 × 26.3 cm (7⅛ × 10⅜ in.). Engraving begun in 1828, published 1856. University of Manchester, The Whitworth Art Gallery. From the *Ports of England* series

The extraordinary phallic rock may be a direct reference to the sixty-six-year-old former prime minister Lord Sidmouth's second marriage to a younger widow. His repressive legislation and his involvement in the causes of the Peterloo Massacre in 1819 earned him widespread unpopularity.

Allusions to historical and political events in Turner's watercolours are sometimes so light as to be barely appreciable. There are, however, notable cases in which a careful interpretation of the details can transform the meaning of the picture. Such an example is the watercolour *Sidmouth, Devon* (pl. 137; cat. 120), made for the *Ports of England* series. The extraordinary rock form in the middleground is overwhelmingly larger than that drawn by Turner on his 1811 tour of Devon.[4] As Eric Shanes has suggested, its phallic shape may be a reference to the well-publicized second marriage in 1823 of the sixty-six-year-old former prime minister Lord Sidmouth (1757–1844) to a widow nearly thirty years his junior.[5] The Tory politician Sidmouth was widely reviled for introducing repressive legislation, including the suspension of habeas corpus in 1817. He was heavily implicated in the causes of the Peterloo Massacre of 1819 – an attack by cavalry forces against a large but peaceful crowd of supporters of political reform – and was a hate figure for the Whigs, the party of Walter Fawkes.

Another example with subtle overtones of political and social reform is *Blenheim House and Park, Oxfordshire* (pl. 138; cat. 123). Shanes first published the suggestion that the painting, made in the late autumn or winter of 1830–31, alludes to coming social change in which the middle and rural classes would challenge the supremacy of the aristocracy. The former groups are represented in the painting by the men, women and children who have shyly emerged through the Blenheim estate's Woodstock town gate on the right, and the latter by the hunting party arriving smartly

from the left, led by a confrontational gentleman with a gun and aggressive dogs.[6] The pose of the man with the gun is comparable to those of the central welcoming figures in *England: Richmond Hill, on the Prince Regent's Birthday* (pl. 106; cat. 73), but in this case the welcome is anything but friendly.

The allusions in Turner's narratives are historical as well as political, for example in the *England and Wales* watercolour *Colchester, Essex* (pl. 139; cat. 121). In the foreground a hare is pursued by a dog, accompanied by wild shouting and waving from a miller's family on the right, and from a horseman on the left. Colchester Castle, behind the trees in the centre of the picture, was the place where Matthew Hopkins (*d.* 1647), the self-styled 'Witchfinder General', passed judgment during the English Civil War. According to rural tradition witches turned themselves into hares, and Turner may have added a visual pun on the supposed blackness of the witch by painting the hare black (hares are brown) and the chasing dog in contrasting white. The seveteenth-century poet Ben Jonson observed: "A witch is a kind of hare/ And marks the weather/ As the hare doth."[7] Furthermore, there is a Turnerian verbal pun here – in Samuel Johnson's *Dictionary* the

138 *Blenheim House and Park, Oxfordshire*, 1830–31, watercolour, 29.6 × 46.8 cm (11⅝ × 18⅜ in.). Engraved 1833. Birmingham Museums & Art Gallery. From the *England and Wales* series

The family groups that shyly emerge through Blenheim's town gate on the right are confronted by an aristocratic hunting party. Turner may here be alluding to coming social change, in which middle and rural classes would challenge the supremacy of the aristocracy.

139 *Colchester, Essex, c.* 1825, watercolour, 28.8 × 40.7 cm (11⅜ × 16 in.). Engraved 1827. London, Courtauld Institute Gallery. From the *England and Wales* series

At Colchester Castle Matthew Hopkins, the 'Witchfinder General', carried out witch trials during the English Civil War. According to rural tradition, witches turned themselves into hares, and in this considered and complex allusion to folklore, local history and liberty, Turner has depicted a hare running across the foreground.

meaning of "to hare" was "to fright, to hurry with terror"; the hare, in fear for its life, is hurrying with terror directly below Colchester Castle, where so many 'witches' were imprisoned, tried and summarily sentenced to death.

The narrative details in Turner's landscape watercolours – the Greek flag in *Nottingham*, the running hare in *Colchester* and perhaps even the phallic rock in *Sidmouth* – might all have been added as finishing touches, long after the main elements of the composition were set down. This suggests that Turner ruminated deeply about his subjects while he was painting, and reveals also the degree of his occasional knowledge of the local history of his subjects.

The references in *Wycliffe, near Rokeby* (pls. 140, 141; cat. 119, 125) are to both historical and contemporary events. In the early nineteenth century Wycliffe Hall was thought to have been the birthplace of John Wycliffe, the fourteenth-century religious reformer, who produced the first translation of the Bible in English. Discussing the picture with John Pye, its engraver, Turner revealed that the geese represented old superstitions that were being driven away by the Reformation of the Church, and the burst of light over the house, present in the engraving but not in the watercolour, should be interpreted as "the light of the glorious Reformation".[8]

When Charles Heath commissioned the engraving for *England and Wales*, Turner had some extra proofs taken, with a new title, *The Birthplace of John Wycliffe (The Morning Star of Liberty) near*

140 John Pye after J M.W. Turner, *The Birthplace of John Wycliffe (The Morning Star of Liberty) near Rokeby, Yorkshire*, 1823, engraving proof with inscription, London, British Museum

This is the only known proof bearing an inscription that provides a history of the dissemination of the Bible in English. It ends with a politically dangerous reference to the trial of the radical Humphrey Boyle in 1822.

Rokeby, Yorkshire, and a long text supplied by him or another engraved in the lower margin. The text provides a brief history of the dissemination of the Bible in English, from Wycliffe's first translation in the fourteenth century to the work of an unnamed society for the distribution of the Bible. It ends with a reference to the trial in May 1822 of the radical Humphrey Boyle on charges of sedition, disaffection and profanity. Boyle refused to give his name in court, and the fact that he is named in the text suggests that somebody involved in the production of the print had some inside knowledge of radical circles and their apparatus of publicity.[9] This may have been Turner himself, but it may equally have been Walter Fawkes. But whoever named Boyle, Turner's approval of the text was a significant piece of political protest, and as near as he got to action.[10] Only "three or four" presentation proofs of this state were made, suggesting that Turner or Pye may prudently have thought better of circulating the print in this form.[11] They may, however, have been exercising a quite different and more commercial sort of prudence, knowing that the copper plate would wear out sooner if too many presentation proofs were made.

One of the very few oil paintings in the Turner Bequest (Tate, London) with a meaning not yet fully explained is the canvas known as '*Death on a Pale Horse*' (pl. 142; cat. 117) – a title given when the

141 *Wycliffe, near Rokeby, c.* 1816–20, watercolour, 29.2 × 43 cm (11½ × 16⅞ in.). Engraved 1823. Liverpool, Walker Art Gallery. From the *History of Richmondshire* series

Wycliffe Hall was thought to be the birthplace of John Wycliffe, the fourteenth-century religious reformer who produced the first English translation of the Bible. Turner revealed to his engraver that the geese represented old superstitions being driven away by the reformation of the church.

work was catalogued after Turner's death. In rapid and light brushwork it depicts the head and shoulders of a rearing horse carrying away what appears to be a decomposing corpse wearing a coronet. A landscape below the main figure may represent a series of buildings or a city, but this is by no means clear. Interpretations of the work have varied from its being a response to Turner's father's death in 1829, a subject painting of imagery from the Book of Revelation, or a reference to the liberation of Greece, the form of the horse's head being modelled on a horse in the Parthenon frieze (part of the Elgin Marbles sold to the nation in 1816). Another suggestion is that it alludes to the unexpected, unwelcome and all-encompassing event that immediately preceded the passing of the Reform Bill: the widespread outbreak of cholera in Britain over the winter of 1831–32. Many thousands of people died of the disease in Scotland, in the North of England and particularly in London, and it is clear that Turner, for one, was frightened of catching it.[12] It may be reasonable to suggest, therefore, that the picture is an acknowledgement of the power of disease, with the coronet

142 *'Death on a Pale Horse'*, 1831–32, oil on canvas, 60 × 75.5 cm (23⅝ × 29¾ in.), London, Tate

The meaning of this oil painting has never been fully explained. It may be a response to the widespread outbreak of cholera in Britain over the winter of 1831–32.

symbolizing the fact that cholera is no respecter of rank. It is a small step from that suggestion to the idea that the painting also alludes to the possible consequences of a failure of the Reform Bill.

Turner's poetry, though composed extensively in the late 1800s and early 1810s, was limited in the 1830s to near-illegible, scribbled verses of various lengths in the sketchbooks, and to extracts from a poem that now exists only in fragments, 'Fallacies of Hope'.[13] Some of Turner's earlier poetry, however, reflects his passion for liberty and the sanctity of nationhood, although one does have to search quite hard for it. In the 'Devonshire Verses' of 1811, for example, are the lines:

> … on a rocky rampart stood
> A Guardian once like others thro the land
> Where native valour dare[s] to make a stand
> Against [?despotism] and Rome … fought
> The prize of valour gaind though dearly bought
> Thus wrought their nature by progressive degrees
> As morning fogs that rising tempt the breeze.[14]

143 *A Frontispiece (at Farnley Hall)*, 1815, pen and ink, watercolour, 17.8 × 24.2 cm (7 × 9½ in.), Oxford, Ashmolean Museum

A watercolour painted to introduce the series of *Historical Vignettes* and *Fairfaxiana* made by Turner for Walter Fawkes.

When the radical politician and writer John Cam Hobhouse (1786–1869) stayed at Farnley Hall with Walter Fawkes in 1823, Turner was a fellow guest. Hobhouse was very surprised to find "the most celebrated landscape painter of our time – I mean Turner, who was employed in making designs for a museum intended to contain relics of our civil wars and to be called *Fairfaxiana*."[15] Had he been a regular guest at Farnley, Hobhouse might not have been quite so taken aback, as Turner was often seen there painting subjects that, for an artist of his stature, might have seemed to an outsider to be absurd. Studies of birds, interiors of Farnley Hall and informal pictures of life at Farnley (pls. 62, 64; cat. 55, 56) all came from his brush during his visits, the nearest to holidays that he ever had. The *Historical Vignettes* and *Fairfaxiana* watercolours (pls. 143–47; cat. 127, 128), which the Fawkes family bound together into an album in 1912, celebrate the evolution of liberty and the rule of law in Britain from the Norman Conquest in 1066 to the English Civil War and the 'Glorious Revolution' of 1688. Bound together they form two distinct sequences: the *Historical Vignettes* (fols. 1–12) and *Fairfaxiana* (fols. 13–17 and the Ashmolean sheet). In their content and narrative they focus both on the presence at Farnley of relics from the Civil War left by Walter Fawkes's forebear, the Parliamentarian general Thomas Fairfax (1612–1671), and on Fawkes's and Turner's telling of British history. Before the watercolours were bound, the frontispiece to the *Fairfaxiana* had long disappeared from Farnley and had come into

   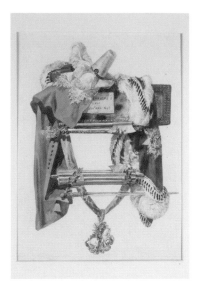

John Ruskin's collection.[16] Ruskin subsequently presented it to the Ashmolean Museum, Oxford (pl. 143; cat. 128).

144, 145 *Historical Vignettes*, pencil and watercolour, 1815–mid-1820s, from the *Historical Vignettes* and *Fairfaxiana* album. Private collection

The twelve *Historical Vignettes* foreshadow, in their small size and emblematic character, the long series of vignettes that Turner painted as illustrations for literature from about 1830. They are atmospheric and allusive, and their power lies in Turner's ability to render in watercolour the telling eloquence of objects. There is wit and humour in the images: in the first of the series Turner added graffiti, including "WALTER" and "Abbott slept in this chair" (pl. 144; cat. 127(i)), to the royal thrones in Westminster Abbey. In the second a small red silk bag is sewn to the sheet representing Agincourt (cat. 127(ii)). It contained the gold coin, depicted on the page, that was found on the battlefield at Agincourt in France and presented to Fawkes by Major General Sir Edward Barnes in 1823.[17] In the *Fairfaxiana* swords, an oak cupboard, a wheeled chair, documents, Fairfax's hat and many other items found at Farnley all feature (pl. 146), as do long texts in both sections, some written in the tiniest of handwriting, that are either transcriptions of documents, or exhortations. The last sheet in the *Fairfaxiana* shows the Fairfax oak cabinet, with painted doors that open and shut, containing documents, the swords of Oliver Cromwell, Fairfax and General John Lambert, and portraits of Cromwell and Fairfax, among other things (pl. 147; cat. 127 (xvii)). It is not clear if either the *Fairfaxiana* or the *Historical Vignettes* are complete, or if Fawkes and Turner planned to make more pages for either. Two pages in the *Historical Vignettes* are blank except for a painted frame, inscribed "OLIVER CROMWELL" and "RICHARD CROMWELL" respectively, and to which small portrait engravings were to be affixed (pl. 145).

Fawkes was a sincere and committed politician. He campaigned with William Wilberforce (1759–1833) against slavery, fought for parliamentary reform, supported the radical MP Sir Francis Burdett without compromise, and spoke at the Crown and Anchor Tavern in the Strand,

London, in 1812 at a meeting to celebrate the tenth anniversary of Burdett's election to Parliament. The plaster bust of Burdett by Sir Francis Chantrey (1781–1841), displayed in the drawing-room at Farnley, is clearly visible in Turner's gouache of the interior.[18] The friendship that Turner and Fawkes shared was so long and mutually fulfilling that their political views must have been compatible. The Britain of liberty and democracy that Fawkes worked to achieve was also, as implicit in his paintings, Turner's Britain.

The overall intention behind the *Historical Vignettes* and *Fairfaxiana* has not previously been determined. The album is comparable with the set of bird studies that Turner painted for Fawkes, and which were used as illustrations to Fawkes's 'Natural History' volumes,[19] lists of birds and animals shot at Farnley, and with collected material such as feathers and eggs.[20] Fawkes

was a trenchant writer on politics, publishing *Chronology of the History of Modern Europe* (1810),[21] *A Speech on Parliamentary Reform* (1812) and *The Englishman's Manual; or, A Dialogue between a Tory and a Reformer* (1817). Turner had provided frontispieces for the *Chronology*, a plain reference book of 250 tables listing kings and queens of Europe,[22] which reflects Fawkes's passion for order and classification rather than any skill of his as a historian or interpreter of evidence. It seems most likely that the *Historical Vignettes* were intended as page illustrations to an unwritten history of Britain by Walter Fawkes, while *Fairfaxiana* was a celebration of family history. Given the catastrophic state of Fawkes's finances in the late 1810s and 1820s, however, any further publication by him was a forlorn hope. He was, as Turner was probably aware, nearly bankrupt.[23] Nevertheless, the two men persisted in creating the collections together, and Turner left them with the Fawkes family when Walter died.

Two years after the Reform Bill had been passed, the Houses of Parliament were destroyed by a fire that broke out in the early evening of 16 October 1834. A stove in the House of Lords, in which a large quantity of wooden tally sticks was being burned, was left untended. Despite smoke being noticed in the chamber during the afternoon, nobody took the slightest action and the fire was left to smoulder until it was too late.[24] Thousands of people came to watch the huge conflagration from the banks of the Thames and from small boats. Among them was Turner. He appears to have made some studies on the spot,[25] moving from near the fire to further away across the river, but he took his time before making a considered response. His response came over the following six months in four works that draw the viewer from the heart of the firefighting action in Old Palace Yard, Westminster – depicted in the watercolour *The Burning of the Houses of Parliament* (London, Tate)[26] – to two positions increasingly distant from the blaze – the south bank of the Thames and the south end of Waterloo Bridge. These are the points from which the views in

146, 147 *Fairfaxiana*, pencil and watercolour, 1815–mid-1820s, from the *Historical Vignettes* and *Fairfaxiana* album. Private collection

Turner's two oil paintings, both titled *The Burning of the Houses of Lords and Commons, 16th October 1834* (pls. 149, 150), are taken. The gap between the event and Turner's depictions of it allowed him plenty of time to ruminate, a process intensified by his act of painting the subject four times.

The watercolour was no doubt painted quietly in his studio, and was perhaps the first of the series. But for the first oil (pl. 149) Turner took the extraordinary decision to rough out the image on canvas, take the canvas in early January 1835 to the British Institution in Pall Mall, and paint it on one of the preparatory 'Varnishing Days' in front of an audience of fellow artists and members of the institution.[27] The occasion was the annual winter exhibition of the British Institution, an organization that was controlled by a committee of aristocratic and landed connoisseurs as a rival to the artist-controlled Royal Academy. Turner had not exhibited there since 1814, when he had had a spat with the management. The patrons and directors of the British Institution were just that section of British life – Tory peers, bishops, landed gentry – that had resisted reform and had wanted to keep their grip on the 'rotten' and 'pocket' boroughs. That Turner should choose this moment, and this subject, for his return to the British Institution was his way of sending the stark message to the heart of the Establishment that the old order was on notice. A fellow artist, Edward Rippingille, watched Turner painting and wrote of how he had been hard at work on the picture for hours:

> he never ceased to work, or even once turned from the wall on which his picture hung. … Presently the work was finished: Turner gathered his tools together, put them into and shut [his] box, and then, with his face still turned to the wall, and at the same distance from it, went sliding off, without speaking a word to anybody, and when he came to the staircase in the centre of the room, hurried down as fast as he could.[28]

Before an audience of his peers Turner created a picture of a dreadful fire that had symbolized the destruction of an old, unjust order. But to the members of the British Institution it was also the most direct, least coded warning that Turner had yet painted: this conflagration had indeed actually happened, but it is also what might have happened if reform had not occurred, and might so happen again if the Establishment did not listen to the people of Britain. Walter Fawkes had also used a fiery metaphor in 1812 when he addressed the meeting at the Crown and Anchor Tavern to celebrate the anniversary of the election of Burdett. Quoting the writer and politician Edmund Burke (1729–1797), Fawkes said:

> Early Reformations are made when the blood is in a cool state – late Reformations are made in a state of inflammation. In this state the people see nothing respectable in government – they see its abuses but they see nothing else. They fall into the temper of a populace, indignant at the conduct of a house of ill fame. They never think

148 James T. Willmore after J.M.W. Turner, *Destruction of both Houses of Parliament by Fire Oct. 16, 1834*, 1835, engraving, 10.6 × 8.7 cm (4⅛ × 3⅜ in.), Birmingham Museums & Art Gallery. Engraving for *The Keepsake*, 1835

149 *The Burning of the House of Lords and Commons, 16th October 1834*, exhibited 1835, oil on canvas, 92 × 123 cm (36¼ × 48½ in.), Philadelphia Museum of Art, The John Howard McFadden Collection

Turner's first version of the subject. The artist painted the picture in front of an audience of fellow-artists at the British Institution on 'Varnishing Day', prior to the opening of the exhibition in January 1835. As well as being a record of an actual event, Turner's painting also symbolized the destruction of the old, unjust order by the force of political reform.

of correcting, they go to work the shortest way – they abate the nuisance but they pull down the house.[29]

Turner could not leave the subject of the burning of the Houses of Parliament alone, despite the continuing pressure on him to produce other oil paintings for exhibition and watercolours for engraving – one of the latter, engraved by James Willmore, was yet another view of the fire (pl. 148; cat. 126). Turner delivered the second oil of the subject to the Royal Academy in late April 1835. The work has the same title as the earlier oil,[30] but takes a panoramic view, from the end of Waterloo Bridge about eight hundred yards downstream from the Houses of Parliament. The crowds just visible in the first oil near the burning buildings are out of sight, and we witness now the Houses of Parliament left to burn, the immense flame filling the sky with light, reflecting in the river and consuming this potent symbol of the works of man. The continuing power of Turner's *Burning of the Houses of Lords and Commons* is such that the imagery, particularly in the second version (the Cleveland Museum of Art canvas; pl. 150), has remained a weapon in the armoury of modern political cartoonists. Steve Bell, in his evocation of the end of John Major's Conservative government, parodied the painting in *The Guardian* newspaper in May 1997, and it was the source for Dave

Brown's cartoon of November 2002 in *The Independent* newspaper linking the Queen's speech at the State Opening of Parliament with the then current firefighters' strike.[31]

Across the river from The Ship and Bladebone, an inn that Turner owned and visited regularly, in Wapping, London, was the yard of the shipbreaker and timber-merchant John Beatson in Rotherhithe.[32] In 1838 the former 98-gun ship of the line, *Temeraire*, was towed there to be broken up. The ship had been built at Chatham, in Kent, where she was launched in 1798, and served first as the flagship of the Channel fleet off Brest in France.[33] Soon after the Peace of Amiens was announced in October 1801, some of her crew refused to weigh anchor and set sail for a new naval station in the West Indies. They chanted "No, no, no" and "England, England" in response to their orders. This was a clear act of mutiny for which fourteen of the ringleaders were court-martialled and hanged, eight of them from *Temeraire's* own yardarm.

It was at the Battle of Trafalgar on 21 October 1805 that the ship and her crew had their greatest moment. There they fought under the command of Captain Eliab Harvey, with twenty-six other ships of the line, against the combined Spanish and French fleets. Her position was directly astern of Horatio Nelson's flagship, *Victory*, and as the battle intensified *Temeraire* saved *Victory* by firing a broadside at the French ship *Redoubtable*, approaching from the larboard (left) side, and then by firing another from the starboard (right) side at *Fougueux*. The *Temeraire* was severely damaged, but both French ships were crippled and taken, one lashed on each side of her. As Captain Harvey described this part of the battle in his log:

> Lashed both Ships to the Temeraire being totally a Wreck. Fell off and had the opportunity of raking the Enemies first rate for half an hour with some of the Foremost guns, the Ship lashed on the Larbd side, her Main Mast Yd and all the Wreck fell on the Temeraire's poop which entirely encumbered the after part of the Ship.[34]

On her journey home under tow via Gibraltar, *Temeraire's* two prizes had to be cut away in a storm and were lost to the sea. But she was refitted in Portsmouth dockyard, and in 1807 set sail to rejoin the English fleet off Toulon. In 1812 she was decommissioned, and served thereafter first as a prison ship at Plymouth, Devon (1813–20), and then as a victualling, training and receiving ship off Sheerness, Kent. Her guns were fired for the last time on 28 June 1838 to mark Queen Victoria's coronation. Only two weeks later the ship was dismasted, had her fittings removed, and was sold to John Beatson.

With one tug pulling, and another attached to her stern as a brake, on 5 and 6 September 1838 *Temeraire* was taken the fifty miles from Sheerness to Rotherhithe. Many apocryphal stories claimed that Turner saw her final journey,[35] but they must all be reflections after the event, developed after his painting – *The Fighting 'Temeraire', tugged to her Last Berth to be broken up, 1838* (pls. 133,

150 *The Burning of the Houses of Lords and Commons, 16th October 1834,* exhibited 1835, oil on canvas, 92.5 × 123 cm (36⅜ × 48½ in.), Cleveland Museum of Art, Ohio

Turner's second version of the subject, painted only a few weeks after pl. 149 for the Royal Academy exhibition in late April. The viewpoint is down-river from the first version. The strength of the blaze is graphically conveyed by its contrast with the puny lights on the riverboats.

151; cat. 118) – had been exhibited at the Royal Academy the following summer. In fact the artist was probably in Margate or France when *Temeraire* was towed to the breakers – he was seen coming back from Margate on the steamship *City of Canterbury* on 23 September.[36] However, Turner would have seen press reports describing the huge hulk, which was the largest vessel ever to have been tugged so far up the Thames. *The Times* reported: "The majestic appearance of this fine ship excited much interest and curiosity; every vessel she passed appeared like a pygmy."[37] On arrival at Beatson's wharf she became immediately an object of curiosity, and her great moment at Trafalgar had not been forgotten:

> the wharf, and the pier-head of the Surrey Canal dock, have been often crowded
> with people, more particularly on Sunday afternoons, to see the remains of the noble
> vessel which acted so distinguished a part at the memorable battle of Trafalgar.[38]

Whether he saw the journey of *Temeraire* up the Thames or not, Turner would have known or guessed from his own experience exactly how the ship was hauled up the river, even if he did choose to omit the second tug from his painting. He also had every opportunity, like the crowds

reported in *The Times*, to see the hulk on a Sunday afternoon, or at any time from the opposite bank of the river at Wapping, and no doubt did so.

Turner's painting of *Temeraire*'s final journey is concerned with infinitely more than the end of an old boat: it is a poem with balance, structure, colour, weight, and, above all, metaphor and allusion; further, it reflects on change in human affairs and on the passing of time. It is a scene at early evening with the sun setting – it must be sunset and not sunrise, because there is a new moon which cannot be visible at sunrise. Thus the old and the new are together in the sky, as they are on the river. The tug, flying a white flag – a universal sign of surrender – pulls the ghostly hulk fitted with three masts. These create a series of strong verticals that together create a diagonal, and also transform the hulk, in reality dismasted before it left Sheerness, back into a

151 *The Fighting 'Temeraire', tugged to her Last Berth to be broken up, 1838*, exhibited RA 1839, oil on canvas, 91 × 122 cm (35⅞ × 48 in.), London, National Gallery

Turner's powerful painting of a contemporary event transformed into an image of national heroism and endurance. Here he evokes the end of 'the wooden walls of England', as oak-built men-o'-war had been known from the seventeenth century.

sailing ship. A funnel on the tug is shown further forwards than it would be in reality, enabling Turner to show its smoke obscuring the jackstaff, that part of the rig from which the Union Jack is flown on a ship in harbour. In obscuring that part of the ship, Turner is alluding to the lines he added to the painting's entry in the 1839 Royal Academy catalogue: "The flag which braved the battle and the breeze,/ No longer owns her." Turner's words here were adapted from the first verse of Thomas Campbell's poem (later set to music) that begins:

Ye Mariners of England!
That guard our native seas,
Whose flag has braved, a thousand years,
The battle and the breeze –
Your glorious standard launch again
To match another foe!

It might further be observed that the colours of the Union Jack – red, white and blue – are all significant elements in the painting, which also contains the horizontal, vertical and diagonal lines that feature on the flag. The painting achieves balance in both content and form: sail and steam; air and water; silence and noise; dignity and presumption; steadiness and urgency; the temporal and the eternal; change and adaptability; the past and the present, and, by implication, the future.

Turner did not try very hard to sell the painting;[39] he waited a short while for approaches but never sold it, despite in 1848 being offered first £5000, and then a blank cheque, by the American collector James Lenox.[40] Nor would he lend it again, after it had been out of his studio in 1844 to be engraved by James Willmore. He drafted a letter in a sketchbook saying, "no considerations of money or favour can induce me to lend my Darling again."[41] The full title Turner gave to the picture, *The Fighting 'Temeraire', tugged to her Last Berth to be broken up, 1838*, describes an event rather than the subject itself. This was a lifelong characteristic: many titles of exhibited works are descriptive, introductory and scene-setting (see, for example, cat. 31, 73). Thus the title of this picture is a little history in itself, a threnody with universal resonance: an epithet, a name, a journey, a birth, a death and a date. With his love of jokes and wordplay, we should not allow the consonance of the words "berth" and "birth" to pass unmarked. In 1838, the year of the coronation of the new queen, Turner is marking for his fellow countrymen the final pageant of the Napoleonic Wars, now part of history.

CHAPTER VI

The New Moon

In the 1840s Turner's priorities, as he aged and lapsed in and out of illness, were changing with new influences. Having been interested enough in the reform movement in the early and mid-1830s to draw it into his paintings, what political fire had once been in his belly had long since burnt itself out. There may perhaps be a hint of the old campaigner in the circumstances behind a letter sent to Turner by Arthur Wellesley, Duke of Wellington, in early November 1841. There had been a destructive fire in the Tower of London on 30 October that had burned for six days: according to *The Times*, the fire "exceeded in grandeur even the great fire at the House of Commons".[1] George Cruikshank and other artists had been allowed to sketch the ruins, but in the letter Turner was curtly refused entry by the duke, who was then Constable of the Tower.[2] One is tempted to the conclusion that a reason for this was that Turner's paintings *The Burning of the Houses of Lords and Commons* had had the required effect. By all appearances Turner had hung up his hat as a quasi-political commentator, his final and most furious commentary on contemporary events being *Slavers Throwing Overboard the Dead and Dying – Typhon Coming on* (exh. 1840; Boston MA, Museum of Fine Arts).[3] References to the modern world that Turner made in his paintings after 1840 are focused not on the great political issues, such as the Chartist movement for political and social reform, or revolution in Europe, but on such intangibles as the tension between man, his new technologies and nature.

The tiny smudge on the horizon in *The New Moon; or, 'I've lost My Boat, You shan't have Your Hoop'* (pls. 152, 153; cat. 129), exhibited in 1840, signals more than just the distant presence of a steamboat off Margate, Kent. It is a small note of optimism in a visionary painted world in which the cycles of the sun and the moon, a busy port on the horizon, larking dogs and squabbling children all unite in the ineradicable presence of technical progress. This painting is Turner's evocation of the peaceable kingdom, but one that is shot through with the constant reality of disagreement: one squabbling child is saying to the other, as the painting's full title indicates, "I've lost my boat, you shan't have your hoop." Painted in the same range of colours as *The Fighting 'Temeraire'* (pl. 151; cat. 118), *The New Moon* is Turner's final exhibited statement on the tranquility of the English landscape, and plucks for the last time at the chromatic chords that we saw first in *England: Richmond Hill, on the Prince Regent's Birthday* (pl. 106; cat. 73).

152 *The New Moon*, 1840, detail of pl. 153

153 *The New Moon; or, 'I've lost My Boat,*
You shan't have Your Hoop', exhibited RA
1840, oil on panel, 65.5 × 81.5 cm
(25¾ × 32 in.), London, Tate

Despite the evident calm, Turner
depicts a treacherous cross-current
in the wave to the left, which subtly
underlines the quarrelsome tone in
the title. A steamboat on the horizon
heralds the modern industrial age that
the squabbling children will inherit.

154 *Morning after the Wreck*, 1840s, oil on canvas, 38 × 61 cm (15 × 24 in.), Cardiff, National Museums and Galleries of Wales

A moving amalgam of Turner's lifetime's experience of seashore activity, as depicted so sharply in pls. 110 and 129. This blurred merging of images evokes memories of the end of the age of the great wooden sailing ships.

In the final decade of Turner's life, Britain as a subject for painting effectively disappeared from the artist's exhibited work. Indeed, the last landscape of a named English place that he showed at the Royal Academy, *St Michael's Mount, Cornwall* (London, Victoria and Albert Museum), was exhibited as early as 1834. Instead, when he came to paint Britain in oil in works for public viewing, as he had in watercolour in the rapidly waning *England and Wales* series, he produced canvases with far deeper levels of meaning than evocation of place. The prime examples of this new approach are *Rain, Steam, and Speed – the Great Western Railway* (exh. 1844; London, National Gallery) and *The New Moon*.

After the appearance of *The New Moon* at the Royal Academy in 1840, where it was greeted with puzzlement,[4] Turner began gradually to extinguish all sense of place in his paintings of British landscape subjects. There is a hint of the form of a harbour in *Morning after the Wreck* (pl. 154; cat. 130), in which a ghostly ship passes in full sail, haunting the foreshore as people pick over tangled wreckage. Though undoubtedly inspired by something Turner had seen from the Kent coast, we are nowhere in particular, just at the end of an era.

The extinguishing of the sense of place became complete in the two landscapes *The Falls of the Clyde* (pl. 155; cat. 132) and *Landscape with river and distant mountains* (pl. 156; cat. 133). In the former, Turner returned to a subject and composition that had first engaged him on his 1801 tour of Scotland, and that he had painted in watercolour in 1802 as *The Fall of the Clyde, Lanarkshire: Noon. – Vide Akenside's Hymn to the Naiads* (pl. 52; cat. 31). Turner did not title the late oil painting, which is a version of the *Liber Studiorum* plate engraved from the 1802 watercolour. It was produced during a long period of introspection in which Turner reminded himself of early subjects by looking again at his *Liber Studiorum* prints and by having some of them reprinted.[5] We are not, however, in any place in this picture, barely even in a landscape, but surrounded by an elemental mix of earth, air and water. Other *Liber Studiorum* subjects to which Turner returned in old age include *Walton Bridges*

155 *The Falls of the Clyde*, 1840s, oil on canvas, 89 × 119.5 cm (35 × 47 in.), Port Sunlight, Lady Lever Art Gallery

A reprise of a subject from Turner's youth (pl. 52), painted in the artist's old age when he reflected on the past in a number of ruminative canvases. So vague is the landscape that we have to take the title on trust.

156 *Landscape with river and distant mountains*, 1840s, oil on canvas, 92 × 122.5 cm (36¼ × 48¼ in.), Liverpool, Walker Art Gallery

A luminous image of distant memory, perhaps the Thames of Turner's youth.

(pl. 57; cat. 42) and *Norham Castle* (*c.* 1840–50; London, Tate), which, despite its deserved fame as an image, is nowhere on this planet, just a blue rock and an unearthly cow. *Landscape with river and distant mountains* is not quite so far removed from reality. There may in this painting be a haunting from a Thames-side subject of about 1805–06, but shown here is a landscape dissolved in bright light, a visual effect now familiar from overexposed photographs. While a number of late Turners, particularly some Venetian subjects, are unfinished, their luminous forms mapped out by blocks of underpaint, we can be fairly confident that in *Landscape with river and distant mountains* the artist took the abstraction of the image as far as he wanted, or was able, to go.

As an old man (he was seventy in 1845) Turner was increasingly conscious of his mortality, and late letters reflect his state of health. Writing to John Ruskin's father in May 1845, for example, he admitted that "I have been so unwell that I was obliged to go away from Town to revival by a little change of fresh air."[6] These periods of weakness, increasingly frequent throughout the 1840s, will inevitably have taken their toll on his painting, and on his ability and desire to create 'finish'. Sophia Booth, his Margate landlady and also his friend and lover, looked after Turner carefully, presumably accompanied him back and forth between the east Kent coast and London, and organized regular visits by his doctor.[7] Yet the declining state of Turner's health must have been the reason why his pattern of exhibiting regularly at the Royal Academy began, after a lifetime's involvement, to falter. He caught cholera in 1848–49, and although he miraculously survived, this illness and his continuous physical weakening caused Turner to exhibit only one painting (and that a reworked old canvas) in 1847, nothing in 1848, and another reworked canvas and a much earlier painting in 1849.[8] The 1847 painting, *Hero of a Hundred Fights* (pl. 157), was a hymn to that giant figure in British history the Duke of Wellington, and depicts the opening of a furnace and the emergence of a bronze cast of an equestrian statue of the duke.[9] Turner plays with reality here – a statue of this huge size cannot be cast whole – but his artistic licence allows him this final piece of theatricality. In 1850 Turner made a magnificent final rally, and exhibited his last group of four canvases on the theme of Dido and Aeneas as his farewell to that subject of Carthaginian history that had preoccupied him throughout his exhibiting life.

Despite his age and growing frailty Turner maintained his engagement with the wider world. He attended Royal Academy functions; was seen regularly in his favourite armchair in a dark corner of the Athenaeum Club, London; and appears to have remained politically aware to the end, as the poet Francis Palgrave (1824–1897) observed:

> Within a few months before we lost him … Turner talked of … the tangle of politics neither wittily, nor picturesquely, nor technically; but as a man of sense before all things.[10]

He retained an active interest in new technologies, and was taken at least twice to see the Crystal Palace – home of the 1851 Great Exhibition – then under construction in Hyde Park. He wrote in January 1851 to tell Walter Fawkes's son Hawkesworth that the as yet unglazed iron framework was "towering over the galleries like a giant".[11]

Turner's interest in technology in his last decade went beyond an appreciation of iron-frame architecture and steam-powered transport to embrace the new and exciting science of photography. Confusing though the arrival of photography may have been to many of his younger contemporaries (the techniques of photography had been revealed in Paris and London in January 1839), Turner showed a close and constructive interest in it from the early 1840s. It may have led him to an understanding that the art of painting would never be the same thereafter. Turner made it his business to get to know John J.E. Mayall (1813–1901), a young maker of daguerrotypes (an early type of photograph) from Yorkshire who had spent some years in the

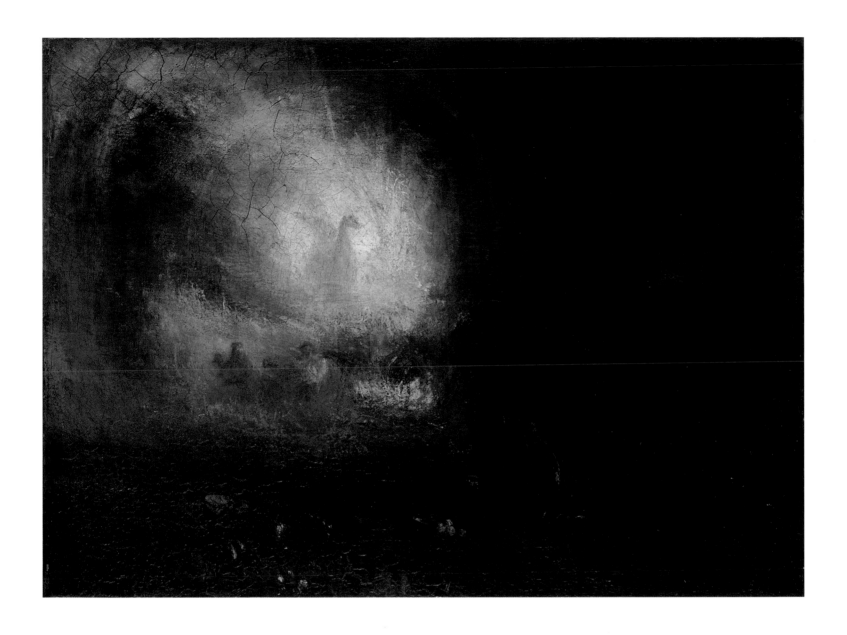

157 *The Hero of a Hundred Fights,*
c. 1806–07, reworked and exhibited
1847, oil on canvas, 91 × 121 cm
(35⅞ × 47⅝ in.), London, Tate
Old and new technology combine
in this early painting of a mill or
foundry. Turner reworked it in 1847
to depict the opening of the furnace
where an equestrian statue is being
cast of the Duke of Wellington,
the 'hero of a hundred fights'.

early 1840s training in Philadelphia. In 1847 Mayall set up a portrait studio and lens-grinding workshop in the Strand, London, and Turner became one of his early customers.[12] Remaining incognito throughout, Turner sat for Mayall, inspected his equipment, watched him grind lenses, talked about the nature of light and became fascinated by the daguerrotypes of Niagara Falls that Mayall had taken when he was working in the United States. Turner was particularly impressed by the way in which these daguerrotypes even registered the presence of a rainbow.[13]

In the 1840s photography was a technology that all the visual arts would have to accommodate. Some younger artists, such as William Lake Price (1810–1891), who trained as a watercolour painter, turned increasingly to photography as an end in itself. For John Brett (1830–1902), photography became a means of gathering information for paintings. Turner was too old to take

158 *Off Deal*, 1840s, oil on paper
on millboard, 24.5 × 32 cm
(9⅝ × 12⅝ in.), Stockholm,
Nationalmuseum

Turner was about seventy years
old when he painted this haunting
evocation of a wintry shoreline
crowded with people and boats
pitted against the elements.

up photography himself, but it remains the case that as his role in recording specific views in the British landscape drew to an end when the publication of the *England and Wales* series foundered in 1838, so, coincidentally, photography became a reality when the principles behind it were made public early the following year. The decline in custom for his engraved British landscape subjects gave Turner the time and inclination to work from Venetian, French, German and Swiss landscapes. But along with the change of subject-matter came a distinct alteration in Turner's approach to landscape. From the careful delineation and recording of the character of landscape, of the kind seen, for example, in the pair of *Gibside* watercolours (pls. 96, 97; cat. 81, 82) – techniques that the camera could now begin to rival – in his 1840s Continental watercolours there is a new luminosity, a fractured quality of light, and evidence of calligraphic working-up of the texture of the landscape with penwork of the same sensitivity as the minuscule lettering in the *Fairfaxiana* pages (pls. 143, 144; cat. 127, 128). This is all picture-making of a kind that photography then simply could not do. The advent of photography gave Turner the following wind to make one last adjustment to his perception of the world.

In England Turner's subjects became gradually more confined to the seashore. Rather than being views from a boat offshore, as in *The Mouth of the River Humber* (pl. 9; cat. 85), Turner's late marine paintings, whether in watercolour or oil, are scenes from the beach or near it.[14] During the 1840s, perhaps in the early part of the decade, Turner painted a group of eighteen or nineteen canvases, each of the standard size of three feet by four feet, to which he did not, as far as is known, give titles. They are painterly evocations of a cold, usually rough, sea, and the titles they were given in the twentieth century refer to salient features in an attempt to distinguish them one from another. This book contains *Rough Sea* (pl. 159; cat. 134); others, also in the Turner Bequest at the Tate, include *Seascape with distant coast*, *Seascape with buoy* and *Wreck, with fishing boats*.[15] Yet others (generally but not exclusively those that escaped the Turner Bequest soon after the artist's death)[16] are now identified by placenames that are too specific, and can be discounted as meaningless; these include *Margate (?) from the sea* (London, National Gallery), *Seascape: Folkestone* (USA, private collection), *Off the Nore: Wind and Water* (New Haven CT, Yale Center for British Art)[17] and *Off Deal* (pl. 158; cat. 131).

Given the artist's lifetime practice of painting in his studio from notes made on the spot, it is safe to assume that this group of pictures was painted indoors, probably in London. Despite the fact that they are so intensely evocative of the sea in winter, the idea that they were painted on the shore can be ruled out immediately – this had never been Turner's habit for such large canvases; they would have been far too large for an elderly man to handle on the beach; and no blown sand has been found in the paint. Thus, like Turner's landscapes for engraving painted in the studio from on-the-spot sketches, they are products of intertwined memory and experience. But in contrast to the studies of specific places, the memory Turner has engaged here was accumulated over a lifetime.

Although he lived as a youth near the ships going up and down the Thames, and by the open sea at Margate, Turner made his first journeys as an artist into the interior of Britain – to Bristol,

South and North Wales, the Midlands, the North of England and Scotland. He made his name and his early living as a painter of widely varied watercolour landscapes of inland Britain. Watercolours of marine subjects were few until he began his paintings for the *Southern Coast* series in 1811.[18] Nevertheless, Turner's first exhibited oil painting was a seascape, *Fishermen at Sea* (exh. 1796; London, Tate), and in early sketchbooks, notably the 'Wilson' sketchbook of 1797,[19] there are spirited sea studies that foreshadow other early marine oils and the *Southern Coast* images. Although sea subjects in oil only comprise about one third of the extant paintings across his entire career, from the 1840s there are more than twice as many seascapes in oil as landscapes, and in the case of works on paper the interior of Britain as a subject disappears.

Thus, with some exceptions that prove the rule, the direction in which Turner moved during his life as an artist was from the interior of Britain to its edge: from looking in, to looking out. When he looked out to sea in his late paintings it was not only at the bleakly empty horizon, but at all human life on the inshore wave, from the scattered wreckage in *Morning after the Wreck* (pl. 154; cat. 130) to the scudding sailing boats in *Off Deal* (pl. 158; cat. 131). Turner continued his mission as an observer of his compatriots and their integration with the landscape and seascape of Britain until he died.

159 *Rough Sea*, 1840s,
oil on canvas, 91.5 × 122 cm
(36 × 48 in.), London, Tate

Turner's last subjects become
gradually more confined to the
seashore, looking towards the
horizon. The direction in which
Turner moved during his career
was from the interior of Britain
to its edge: from looking in,
to looking out.

Map of Turner's Tours of Britain

.... 1794
———— 1797
———— 1798
– – – 1801
———— 1811
———— 1816
– – – 1830
———— 1831

Novar

Elgin

Inverness

Isle of Skye

Blair Athol

Fort William

Tobermory

Staffa   Mull   Oban

Inveraray

Loch Lomond   Stirling

Greenock

Glasgow   Edinburgh   Berwick-upon-Tweed

Lanark   Norham   Lindisfarne

Abbotsford & Melrose   Kelso   Dunstanburgh Castle

Langholm

Gretna Green   Newcastle upon Tyne   North Shields   South Shields

Penrith   Durham

Appleby   Barnard Castle   Middlesborough

Kendal   Richmond   Whitby

Askrigg   Scarborough

Lancaster   Farnley   Harewood

Browsholme   Skipton   York

Leeds   Beverley

Wakefield   Brocklesby

Doncaster   Louth

Conway   Chesterfield   Lincoln

Denbigh   Chester   Matlock   Newark

Caernarvon   Wrexham   Grantham

Nottingham   Boston

Dolgellau   Great Yarmouth

Shrewsbury   Ashby

Penegoes   Ludlow   Wolverhampton   Ely

Aberystwyth   Bridgenorth   Birmingham   Huntingdon

Dudley   Coventry   Cambridge

Cardigan   Worcester   Warwick

Brecon   Oxford

Abergavenny   Monmouth

Cyfarthfa   London

Bristol   Windsor   Margate

Ilfracombe   Bridgwater   Wells   Stonehenge

Barnstaple   Salisbury   Petworth

Bude   Lyme Regis   Portsmouth

Padstow   Exeter   Christchurch

Bodmin   Weymouth   Corfe Castle

Fowey   Plymouth   Dartmouth

Land's End

Timeline

1775

Joseph Mallord William Turner born at 21 Maiden Lane, Covent Garden, London. In adult life he claimed that his birthday was 23 April, St George's Day and also Shakespeare's birthday.

James Watt and Matthew Boulton of the Soho Manufactory, Birmingham, enter into a partnership to supply steam engines.

1776

Declaration of Independence by the thirteen British colonies on the eastern seaboard of America.

1779

A steam engine to the design of James Watt is installed to pump water at Smethwick on the Birmingham Canal.

1781

The Iron Bridge at Coalbrookdale is opened to traffic on New Year's Day.

1781–82

The Turner family moves across the road to 26 Maiden Lane. Turner is sent to Brentford to stay with his uncle and aunt. In subsequent years he was sent to stay in Margate and Sunningwell, near Oxford.

1783

The Treaty of Versailles brings to an end the American War of Independence, and recognizes the United States as a sovereign nation.

Richard Arkwright builds Masson Mill at Cromford, an elegant cotton mill in the style of a country house.

1786

Colours the plates in Henry Boswell's *Picturesque Views of the Antiquities of England and Wales* (cat. 1).

1787

Paints his earliest surviving signed and dated watercolours.

1789

Admitted to the Royal Academy Schools as a student.

The storming of the Bastille on 14 July, a crucial event in the early stages of the French Revolution.

Publication of Songs of Innocence *by William Blake (1757–1827).*

1790

Exhibits his first work at the Royal Academy, the watercolour *Archbishop's Palace, Lambeth* (Indianapolis Museum of Art).

1791

Travels to Bristol to stay with the Narraways, friends of his father, and sketches in and around Bristol, Malmesbury and Bath (cat. 3–6). Takes a part-time job painting stage scenery at the Pantheon, Oxford Street, London.

Franz Josef Haydn arrives for the first of two stays in England, during which time he composes Symphonies Nos. 99–104.

Death of John Wesley, the founder of the Methodist church.

Rioters wreck the house at Fairhill, Birmingham, of Joseph Priestley (1733–1804), theologian and scientist.

1792

Enters the Life Class at the Royal Academy. Sketching trip to South and Central Wales.

Publication of the second part of Tom Paine's The Rights of Man, *after which the author flees to France.*

1793

Awarded the Greater Silver Palette by the Society of Arts for "Drawing of Landscapes".

Britain enters into war with France, which, with brief intervals, continues until 1815.

1794

Makes his first tour to the Midlands, and on into North Wales (cat. 7–14). First engraving of a commissioned work published in the *Copper-Plate Magazine*. First press notice.

1795

Tours South Wales and the Isle of Wight (cat. 15). Engraving after his drawing of Birmingham (cat. 14) published in the *Copper-Plate Magazine*.

Death of Josiah Wedgwood, pioneer of the pottery industry and canal entrepreneur.

1796

Exhibits his first oil painting at the Royal Academy, *Fishermen at Sea* (London, Tate). Watercolours of Salisbury subjects commissioned (cat. 32–34).

The Ditherington Flax Mill, Shrewsbury – the first multi-storeyed iron-framed building – is completed.

1797

Tours the North of England and the Lake District (cat. 16–18, 23, 24).

On 22 February a small force of French soldiers lands at Fishguard, but quickly retreats.

1798

Makes sketching trips to Malmesbury, Bristol, North Wales, and to Knockholt in Kent (cat. 22), where he paints in oils in the open air. Poetic quotations published in RA catalogue for the first time. *Morning amongst the Coniston Fells* exhibited (cat. 23).

S.T. Coleridge and William Wordsworth publish Lyrical Ballads.

1799

Painting at Fonthill Abbey for William Beckford (cat. 35, 36). Elected Associate of the Royal Academy. Moves to rooms in Harley Street, London. Sarah Danby becomes his lover. His mother is admitted to St Luke's Hospital, Old Street, on grounds of "madness". First watercolours of Oxford subjects commissioned for engraving. Series continues until 1809 (cat. 37–39).

1800

His mother is moved from St Luke's to Bethlem Hospital for the Insane. Turner's earliest known poetry published in RA catalogue, with his painting *Dolbadern Castle* (cat. 25). His daughter Evelina is born (or 1801).

1801

First tour to Scotland, and on to the Lake District (cat. 27–31).

On 1 January the Act of Union between the parliaments of England and Ireland becomes effective.

1802

Elected to the Royal Academy. July–October: trip to France, through Calais and Paris, and to Switzerland and Aosta, Italy.

1803

Festival upon the Opening of the Vintage of Macon (cat. 40) exhibited. Becomes a member of the Royal Academy Council.

1804

Death of his mother at Bethlem Hospital. He opens his own picture gallery at his house at 64 Harley Street. Reacts angrily to Royal Academy rules and management. Begins a period of painting out of doors on the Thames. Rents Sion Ferry House, Isleworth (until 1806).

1805

Painting out of doors on the Thames. Does not show at the RA this year.

Naval victory at Trafalgar frees Britain from the threat of invasion by Napoleon's French army.

The Pontcysyllte Aqueduct, an iron trough 1000 feet long and 127 feet high, opens on the Ellesmere Canal.

The opening of the Blisworth Tunnel in Northamptonshire, which enables vessels to travel between Birmingham and London entirely by canal.

1806

Begins making engravings of his own compositions for his *Liber Studiorum* (cat. 72). Rents a house at West End, Hammersmith. Buys property at Lee Clump, near Great Missenden, Bucks.

1807

First volume of *Liber Studiorum* published. Elected Professor of Perspective at the RA.

Sir John Soane completes the Tivoli Corner of the Bank of England, between Princess Street and Lothbury.

The slave trade is abolished in the British Empire.

1808

Paints views of Tabley Hall for Sir John Leicester. Travels into North Wales. Makes his first visit to Farnley Hall, near Leeds, home of Walter Fawkes, and begins his long series of watercolours of Wharfedale views (cat. 54–59). *Pope's Villa at Twickenham* is exhibited at Turner's Gallery (cat. 43).

1809

Visits Petworth House, the Sussex home of Lord Egremont, for the first time. Sketching tour to the North of England to paint Cockermouth Castle, an Egremont property, and Lowther Castle (cat. 50–52). Pair of *Tabley* pictures exhibited (cat. 44, 45) at the RA.

1810

Travels to Rosehill, near Lewes, Sussex, to make drawings for John Fuller, and to Farnley Hall, where he becomes a regular visitor until Fawkes's death in 1825. *Petworth: Dewy Morning* exhibited (cat. 46). Moves to 44 Queen Anne Street.

1811

Gives first series of Perspective lectures at the RA. Writes a long poem about the history and destiny of Britain. Commissioned by the Cooke brothers to make drawings for the *Southern Coast* series of engravings (cat. 61–67, 69–71). Tours the West Country to make sketches for it. John Pye and Charles Heath's engraving *Pope's Villa* published. His second daughter, Georgiana, is born (or 1812).

Completion of The Cob, the great embankment at Porthmadog.

1812

Begins construction of Sandycombe Lodge, Twickenham, to his own design (completed 1813).

Robert Owen of New Lanark publishes his New View of Society.

1813

Second tour of Devon (cat. 48, 49).

1814

First instalment of engravings from *Picturesque Views of the Southern Coast of England* is published.

1815

Visits Farnley Hall. Embarks on his *Fairfaxiana* watercolours (cat. 127, 128).

Battle of Waterloo marks the end of the wars with France.

Establishment of the Holyhead Road Commission.

William Smith publishes his geological map delineating the strata of England and Wales.

1816

Travels to Lancashire and Yorkshire to make sketches for *History of Richmondshire*. Stays at Farnley Hall.

1817

Travels on the Continent for the first time since 1802. Visits Belgium, Holland and the Rhineland. Travels to Raby Castle and Gibside in County Durham on his return. Sells his complete set of watercolours of Rhine scenes to Walter Fawkes.

1818

Exhibits *Raby Castle, the Seat of the Earl of Darlington* (pl. 98) at the RA. Commissioned by Sir Walter Scott to contribute illustrations to *Provincial Antiquities and Picturesque Scenery of Scotland* (cat. 89). Visits Edinburgh and the Lowlands of Scotland.

1819

Last group of *Liber Studiorum* prints is published. Shows sixty watercolours in an exhibition at Walter Fawkes's London house in Grosvenor Place (including cat. 54, 80), and twelve oil paintings at Sir John Leicester's Gallery in Hill Street (including cat. 43–45). *England: Richmond Hill* exhibited (cat. 73). Begins a six-month visit to Italy, staying in Venice, Florence, Rome, Naples and Paestum. Enlarges his Queen Anne Street house to include a new picture gallery.

The massacre of Peterloo, Manchester – a troop of yeomen cavalry charges a crowd demonstrating in favour of parliamentary reform, killing two women and men, and wounding several hundred.

1820

February: returns from Italy. Inherits cottages in Wapping, and begins to convert them into an inn, The Ship and Bladebone. Alterations at 44 Queen Anne Street completed. Watercolours for *Views in London and its Environs* commissioned (cat. 86–88).

Death of King George III after a reign of sixty years.

1821

Travels to Paris and northern France to make studies for series of engravings of Seine views.

1822

William and George Cooke exhibit Turner's watercolours at their gallery in Soho Square. Travels to Edinburgh by sea to paint George IV's visit. Opens his renewed gallery in Queen Anne Street. *Rivers of England* watercolours commissioned (cat. 83–85).

1823

William and George Cooke exhibit Turner's watercolours in their gallery in Soho Square. First set of *Rivers of England* engravings published.

1824

William and George Cooke exhibit Turner's watercolours in their gallery in Soho Square. Travels in East Anglia. Visits Belgium, Luxembourg, Germany and northern France.

1825

England and Wales series commissioned by Charles Heath (cat. 94–110). Tours the Low Countries. Death of Walter Fawkes.

Opening of the Stockton & Darlington Railway.

1826

Visits northern France. Breaks his relationship with the Cooke brothers.

1827

Stays with John Nash at East Cowes Castle, Isle of Wight, and at Petworth with Lord Egremont. First three parts of *England and Wales* published.

1828

Gives his final series of Perspective lectures at the RA. Lord Egremont commissions a series of paintings for the Carved Room at Petworth (cat. 74–76). Second visit to Italy, August to February 1829.

Opening of Thomas Telford's suspension bridge carrying the Holyhead Road across the Menai Straits, the first large-scale suspension bridge.

1829

England and Wales subjects exhibited at the Egyptian Hall, Piccadilly, London, and later in the Birmingham Society of Artists Exhibition, in New Street, Birmingham (cat. 116). Visits Paris, Normandy and Brittany. His father dies, and Turner makes his first will.

Establishment by Sir Robert Peel of the Metropolitan Police.

The Catholic Emancipation Act allows Roman Catholics to become MPs and to participate generally in public life.

1830

Tours the Midlands to gather further sketches for *England and Wales* (cat. 102, 103, 107, 113–15).

Opening of the Liverpool & Manchester Railway.

1831

Summer: travels to Scotland to stay with Sir Walter Scott at Abbotsford, and to gather material for *Scott's Poetical Works* (cat. 90).

The first epidemic of Asiatic cholera to reach Britain breaks out at Sunderland.

1832

Becomes a regular visitor to Margate, where he stays in Mrs John Booth's house near the harbour. Autumn: travels to the Channel Islands, and to Paris. December: at Petworth; Christmas at East Cowes Castle.

Passage of the Reform Act and the first general election held under the new franchise and after the redistribution of seats.

1833

Exhibition at Moon, Boys & Graves of *England and Wales* and the Walter Scott watercolours. Travels down the Rhine and Danube to Munich and Vienna, and on through Switzerland to Venice. Publication of first volume of *Turner's Annual Tour: Wanderings by the Seine*; second and third volumes in 1834 and 1835 respectively. John Booth dies in Margate.

Publication of the first of the 'Tracts for the Times', marking the beginning of the Oxford Movement in the Church of England.

Birmingham Town Hall completed to the design of Joseph Hansom.

Emancipation of slaves in the British Empire.

1834

Turner witnesses the burning of the Houses of Parliament, 16 October.

The Poor Law Amendment Act establishes unions of parishes for the administration of the Poor Law.

1835

Exhibits two paintings of *The Burning of the Houses of Lords and Commons* (pls. 146, 147). Visits Copenhagen, Berlin, Dresden, Prague, Nuremburg, the Rhine and Rotterdam.

1836

Tour of France and Switzerland. Final exhibition of the RA at Somerset House. Revd John Eagles attacks *Juliet and her Nurse* in *Blackwood's Magazine*, prompting a response from the young John Ruskin.

Publication of the first part of Pickwick Papers *by Charles Dickens.*

HMS Beagle *returns from a surveying voyage round the world that the ship's naturalist, Charles Darwin, described as "by far the most important event in my life".*

1837

First RA exhibition in rooms adjacent to the new National Gallery, Trafalgar Square. Travels to Paris. October: at Petworth; November: death of Lord Egremont. Resigns RA Professorship of Perspective.

Accession of Queen Victoria.

1838

Last set of engravings to *England and Wales* published. Unsold prints and plates sold at auction. HMS *Temeraire* sold out of naval ownership and towed to be broken up.

Opening of the London & Birmingham Railway between Philip Hardwick's monumental passenger stations at Euston in London and Curzon Street in Birmingham.

1839

Exhibits *The Fighting 'Temeraire'* at the RA (cat. 118). Travels to Belgium, Luxembourg and Germany. Forty-two works from Walter Fawkes's collection exhibited at the Music Hall, Leeds.

1840

Exhibits *Slavers Throwing Overboard the Dead and Dying* and *The New Moon* (cat. 129) at the RA. Meets John Ruskin for the first time. Travels to Venice, through Rotterdam and down the Rhine, returning through Munich and Coburg.

1841

Travels to Switzerland. Deaths of David Wilkie and Sir Francis Chantrey. Refused access by the Duke of Wellington to the Tower of London to sketch fire damage.

1842

Travels to Switzerland.

1843

First volume of Ruskin's Modern Painters *published.*

Isambard Kingdom Brunel's iron steamship Great Britain *launched at Bristol.*

1844

Exhibits *Rain, Steam, and Speed* (London, National Gallery) at the RA. Final visit to Switzerland. Travels to Portsmouth to witness the arrival of King Louis-Philippe of France on a state visit.

W.E. Gladstone, President of the Board of Trade, pilots through Parliament a bill regulating railways.

1845

Made Acting President of the RA during illness of Sir Martin Archer Shee, and later in the year Deputy President. *Staffa* (New Haven CT, Yale Center for British Art) is bought by the New Yorker James Lenox – the first Turner to go to America. Makes two trips to France, in May to Boulogne and environs, and in the autumn, his last foreign trip, to Dieppe and Picardy. Dines at Eu with King Louis-Philippe.

Friedrich Engels publishes his Condition of the Working Classes in England.

The Albert Dock complex, Liverpool, completed to the design of Jesse Hartley.

1846

Moves to 6 Davis Place, Chelsea, with Mrs Booth.

Failure of the potato crop marks the beginning of the Great Famine in Ireland, and leads Sir Robert Peel's government to repeal import duties on corn.

1847

Repaints a work of *c.* 1798 and exhibits it as *The Hero of a Hundred Fights* (pl. 154) at the RA. Probably makes his first visit to John Mayall's photographic studio in the Strand this year.

1848

Does not exhibit at the RA this year, probably through ill health.

Year of revolutions in continental Europe. A great demonstration for the reform of the political system is held by Chartists on Kennington Common, London, on 10 April.

1849

Repaints a work of *c.* 1807, and exhibits it as *The Wreck Buoy* at the RA, along with a *Venus and Adonis* of *c.* 1804. Ill during much of this year.

1850

Exhibits for the last time at the RA, showing four sequential paintings on the theme of Dido and Aeneas.

1851

Visits the Crystal Palace, under construction in Hyde Park, London. Attends Varnishing Days at the RA, and the Private View and Banquet. Confined through illness to his bed in Chelsea. 19 December, dies at home; 30 December, is buried in St Paul's Cathedral, London.

The Great Exhibition opens in the Crystal Palace on 1 May.

Appendix I

Extracts from a letter published in the Birmingham Journal, *12 December 1829, during the Birmingham Society of Arts exhibition, in which Turner's watercolours were shown for the first time in the city. The letter, dated 1 December 1829, is signed 'X'. I am most grateful to Martin Hampson of Birmingham City Libraries Local Studies and History Department for drawing the letter to my attention. A cutting from the* Birmingham Journal *in which the letter appears is pasted into* Birmingham Society of Arts Catalogues 1828–1830, *Birmingham City Libraries,* L54.61 *(cat. 116). For commentary on this letter, see Chapter IV.*

On the Pictures of J.M.W. Turner Esq R.A.

Of all living artists, Mr Turner is, perhaps, the most profoundly versed in *pictorial effect*, using this term as combining the arrangement of colours, and the distribution of light and shade. Many other artists have studied in the school of Nature, – they are familiar with all the secrets she has ever revealed; but Turner has entered her hidden treasury, and has brought thereout 'things *new*' as well as '*old*'. The speculative astronomers tell us that there may be stars, whose light, travelling at the rate of millions of miles in a minute, has not yet reached our globe; we see them not, but they may be seen hereafter. So I could fancy that Turner has *anticipated* nature – that he has forcibly 'seized the forelock of time', and with a daring hand exhibited effects and combinations which nature has in store, but which she has not yet produced. A picture by him is a new creation; an epic version of a passage in Nature's book. He discerns at once the *capabilities* of the landscape he sits down to paint; and as he rapidly estimates the mode of combining them with the particular feeling the scene is calculated to excite whether as a matter of natural, moral, or historic interest; and these, as well as the identical forms before him, he determines to illustrate.

The theme of a picture, then, in the mind of Turner, is something refined and abstracted; the subject proposed is destined to be the vehicle of some classical and learned combination; some magical vision of taste, imagination and splendour. … And this is one of the peculiar sleights of Turner's pencil; that, as in nature, close observation discerns points and beauties which, on slight notice, are not perceptible …

In all these the capabilities of the scene *permitted*, and the feelings proper to be excited *required*, the effects at the hands of the artist, and he has given them. What is it to the examiner if he cannot *make out* all the *physique*? Could he doubt in nature? Or if he could, is there no difference between the two? Nature is great and varying; a picture is small and unaltering – to many artists it may and ought to be sufficient to give a close transcript of the scene; – to the one in ten thousand it suffices not. – The poet – the *Shakspeare* of art – discerns the best of all *possible* or conceivable moods of nature, and the result is, a feast to the eye; a lecture to the heart and the understanding …

Like the voice of the powerful and instructed singer, in whatever *key* he commences, the tune is built thereon, and is sustained and modulated throughout. Should he then stay his pencil at the precise limit of the real and the visible? The sculptor of the Apollo or the Venus was not to withhold his last touches of imagined beauty, because no totality of existing form could be discovered, from which he might work. Turner does not, however, *invent* new series of colours. His sunshine is never cold; his morning mists are not orange; nor does the influence of his sunsets produce hard or discordant blues. Never does he lay on his tints in affected, incongruous, or inconsequential spots or masses. They who do so, travestie nature. Turner sublimes her. We look at his work, and it seems the creation of impulse, but it is, in fact, an elaborate structure, full of *principle*, and deep consideration, harmonious and elevated throughout …

But he is said to be heedless, in respect of the broad *facts* of natural effects and *chiaro oscura*. If the 'balance of power' requires a light, on the shaded side of the building – he will throw one there. If a bright spot would effectually relieve a dark mass, he introduces a figure illuminated on the side the farthest from the source of light. The charge, however, is often brought by ignorance and inobservation. His bold and skilful use of *reflected* lights permits him to introduce these reliefs when they touch the very verge of the possible; – and if he does occasionally transgress, he gives – shall I say it – in the emanation of his genius, something more valuable, *in that instance*, than truth itself.

Yet must he not be imitated. He himself bears 'a charmed life', and may venture unhurt, where the fame of others would incur inevitable destruction. He alone may play with the lion and the leopard – and yet live. He possesses that 'poet's eye', that master's hand, which can give to the most unprecedented combinations, 'a local habitation' and a familiar beauty; and the most sincere and *attentive* peruser of his works, perceives that the longer they are dwelt on, the more intelligent and delightful they become. They are found to be true, *in* and *to* themselves, entire, harmonious, consistent. True also to *nature*, in her loveliest and most potential aspects – ideal abstractions of *conceivable* perfections.

Appendix II

Rubric published beneath the engraving Wycliffe, *near Rokeby (cat. 125; see Chapter V)*

The Birth Place of John Wickliffe (*The Morning Star of Liberty*) near Rokeby, Yorkshire
margin left: Drawn by J.M.W. Turner R.A
margin right: Engraved by John Pye 1823

In the fourteenth century he translated the scriptures into English and was persecuted for his opposition to the Clergy. A law was passed in the 2nd Year of Henry 5th by which whomsoever they were that should read the Scriptures in their Mother tongue (which was then called Wickleu's learning) they should forfeit land, Cattle, body, life and goods, for their heirs for ever and be condemned for heretics to God, enemies of the Crown and most errant traitors to the land – In 1543, it was enacted that no woman (except noblewomen and gentle-women who might read to themselves alone, and not to others, for which indulgence they were indebted to the courtesy of Cranmer) nor Artificiers, 'prentices, journeymen, serving men, nor labourers were to read the Bible or new Testament in English to himself, or to any others privately or openly upon pain of one months imprisonment – In 1804 a Society was established in London for the distribution of Bibles and to encourage the reading of it thro all classes of people it was translated by the Society into 126 different languages and dialects the expenditure of which for the Year 1818 amounted to £125,335. The Society issued 2,617,268 Bibles and Testaments in the course of 14 years – On the Trial of Humphrey Boyle in May 1822 at the Old Bailey before Mr Common Serj[t]. Denman Woman and Boys were ordered to quit the court while the defendant read extracts from the Bible.

Notes

ABBREVIATIONS IN THE NOTES

BJ
Martin Butlin and Evelyn Joll, *The Paintings of J.M.W. Turner*, 2 vols., New Haven CT (Yale University Press), revised edn. 1984

FD
The Diary of Joseph Farington RA 1793–1821 (ed. Kenneth Garlick, Angus Macintyre and Kathryn Cave), 16 vols., New Haven CT (Yale University Press), 1978–84

Finberg
A.J. Finberg, *The Life of J.M.W. Turner*, Oxford (Clarendon Press) 1939, revised edn. 1961

Gage
John Gage, *Collected Correspondence of J.M.W. Turner*, Oxford (Clarendon Press) 1980

Hamilton 1997
James Hamilton, *Turner – A Life*, London (Hodder and Stoughton) 1997

Herrmann 1990
Luke Herrmann, *Turner Prints – The Engraved Work of J.M.W. Turner*, Oxford (Phaidon) 1990

Hill 1984
David Hill, *In Turner's Footsteps – Through the Hills and Dales of Northern England*, London (John Murray) 1984

RA
Royal Academy of Arts, London

Shanes 1990
Eric Shanes, *Turner's England 1810–38*, London (Cassell) 1990

TB
Turner Bequest

Thornbury
Walter Thornbury, *The Life and Correspondence of J.M.W. Turner RA*, 1862. The edition cited here is the revised edition, London (Chatto & Windus) 1897

V&A
Victoria and Albert Museum, South Kensington, London

W
Andrew Wilton, *J.M.W. Turner, his Art and Life*, Fribourg 1979 [The prefix W refers to the catalogue of watercolours in this volume.]

Wilton 1987
Andrew Wilton, *Turner in his Time*, London (Thames & Hudson) 1987

Wilton 1990
Andrew Wilton, with transcriptions by Rosalind Mallord Turner, *Painting & Poetry – Turner's 'Verse Book' and his Work 1804–1812*, exhib. cat., Tate Gallery, London, 1990

INTRODUCTION

1 William Reynolds to William Rathbone, 23 February 1777, Liverpool University Library, Rathbone Papers, II.1.28; B. Trinder, *The Industrial Revolution in Shropshire*, 3rd edn., Chichester (Phillimore) 2000, pp. 106–08; J. Hamilton, *Turner and the Scientists*, London (Tate) 1998, pp. 115–128.

2 E. Beazley, *Madocks and the Wonder of Wales*, London (Faber) 1967, pp. 69–81.

3 B. Trinder, *The Making of the Industrial Landscape*, 3rd edn., London (Orion) 1997, pp. 96–99.

4 M. Stratton and B. Trinder, 'The Foundations of a Textile Community: Sir Robert Peel at Fazeley', *Textile History*, XXVI, 1995.

5 M.K. Ashby, *Joseph Ashby of Tysoe*, Cambridge (Cambridge University Press) 1961, p. 56.

6 M. Baty, 'Nuneham Courtenay: An Oxford 18th Century Deserted Village', *Oxoniensia*, no. 33, 1968.

7 T. Mozley, *Reminiscences: Chiefly of Towns, Villages and Churches*, London (Longmans Green) 1885, p. 208.

8 *The Victoria County History of Staffordshire*, Oxford (Oxford University Press) 1996, X, p. 4.

9 R. Samuel, 'Quarry Roughs: Life and Labour in Headington Quarry, 1860–1920', in *Village Life and Labour*, ed. R. Samuel, London (Routledge & Kegan Paul) 1975, pp. 139–244.

10 E. Royle, *Robert Owen and the Commencement of the Millennium*, Manchester (Manchester University Press) 1998, pp. 72–88, 118–48.

11 A.M. Hadfield, *The Chartist Land Company*, Newton Abbot (David and Charles) 1970; P. Searby, 'Great Dodford: The Later History of the Chartist Land Scheme', *Agricultural History Review*, XVI, 1968, p. 33.

12 M. Rutherford, *The Revolution in Tanner's Lane*, London (Hodder and Stoughton) 1887, pp. 153–67.

13 *Banbury Guardian*, 13 May 1852; P. Borsay, 'Health and Leisure Resorts 1700–1840', in *The Cambridge Urban History of Britain*, II: 1540–1840, ed. P. Clark, Cambridge (Cambridge University Press) 2000, pp. 775–804.

14 B. Trinder, *The Making of the Industrial Landscape*, 3rd edn., London (Orion) 1997, pp. 170–201.

15 M. Berg, *The Age of Manufactures*, 2nd edn., London (Routledge) 1994, pp. 198–201, 232–34.

16 B. Trinder, 'The Textile Industry in Shrewsbury in the Late Eighteenth Century', in *Industry and Urbanisation in Eighteenth Century England*, ed. P. Clark and P. Corfield, Leicester (Centre for Urban History, University of Leicester) 1994, pp. 80–93.

17 A. Young, *Tours in England and Wales*, London (LSE Reprints) 1932, pp. 140, 253, 269.

18 R. Holmes, *Redcoat: The British Soldier in the Age of Horse and Musket*, London (Harper Collins) 2001, p. 265.

19 A. Brodie, J. Croom and J.O. Davies, *English Prisons: An Architectural History*, Swindon (English Heritage) 2002, p. 55.

20 A. Somerville, *The Autobiography of a Working Man*, London (Macgibbon and Kee) 1967, p. 139.

21 N. Scarfe, *Innocent Espionage*, Woodbridge (Boydell) 1995, p. 183.

22 C.P. Moritz, *Journeys of a German in England in 1782*, trans. R. Nettel, London (Eland) 1983, pp. 178–79.

23 W. Champion, 'John Ashby and the History and Environs of the Lion Inn, Shrewsbury', *Shropshire History and Archaeology*, LXXV, 2000, pp. 49–84.

24 B. Trinder, 'The Holyhead Road: An Engineering Project in its Social Context', in *Thomas Telford: Engineer*, ed. A. Penfold, London (Thomas Telford) 1980, pp. 41–61; see also J. Quartermaine, B. Trinder and R. Turner, *Thomas Telford's Holyhead Road*, London (Council for British Archaeology) 2003.

25 M. Lewis, *Early Wooden Railways*, London (Routledge & Kegan Paul) 1970, pp. 280–300.

26 A. Somerville, *The Autobiography of a Working Man*, London (Macgibbon and Kee) 1967, p. 245.

27 M. Prior, *Fisher Row: Fishermen, Bargemen and Canal Boatmen in Oxford 1500–1900*, Oxford (Clarendon Press) 1982, 206–33.

28 R. Hayman, 'Aberdulais Falls', *Industrial Archaeology Review*, VIII, 1986, pp. 147–65.

29 K. Falconer, *Guide to England's Industrial Heritage*, London (Batsford) 1980, p. 262.

30 B. Trinder, *The Industrial Archaeology of Shropshire*, Chichester (Phillimore) 1996, p. 44.

31 B. Trinder, *The Market Town Lodging House in Victorian England*, Leicester (Friends of the Centre for English Local History) 2001, pp. 30–31; M. Prior, *Fisher Row: Fishermen, Bargemen and Canal Boatmen in Oxford 1500–1900*, Oxford (Clarendon Press) 1982, pp. 206–33; R. Samuel, 'Quarry Roughs: Life and Labour in Headington Quarry, 1860–1920', in *Village Life and Labour*, ed. R. Samuel, London (Routledge & Kegan Paul) 1975, pp. 139–244.

CHAPTER I

1 Thornbury, p. 8.

2 John Ruskin, *Modern Painters*, 5 vols., London 1843–60, V, part xi, chapter ix, paragraph 5.

3 According to family legend. Fred Turner, *History and Antiquities of Brentford*, Brentford (W. Pearce & Co.) 1922, p. 126.

4 Shanes 1990, p. 17.

5 For example, *A View of the City of Oxford*, TB III-B; ill. Colin Harrison, *Turner's Oxford*, Oxford (Ashmolean Museum) 2000, pl. 2.

6 TB VI, p. 20a.

7 Finberg, p. 46.

8 Wilton 1987, pp. 45, 119.

9 Curtis Price, 'Turner at the Pantheon Opera House', *Turner Studies*, VII, no. 2, pp. 4–8.

10 But his painting of a miniature self-portrait in the late 1780s suggests that he had some experience even there.

11 'North of England' sketchbook; TB XXXIV, fols. 16, 29, 30, 80, 86.

12 'Matlock' sketchbook, TB XIX.

13 *ibid*, fols. 2–6. The handwriting is comparable with that of Joseph Farington, who had been to the Midlands in 1789.

14 For example, in the sketchbooks 'South Wales', 1795, TB XXVI; 'Dinevor Castle', 1798, TB XL; 'Dolbadern', 1799, TB XLVI. This practice continued into the 1820s.

15 'Matlock' sketchbook, fol. 3.

16 Ian Warrell, *Turner in the North of England*, London (Tate), 1997.

17 There are lists of "Order'd Drawings" with names of purchasers in the 1795 sketchbooks 'South Wales', TB XXVI, fol. 5; and 'Isle of Wight', TB XXIV, inside cover.

18 Malachy Postlethwayt, *Universal Dictionary of Trade and Commerce*, 1774, II, art. 'Roads'.

19 J.M. Robinson, *Temples of Delight: Stowe Landscape Gardens*, London (National Trust) 1990; Katharine Eustace, 'The Politics of the Past: Stowe and the development of the historical portrait bust', *Apollo*, CXLVIII, no. 437, July 1998, pp. 31–40.

20 *Observations Relative Chiefly to Picturesque Beauty: Made in the Year 1776, on Several Parts of Great Britain, particularly the High-lands of Scotland*, 2 vols., 1789; *Observations on the River Wye, and Several Parts of Wales, &c Relative Chiefly to Picturesque Beauty*, 1782; *Three Essays: On Picturesque Beauty; On Picturesque Travel; and On Sketching Landscape; to which is Added a Poem, On Landscape Painting*, 1792; *Observations on the Coast of Hampshire, Sussex, and Kent: Relative Chiefly to Picturesque Beauty; Made in the Summer of the Year 1774*, 1804.

21 Letter to William Mason, 25 April 1772. Quoted in Bernard Denvir, *The Eighteenth Century: Art, Design and Society 1689–1789*, London (Longman) 1983, p. 261.

22 *Observations on the River Wye …*, p. 18.

23 My thanks to Christine Stevens of St Fagan's Museum of Welsh Life, Cardiff.

24 *St James's Chronicle*, 13 May 1794.

25 Thomas Green, *Extracts from the Diary of a Lover of Literature*, Ipswich 1810, under 3 June 1799.

26 John Milton, *Paradise Lost*, V.

27 The Golden Section is the measure of harmonic proportion that originated in the circle of Pythagoras (sixth century BC): the ratio of the shorter to the longer is the same as the longer to the sum of the shorter and longer; or a:b = b:a+b. See the entry on Golden Section in *Dictionary of Art*, ed. Jane Turner, London (Grove) 1996, XII, p. 871.

28 James Thomson, *The Seasons*: 'Summer', ll. 1648–54 (Turner omits ll. 1651–52).

29 Wilton 1990, cat. 1.

30 Hamilton 1997, p. 42; Wilton 1987, p. 44.

31 TB LXXVIII, fol. 1.

32 'Swans' sketchbook, 1798, TB XLII, fol. 139.

33 FD, 22 April 1798.

34 FD, 9 February 1799.

35 RA Council minutes, 22 December 1796.

36 FD, 5 January 1798.

37 FD, 6 July 1799.

38 Turner himself listed these as follows: [Views of Salisbury] "1. Bishop's Palace; 2. St Thomas's Church; 3. Ancient Arch in Mr Wyndham's Garden; 4. Close Gate; 5. Ancient Market Place; 6. New Council Room; 7. St Ed [….] Church by the Market Place; 8. Wilton House; 9. St Edmund's Church; 10. Poultry Cross." [In the cathedral] "1. Chapter House; 2. Ditto; 3. Cloisters; 4. General View of Church from Bishop's Garden; 5. East Front; 6. West ditto; 7. North ditto; 8. Transept; 9. Choir – Audley Chapel; 10. Entrance from West Door." TB CCCLXVIII-A.

39 TB III-B; Colin Harrison, *loc. cit.*

40 FD, 30 October 1799; BJ35a–j.

41 See Eric Shanes, *Turner's Watercolour Explorations*, London (Tate) 1997.

42 It has been suggested that the drawing of the façade of Hafod (pls. 45, 46; cat. 19) may be by another hand, but I see no reason to doubt it. See W331.

43 See those listed at W327–34.

44 Turner's 'Verse Book', *c.* 1805–10, p. 13; private collection. Transcribed in Wilton 1990, p. 150. See also pp. 30–32.

45 'Salisbury' sketchbook, TB XLIX, inside front cover.

46 Hamilton 1997, pp. 61–63, 87–88.

CHAPTER II

1 'Hymn to the Naiads: Argument and Poem', in *The Poetical Works of Mark Akenside*, ed. R. Dix, Teaneck NJ (Fairleigh Dickinson University Press) 1996, pp. 359–78.

2 Joshua Reynolds, *Fourteenth Discourse*, 10 December 1788.

3 Hamilton 1997, p. 88.

4 FD, 2 and 3 May 1803.

5 *British Press*, 6 May 1803; in this context "the first" should be read with its contemporary meaning, 'the best, greatest'.

6 The painting was redisplayed in the late 1970s at the Mappin Art Gallery, Sheffield, with a photograph of Richmond Hill nearby; see also Hamilton 1997, pp. 74, 80.

7 Another watercolour rendering is *Richmond Hill, c.* 1820–25 (Liverpool, Lady Lever Art Gallery), W518.

8 For an overview of the political situation at the RA *c.* 1802, see Eric Shanes, 'Dissent in Somerset House: Opposition to the Political Status Quo within the Academy around 1800', *Turner Studies*, X, no. 2, 1990, pp. 40–46.

9 26 March 1803 and 4 April 1803.

10 For one meeting only, 4 April 1803.

11 26 March, 4 April, 8 April 1803.

12 8 April 1803.

13 14 April 1803.

14 Carried unanimously, 21 April 1803.

15 FD, 24 December 1803.

16 FD, 30 April 1803.

17 See Hamilton 1997, Appendix 1, on the destruction of Trimmer's papers.

18 TB XC *passim*.

19 *Gentleman's Magazine*, supplement for 1808, p. 200.

20 Eric Shanes gives a rich explication of the picture in *Turner's Human Landscape*, 1990, pp. 24–28; as does Wilton 1990, pp. 50–53.

21 John Landseer, *Review of Publications of Art*, June 1808. Quoted at BJ72.

22 W.G. Rawlinson, *The Engraved Work of J.M.W. Turner*, London (Macmillan) 1908, I, p. xxvi.

23 'Verse Book', p. 11; transcribed in Wilton 1990, p. 150.

24 'Verse Book', p. 35; transcribed *ibid.*, p. 152.

25 *Repository of Arts*, I, p. 490. Here, "pencil" means paint brush.

26 Gillian Forrester, *Turner's Drawing Book – The Liber Studiorum*, 1996.

27 Following advice given to Turner by William Wells, quoted in Finberg, p. 128; Hamilton 1997, p. 98.

28 Letter from Charles Lyell to Dawson Turner, 18 April 1815, Dawson Turner Papers, Trinity College Library, Cambridge.

29 FD shows that they sat together at the dinners in 1813, 1814, 1815, 1818 and 1821. Table plans are not reproduced in the Yale edition of Farington's diary, but are listed in a typescript of the diary in the Clore Library at the Tate, London.

30 Ruskin, *Modern Painters*, IV, p. 262 – v. 16.29.

31 *Literary Gazette*, 22 May 1819.

32 W. Carey, *Some Memoirs of the Patronage and Progress of the Fine Arts*, 1826, p. 147. Quoted in Gage, p. 254.

33 Hamilton 1997, p. 207.

34 Letter from Anna Maria Crompton to William Rookes Crompton, 22 April 1810; *Letters and Papers of Henrietta Matilda Crompton and her Family*, ed. M.Y. Ashcroft, North Yorkshire County Record Office Papers, no. 53, 1994, p. 251.

35 The paintings hung together for less than ten years, being separated in 1827 when *Calm Morning* (cat. 45) was sold at auction to Lord Egremont. Since then they have been shown together only once, at Turner's bicentenary exhibition at the Royal Academy, 1974–75.

36 *Manchester Guardian*, 29 Aug 1829. "Gamboge" is a bright yellow pigment that Turner used much from the late 1820s; "maguilp" (or "megilp") is an oily medium used by Turner later in his career, which darkened drastically; "quackery" is self-explanatory.

37 Hamilton 1997, pp. 100, 134–38, 209, 282.

38 *Oxford Companion to J.M.W. Turner*, ed. Martin Butlin, Evelyn Joll and Luke Herrmann, 2001. See entry 'Finance and Property' by N.R.D. Powell.

39 'River and Margate' sketchbook, TB XCIX, pp. 48–47a. See Hamilton 1997, p. 208.

40 'Windmill and Lock' sketchbook, ?1811, TB CXIV, fol. 50a.

41 'Perspective' sketchbook, TB CVIII, *c.* 1809, fols. 23r–24r.

42 The other artists were (in order of appearance) Samuel Owen, William Collins, Edward Blore, Luke Clennell, James Hakewill, William Havell, Henry Eldridge, Louis Francia, Peter de Wint, Joshua Cristall, William Alexander, William Westall and Samuel Prout.

43 'Devonshire Coast No. 1' sketchbook, TB CXXIII, fols. 18v–204v. See also Hamilton 1997, pp. 142–46. Transcribed in Wilton 1990, p. 170.

44 Verse 8, fol. 30v.

45 Verse 20, fol. 58v.

46 Verse 21, fol. 60v.

47 Verse 31, fol. 90v.

48 John Opie, *Lectures on Painting Delivered at the Royal Academy of Arts. With a Letter on the Proposal for a Public Memorial of the Naval Glory of Great Britain …*, 1809. Turner owned a copy of this book. See Wilton 1987, p. 247.

49 Verse 60, fol. 176v.

50 Gage, p. 49 and n. 3.

51 Richard Ayton, *A Voyage Around Great Britain, undertaken in the Summer of the Year 1813 and commencing from the Land's End, Cornwall, with a Series of Views Illustrative of the Character and Prominent Features of the Coast, Drawn and Engraved by William Daniell, ARA*, 8 vols., 1814–25.

52 Verse 37, fol. 110v.

53 Sam Smiles, 'Picture Notes – St Mawes', *Turner Studies*, VIII, no. 1, 1988, pp. 53–57.

54 Quoted in Herrmann 1990, p. 89.

55 Sam Smiles, 'The Devonshire Oil Sketches of 1813', *Turner Studies*, IX, no. 1, 1989, pp. 10–26.

CHAPTER III

1 Turner to James Holworthy, 31 July 1816; Gage, p. 65.

2 FD, 15 and 17 May 1816; Shanes 1990, pp. 10–11.

3 A full account of this trip is in David Hill, *In Turner's Footsteps – Through the Hills and Dales of Northern England*, 1984.

4 Hill 1984, p. 43.

5 Letter from Turner to W.B. Cooke, 28 Aug 1816; Gage, p. 66. V&A MS 86.CC.20.II.

6 Sketchbooks 'Yorkshire 2', TB CXLV; 'Yorkshire 4', TB CXLVII; 'Yorkshire 5', TB CXLVIII.

7 'Yorkshire 4' sketchbook, TB CXLVII, fol. 35a.

8 Eric Shanes, *Turner's Human Landscape*, 1990, pp. 84–85.

9 Hill 1984, p. 84.

10 'Itinerary Rhine Tour' sketchbook, TB CLIX, fol. 100, has Turner's fairly clear diary of this trip. See also Finberg, p. 249.

11 'Raby' sketchbook, TB CLVI.

12 Turner to James Holworthy, 21 Nov 1817 [written from Farnley]; Gage, p. 70.

13 Gage, *Colour in Turner*, 1969, Appendix III, p. 214.

14 Turner lists Antwerp sights to be seen in his 'Itinerary Rhine Tour' sketchbook, TB CLIX, fol. 9.

15 *Sun*, 12 May 1818.

16 Thornbury, pp. 192–93.

17 Shanes 1990, p. 11 and n. 38.

18 These were *Picturesque Views on the Southern Coast of England*, for the Cooke brothers; *The Rivers of Devon*, for the Cooke brothers; *Views in Sussex and Related Drawings*, for Jack Fuller, John Murray and the Cooke brothers; *Loidis and Elmete*, for Thomas Whitaker; *The General History of the County of York* (appearing as *The History of Richmondshire*), for Thomas Whitaker and Thomas Longman; *The History of Durham*, for Robert Surtees; and *Views in London and its Environs* for the Cooke brothers.

19 See Eric Shanes, 'Turner's "unknown" London series', *Turner Studies*, I, no. 2, 1981, pp. 36–42.

20 James Hamilton, *Faraday – The Life*, 2002, pp. 139–40.

21 W.B. Cooke to Turner, 1 Jan 1827; Gage, p. 121.

22 Jean Golt, 'Beauty and Meaning on Richmond Hill', *Turner Studies*, VII, no. 2, pp. 9 ff.; Charles Stuckey, 'Turner's Birthdays', *Turner Society News*, no. 21, April 1981, pp. 4–6.

23 Jean Golt, *op. cit.* See also Andrew Loukes, 'Turner and Cricket', in *Catalogue of Cricket Literature*, Bodyline Books, VI (Spring 1999), pp. 1–4, for an alternative account that suggests a reason for the presence of the royal barge on the river, and the significance of the cricket match on Petersham Meadow in the middle distance.

24 *The Battle of Trafalgar* (1822–24; London, National Maritime Museum; BJ252). Commissioned for St James's Palace.

25 The fullest accounts of Turner at Petworth are Martin Butlin, Mollie Luther and Ian Warrell, *Turner at Petworth – Painter and Patron*, London (Tate) 1989; also Christopher Rowell, Ian Warrell and David Blayney Brown, *Turner at Petworth*, London (Tate) 2002.

26 TB CCXLIV, 1-116.

27 *Spilt Milk* and *Landscape near Petworth*; see Rowell, Warrell and Blayney Brown, *Turner at Petworth*, 2002, figs. 101 and 172.

28 Rowell, Warrell and Blayney Brown, *Turner at Petworth*, 2002, pp. 127–29.

29 In an early arrangement, *A Ship Aground* and *The Chain Pier, Brighton* were paired on one side of the fireplace, with the two Petworth Park subjects on the other. See Rowell, Warrell and Blayney Brown, *op. cit.*

CHAPTER IV

1 Letter from Charles Heath to Dawson Turner, 19 February 1825; Dawson Turner Papers, Trinity College Library, Cambridge. Quoted in Shanes 1990, p. 13.

2 Published on the back cover of the wrapper of *England and Wales, from Drawings by J.M.W. Turner Esq RA with Descriptive and Historic Illustrations by H.E. Lloyd Esq*, no. 3, 1827.

3 TB XXXIV, fol. 80.

4 *ibid.*, fol. 86.

5 'Yorkshire 5' sketchbook, TB CXLVIII, fol. 35v.

6 'Lancashire and North Wales' sketchbook, TB XLV, fol. 42.

7 The full catalogue of the 1829 Egyptian House exhibition is published in Gage, Appendix II, pp. 237–38.

8 The only earlier instances are of one oil painting exhibited at Plymouth, 1815; and two watercolours at the Northern Academy of Arts, Newcastle upon Tyne, 1828. Turner's work continued to be seen in Birmingham, in 1830 (two watercolours); 1832 (five engravings); 1834 (two watercolours, including *Rye, Sussex* (pl. 83; cat. 64), and five engravings); and 1835 (one work). I am grateful to Gordon Thomas, Archivist to the Royal Birmingham Society of Artists, for this information.

9 *Aris's Gazette*, 9 November 1829. I am grateful to Martin Hampson of Birmingham Libraries Local Studies Department for the *Aris's Gazette* references.

10 Turner's exhibits in Birmingham were *Colchester*, no. 388; *Richmond Castle* (i.e. *Richmond, Yorkshire*), no. 424; *Entrance to Fowey Harbour*, no. 356; *Kilgarren Castle*, no. 345; *Stonehenge*, no. 377; and *Lake Albano*, no. 412.

11 *Aris's Gazette*, 16 November 1829.

12 Hamilton 1997, p. 216.

13 This has been considered to be, variously, a view of Gloucester Cathedral, and of the Boston 'Stump'. On visual evidence, however, the case for St Mary's, Warwick, is very strong.

14 For the fullest information about these tours see Ian Warrell, *Turner on the Loire*, London (Tate) 1997; and the same author's *Turner on the Seine*, London (Tate) 1999.

15 See Jan Piggott, *Turner's Vignettes*, London (Tate) 1993.

16 Letter from Turner to Charles Heath, 15 December 1828; Gage, p. 145.

17 Gage, p. 299.

18 *ibid.*

19 Southgate's, 18 June 1839.

20 Alaric Watts, biographical sketch of Turner in *Liber Fluviorum, or River Scenery in France*, 1853, p. xxi. This, at p. xxix, is also the source for the information that Turner took thirty proofs of each engraving.

CHAPTER V

1 A.G.H. Bachrach, *Turner and Rotterdam*, 1974, p. 14.

2 See Shanes 1990, pp. 228–29.

3 *ibid.*, pp. 222–23.

4 'Devonshire Coast no. 1' sketchbook, TB CXXIII, fol. 205.

5 Shanes 1990, pp. 138–39. See also Philip Ziegler, *Addington: A Life of Henry Addington, First Viscount Sidmouth*, London (Collins) 1965, pp. 405–06.

6 *ibid.*, pp. 220–21.

7 Ben Jonson, *Sad Shepherd*, II. iii.

8 W.G. Rawlinson, *The Engraved Works of J.M.W. Turner*, I, no. 177.

9 Humphrey Boyle, *Report of the Trial of Humphrey Boyle*, London (R. Carlile, Koran Society's Office) 1822.

10 Wilton suggests that the text might have been added at the request of Walter Fawkes for circulating among a select group of his radical friends. Wilton 1987, p. 120. Indeed, Fawkes may have been its author.

11 Rawlinson, *loc. cit.*

12 Letter from Turner to Robert Cadell, 25 February 1832; Gage, p. 174. See Hamilton, 1997, p. 258.

13 Fragments were published by Turner as epigraphs to paintings from 1812 until the 1840s. If there ever was a manuscript of a whole or partial work, it is lost. See Hamilton, 1997, pp. 124, 143 and *passim*.

14 'Devonshire Coast No. 1' sketchbook, TB CXXIII, p. 117v.

15 John Cam Hobhouse, *Recollections of a Long Life*, 6 vols., London (W. Clowes & Sons) 1865–67. I, 1786–1816; III, 1910–11, p. 28.

16 'List of Works by Turner at any Time in the Collection of Ruskin', *Works of Ruskin*, XIII, p. 600.

17 The gold coin went missing for some years but was rediscovered at Farnley Hall in 2002 by Nicholas Horton-Fawkes and James Hamilton.

18 A. Yarrington, I.D. Lieberman, A. Potts and M. Baker, 'An Edition of the Ledger of Sir Francis Chantrey, R.A., at the Royal Academy, 1809–41', *Walpole Society*, LVI, 1994, no. 7a.

19 Most are now in Leeds City Art Gallery, while four are in other public collections – see W632–35.

20 Anne Lyles, *Turner and Natural History – the Farnley Project*, London (Tate) 1988; David Hill, *Turner's Birds*, Oxford (Phaidon) 1988.

21 Full title: *Chronology of the History of Modern Europe From the Extinction of the Western*

Further Reading

Empire AD 475 to the Death of Louis the Sixteenth, King of France, AD 1793 in Ten Epochs, York 1810.

22 Repr. Eric Shanes, *Turner's Watercolour Explorations*, London (Tate) 1997, figs. 4, 5.

23 Hamilton 1997, pp. 186 and 224–25.

24 Katherine Solender, *Dreadful Fire! Burning of the Houses of Parliament*, Cleveland Museum of Art, 1984, *passim*, especially pp. 30–42.

25 'Burning of the Houses of Parliament' sketchbooks 1 and 2, TB CCLXXXIII and CCLXXXIV.

26 TB CCCLXIV-373. Shanes 1990, p. 244, has suggested that this was intended as part of *England and Wales*, but the subject is so far out of line with the rest of the series that to argue for its inclusion would be to suggest that Turner was being deliberately and uncharacteristically provocative. The subject was never engraved.

27 The days before the opening of an exhibition at the Royal Academy or British Institution that were made over to artists to put finishing touches, and varnish, to their work.

28 *Art Journal*, 1860, p. 100.

29 Walter Fawkes, *Speech … on Parliamentary Reform, May 23rd 1812*, 1813, p. 15.

30 The difference in the use of "House" in the title of the earlier version and "Houses" in the later one must be nothing more than an unintentional inconsistency, or a printer's error.

31 *The Guardian*, 2 May 1997; *The Independent*, 14 November 2002.

32 Hamilton 1997, p. 283.

33 Judy Egerton, *Turner – The Fighting Temeraire*, 1995, p. 24.

34 Quoted in *ibid.*, pp. 29–30.

35 *ibid.*, pp. 75–77.

36 A silhouette portrait of Turner (Tate, London) is inscribed "taken on board the *City of Canterbury* steamboat, 23 September 1838".

37 *The Times*, 13 September 1838.

38 *The Times*, 12 October 1838.

39 There is a letter from Turner to C.R. Leslie referring to "two Gentlemen who cannot make up their minds" about buying it; Gage, p. 226.

40 W.J. Stillman, *Autobiography of a Journalist*, London (Grant Richards) 1901, I, p. 106.

41 Note in sketchbook, *c.* 1845, in British Museum, 1981-12-12-15, fol. 1v.

CHAPTER VI

1 *The Times*, 1 November 1841.

2 "VM The Duke of Wellington presents his compliments to Mr Turner. The Comg. Officer in the Tower has given orders that no person shall be admitted except on business. It cannot be expected that the Duke should interfere with an order so given without being responsible for the consequences – The Duke declines to take upon himself such a responsibility. London, 3 Nov 1841"; Gage, p. 247.

3 This is one of most widely known paintings by Turner, and is discussed extensively in Turner literature.

4 "It is far below even 'moonshine'", *Blackwood's Magazine*, September 1840; "Unintelligible periphrasis", *The Times*, 6 May 1840.

5 See preamble to BJ509–19, and a letter from Turner to J.J. Ruskin, 15 May 1845; Gage, p. 282.

6 Gage, p. 282.

7 Hamilton 1997, Appendix 3, pp. 343–45.

8 1847: *Hero of a Hundred Fights*, Tate, BJ427; 1849: *The Wreck Buoy*, Liverpool, National Museums and Galleries on Merseyside, BJ428; and a work of *c.* 1803, *Venus and Adonis*, private collection, BJ150.

9 Hamilton 1998, pp. 111–14.

10 Letter from F.T. Palgrave to John Ruskin, quoted in Finberg, p. 434.

11 Letter from Turner to F.H. Fawkes, 31 January 1851, Gage, p. 323.

12 Thornbury, pp. 349 ff.; Hamilton 1997, p. 305.

13 *ibid.*

14 An exception is the 'Channel' sketchbook, New Haven CT, Yale Center for British Art, in use in the 1840s. See Andrew Wilton, 'A Rediscovered Turner Sketchbook', *Turner Studies*, VI, no. 2, pp. 9–23.

15 BJ467, 468, 470.

16 BJ, text vol., pp. 284–94.

17 BJ464, 472, 476.

18 The earliest seem to be *Brighthelmstone* (London, Victoria and Albert Museum), W147; and *Crest of the Wave* (San Marino CA, Huntington Gallery), W150, both *c.* 1796. See also W149, 280 and 281.

19 TB XXXVII.

More books and articles have been written about Turner than about any other British artist, living or dead. The following brief selection of works is intended both as a guide to what is available, and as sources to take the reader further into ideas and issues discussed in this book.

Anthony Bailey, *Standing in the Sun – A Life of J.M.W. Turner*, London (Sinclair-Stevenson), 1997

David Blayney Brown, *Turner in the Tate Collection*, London (Tate Gallery Publications) 2002

Martin Butlin and Evelyn Joll, *The Paintings of J.M.W. Turner*, 2 vols., New Haven CT (Yale University Press), revised edn. 1984

Judy Egerton, *Turner – The Fighting Temeraire*, London (National Gallery) 1995

A.J. Finberg, *The Life of J.M.W. Turner*, Oxford (Clarendon Press) 1939, revised edn., 1961

John Gage, *Colour in Turner – Poetry and Truth*, London (Studio Vista) 1969

John Gage, *Collected Correspondence of J.M.W. Turner*, Oxford (Clarendon Press) 1980

John Gage, *J.M.W. Turner – 'A Wonderful Range of Mind'*, New Haven CT and London (Yale University Press) 1987

James Hamilton, *Turner – A Life*, London (Hodder and Stoughton) 1997

James Hamilton, *Turner and the Scientists*, London (Tate Gallery Publications) 1998

Luke Herrmann, *Turner Prints – The Engraved Work of J.M.W. Turner*, Oxford (Phaidon) 1990

David Hill, *In Turner's Footsteps – Through the Hills and Dales of Northern England*, London (John Murray) 1984

David Hill, *Turner on the Thames*, New Haven CT and London (Yale University Press) 1993

David Hill, *Turner in the North*, New Haven CT and London (Yale University Press) 1996

Evelyn Joll, Martin Butlin and Luke Herrmann, *The Oxford Companion to J.M.W. Turner*, Oxford (Oxford University Press) 2001

Graham Reynolds, *Turner*, London (Thames & Hudson) 1969

William S. Rodner, *J.M.W. Turner – Romantic Painter of the Industrial Revolution*, Berkeley CA (University of California Press) 1997

Eric Shanes, *Turner's England 1810–38*, London (Cassell) 1990

Eric Shanes, *Turner's Human Landscape*, London (Heinemann) 1990

Eric Shanes, with essays by Evelyn Joll, Ian Warrell and Andrew Wilton, *Turner – The Great Watercolours*, London (Royal Academy of Arts) 2001

Sam Smiles, *J.M.W. Turner*, London (Tate Gallery Publications) 2000

Walter Thornbury, *The Life and Correspondence of J.M.W. Turner RA*, 1862; revised edn., London (Chatto & Windus) 1897

Andrew Wilton, *J.M.W. Turner, his Art and Life*, Fribourg, 1979

Andrew Wilton, *Turner in his Time*, London (Thames & Hudson) 1987

Andrew Wilton, with transcriptions by Rosalind Mallord Turner, *Painting & Poetry – Turner's 'Verse Book' and his Work 1804–1812*, Tate Gallery (exhib. cat.) London, 1990

Catalogue

CHAPTER I

Youthful works

1. Henry Boswell, *Historical and Descriptive Accounts of Picturesque Views of the Antiquities of England and Wales*, 1786, volume of engraved plates with hand colouring, 40.5 × 26 × 8 cm (16 × 10¼ × 3⅛ in.), London Borough of Hounslow, Local Studies Collection (Chiswick Library) [pl. 12]

2. *Lincoln*, 1780s, pencil and watercolour, 23.5 × 32.1 cm (9¼ × 12¾ in.), London, Victoria and Albert Museum, Ashbee Bequest [pl. 14]

Works made during and shortly after Turner's first Bristol tour, 1791

3. 'Bristol and Malmesbury' sketchbook, 1791, 19.7 × 26.6 cm (7¾ × 10½ in.), London, Tate; bequeathed by the artist, 1856, TB VI [pl. 16]

4. *Cote House, near Bristol*, c. 1791, watercolour, 29.2 × 25.4 cm (11½ × 10 in.), Bedford, Cecil Higgins Art Gallery, W21 [pl. 17]

5. *Old Hot Wells House, Bristol*, 1791–92, watercolour, 27.3 × 34 cm (10¾ × 13⅜ in.), Bristol Museums & Art Gallery, W19 [pl. 18]

6. *Near the Mouth of the Avon*, c. 1791–92, watercolour, 17.7 × 25.1 cm (7 × 9⅞ in.), Cambridge MA, Fogg Art Museum, Harvard University Art Museums, 1991.19, Gift of David P. Wheatland in memory of Richard Wheatland, Class of 1895 [pl. 13]

Works made during and shortly after Turner's first Midlands tour, 1794

7. *At Chester*, 1794, pencil, 21.5 × 27.3 cm (8½ × 10⅜ in.), Cambridge MA, Fogg Art Museum, Harvard University Art Museums, Gift of James Loeb, Class of 1888, 1907.17 [pl. 21]

8. *In the Main Street, Chester*, 1794, pencil, 21.5 × 27.5 cm (8½ × 10⅞ in.), Cambridge MA, Fogg Art Museum, Harvard University Art Museums, Gift of James Loeb, Class of 1888, 1907.18 [pl. 22]

9. *Old Shops in Chester*, 1794, pencil, 27.1 × 20.3 cm (10⅝ × 8 in.), Oxford, Ashmolean Museum; the Ruskin School of Drawing and Fine Art, University of Oxford [pl. 3]

10. *Wrexham, Denbighshire*, 1794, pencil and watercolour, 23.6 × 32.4 cm (9¼ × 12¾ in.), London, Victoria and Albert Museum, Ashbee Bequest [pl. 23]

11. *Old Bridge, Shrewsbury*, signed and dated 1794, watercolour, exhibited RA 1795, 21.8 × 27.9 cm (8⅝ × 11 in.), University of Manchester, The Whitworth Art Gallery, W82 [pl. 29]

12. *Newark-upon-Trent Castle*, 1794–95, watercolour, 30.5 × 42.9 cm (12 × 16⅞ in.), New Haven CT, Yale Center for British Art W168 [pl. 28]

13. *Wolverhampton Green, Staffs*, exhibited RA 1796, watercolour, 31.8 × 41.9 cm (12½ × 16½ in.), Wolverhampton Art Gallery, W139 [pl. 24]

14. James S. Storer after J.M.W. Turner, *Birmingham*, engraving for John Walker's, *Copper-Plate Magazine*, 1795, 10.7 × 16.6 cm (4¼ × 6½ in.) (image), Birmingham Museums & Art Gallery, bequeathed by G. H. Keen, 1945 [pl. 19]

Works made during and shortly after Turner's tours to South Wales (1795), the North of England (1797), North Wales (1798) and into Kent (1798)

15. *Llandilo Bridge and Dinevor Castle*, exhibited RA 1796, watercolour, 35.6 × 50.2 cm (14 × 19¾ in.), Cardiff, National Museums and Galleries of Wales, W140 [pl. 25]

16. *Wakefield Bridge*, 1797–98, watercolour, 26 × 43 cm (10¼ × 17 in.), London, Trustees of the British Museum, W241 [pl. 27]

17. *St Agatha's Abbey, Easby, Yorks (The Abbey Pool)*, 1797–1800, watercolour, 51.4 × 76.2 cm (20¼ × 30 in.), University of Manchester, The Whitworth Art Gallery, W272 [pl. 20]

18. *The Dormitory and Transept of Fountains Abbey – Evening*, exhibited RA 1798, watercolour, 45.6 × 61 cm (18 × 24 in.), York Art Gallery, York Museums Trust w238 [pl. 32]

19. *Hafod*, c. 1798, watercolour, 61 × 91.5 cm (24 × 36 in.), Port Sunlight, Lady Lever Art Gallery, Board of Trustees of the National Museums and Galleries on Merseyside, W331 [pl. 45]

20. *Ludlow Castle*, 1798–1800, watercolour, 35.6 × 67.1 cm (14 × 26⅜ in.), University of Birmingham, The Barber Institute of Fine Arts, W265 [pl. 5]

21. *A Lime Kiln by Moonlight*, c. 1799, watercolour, 16.5 × 24 cm (6½ × 9½ in.), Coventry, Herbert Art Gallery and Museum, W262 [pl. 30]

22. *A beech wood, Knockholt, Kent*, 1799, oil on paper, 16.5 × 24.1 cm (6½ × 9½ in.), Cambridge MA, Fogg Art Museum, Harvard University Art Museums, Gift of Mr. and Mrs. William Emerson, BJ35c [pl. 39]

23. *Morning amongst the Coniston Fells, Cumberland*, exhibited RA 1798, oil on canvas, 122.9 × 89.9 cm (48⅜ × 35½ in.), London, Tate; bequeathed by the artist, 1856, BJ5 [pl. 31]

24. *Dunstanborough Castle*, c. 1798, oil on canvas, 47 × 69 cm (18½ × 27⅛ in.), Collection of the Dunedin Public Art Gallery, New Zealand, BJ32 [pl. 42]

25. *Dolbadern Castle*, exhibited RA 1800, oil on canvas, 119.5 × 90.2 cm (47 × 35½ in.), London, Royal Academy of Arts, BJ12 [pl. 33]

26. *Lincoln from the Brayford*, 1803–04, watercolour, bodycolour and scraping out, 66 × 102 cm (26 × 40⅛ in.), Lincoln, Usher Gallery, Lincolnshire County Council [pl. 44],

Works made during and shortly after Turner's Scottish tour, 1801

27. *Loch Awe*, 1801, pencil, 34 × 48 cm (13⅜ × 18⅞ in.), London, Tate; bequeathed by the artist, 1856, TB LVIII.15 [pl. 49]

28. *Study of Clouds and Hills, Inverary*, 1801, pencil and watercolour, 26.1 × 41.3 cm (10¼ × 16¼ in.), Oxford, Ashmolean Museum [pl. 48]

29. *Edinburgh from St Anthony's Chapel*, 1801, pencil, 26.3 × 41.3 cm (10⅜ × 16⅛ in.), Cambridge MA, Fogg Art Museum, Harvard University Art Museums, Gift of James Loeb, Class of 1888, 1907.4 [pl. 47]

30. *Kilchern Castle, with the Cruchan Ben Mountains, Scotland: Noon*, exhibited RA 1802, watercolour, 53.3 × 72.2 cm (21 × 28⅜ in.), Plymouth City Museums and Art Gallery, W344 [pl. 50]

31. *The Fall of the Clyde, Lanarkshire: Noon. – Vide Akenside's Hymn to the Naiads*, exhibited RA 1802, watercolour, 74.5 × 195.8 cm (29⅜ × 77⅛ in.), Liverpool, Walker Art Gallery, W344 [pl. 52]

Early commissions: Salisbury, Fonthill and Oxford

32. *Salisbury Cathedral from the Bishop's Garden*, 1797–98, pencil, pen and ink and watercolour, 51.3 × 67.8 cm (30¼ × 21⅝ in.), Birmingham Museums & Art Gallery; presented by the Trustees of the Public Picture Gallery Fund, 1897, W200 [pl. 34]

33. *South view from the Cloisters, Salisbury Cathedral*, c. 1802, watercolour, 68 × 49.6 cm (26¾ × 19½ in.), London, Victoria and Albert Museum;, ex coll. Sir Henry Hoare, Bt, W202 [pl. 36]

34. *Interior of Salisbury Cathedral, looking towards the North Transept*, 1802–05, watercolour, 66 × 50.8 cm (26 × 20 in.), Salisbury and South Wiltshire Museum, W203 [pl. 35]

35. *Fonthill Abbey at sunset*, 1799, pencil and watercolour, 46.8 × 33.1 cm (18⅜ × 13 in.), London, Tate; bequeathed by the artist, 1856, TB XLVII.10 [pl. 40]

36. *Fonthill, from a stone quarry*, 1800, pencil, watercolour and bodycolour, 29.8 × 44.2 cm (11¾ × 17⅜ in.), Leeds City Art Gallery, W340 [pl. 41]

37. *Exeter College and All Saints Church &c from the Turl*, 1803–04, pencil and watercolour, 32.1 × 45 cm (12⅝ × 17¾ in.), engraved for the 1806 *Oxford Almanack*, Oxford, Ashmolean Museum; the Delegates of the Clarendon Press, W297 [pl. 38]

38. *Inside View of the Hall of Christ Church*, 1803–04, pencil, watercolour and scratching out, 32.9 × 44.8 cm (13 × 17⅝ in.), engraved for the 1807 *Oxford Almanack*, Oxford, Ashmolean Museum; the Delegates of the Clarendon Press, W298 [pl. 37]

39. *Oxford from the South Side of Heddington Hill*, 1803–04, pencil and watercolour, 31.6 × 44.8 cm (12½ × 17⅝ in.), engraved for the 1808 *Oxford Almanack*, Oxford, Ashmolean Museum; the Delegates of the Clarendon Press, W302 [pl. 2]

CHAPTER II

Exhibited and commissioned oil paintings

40. *The Festival upon the Opening of the Vintage of Macon*, exhibited RA 1803, oil on canvas, 146 × 237.5 cm (57½ × 93½ in.), Sheffield Galleries and Museums Trust, BJ47 [pl. 53]

41. *Windsor Castle from the Thames*, probably exhibited at Turner's gallery, 1805, oil on canvas, 91 × 122 cm (35⅞ × 48 in.), London, Tate, on loan to Petworth House, Sussex; accepted by HM Govt. in lieu of tax and allocated to the Tate Gallery, 1984, BJ149 [pl. 56]

42. *Walton Bridges*, probably exhibited at Turner's gallery, 1806, oil on canvas, 92.7 × 123.8 cm (36½ × 48¾ in.), Oxford, Ashmolean Museum, Loyd Collection, BJ60 [pl. 57]

43. *Pope's Villa at Twickenham*, exhibited at Turner's gallery, 1808, oil on canvas, 91.5 × 120.6 cm (36 × 47⅜ in.), Sudeley Castle, Gloucestershire, Trustees of the Walter Morrison Picture Collection, BJ72 [pl. 59]

44. *Tabley, the Seat of Sir J.F. Leicester, Bart.: Windy Day*, exhibited RA 1809, oil on canvas, 91.5 × 120.6 cm (36 × 47½ in.), University of Manchester, Tabley House Collection, BJ98 [pl. 71]

45. *Tabley, Cheshire, the Seat of Sir J.F. Leicester, Bart.: Calm Morning*, exhibited RA 1809, oil on canvas, 91.5 × 116.8 cm (36 × 46 in.), London, Tate, on loan to Petworth House, Sussex; accepted by HM Govt. in lieu of tax and allocated to the Tate Gallery, 1984, BJ99 [pl. 72]

46. *Petworth, Sussex, the Seat of the Earl of Egremont: Dewy Morning*, exhibited RA 1810, oil on canvas, 91.4 × 120.6 cm (36 × 47½ in.), London, Tate, on loan to Petworth House, Sussex; accepted by HM Govt. in lieu of tax and allocated to the Tate Gallery, 1984, BJ113 [pl. 70]

Oil studies

47. *The Thames near Walton Bridges*, c. 1806–07, oil on mahogany veneer, 37.1 × 73.7 cm (14⅝ × 29 in.), London, Tate; bequeathed by the artist, 1856, BJ184 [pl. 55]

48. *The Plym Estuary looking North*, 1813, oil on prepared paper, 15.5 × 25.7 cm (6⅛ × 10⅛ in.), London, Tate; bequeathed by the artist, 1856, TB CXXX-L, BJ224 [pl. 87]

49. *The Plym Estuary from Boringdon Park*, 1813, oil on prepared paper, 24.5 × 30.5 cm (9⅝ × 12 in.), London, Tate; bequeathed by the artist, 1856, TB CXXX-E, BJ217 [pl. 88]

Preliminary pencil and watercolour studies

50. *Distant view of Lowther Castle*, 1809, pencil and watercolour, 22.5 × 35.4 cm (8⅞ × 14 in.), Oxford, Ashmolean Museum, W524 [pl. 75]

51. *Distant view of Lowther Castle*, 1809, pencil, 21.3 × 35.7 cm (8⅜ × 14 in.), Oxford, Ashmolean Museum [pl. 74]

52. *Lowther Castle*, 1809, pencil, 22 × 35.3 cm (8⅝ × 13⅞ in.), Oxford, Ashmolean Museum [pl. 73]

53. 'Hesperides I' sketchbook, 1805, 17.1 × 26.4 cm (6¾ × 10⅜ in.), London, Tate; bequeathed by the artist, 1856, TB XCIII [pls. 54, 58]

'Wharfedales' and other subjects for Walter Fawkes

54. *Bolton Abbey, Yorkshire*, 1809, watercolour, 27.8 × 39.5 cm (11 × 15½ in.), London, Trustees of the British Museum, W532 [pl. 68]

55. *Steeton Manor House, near Farnley*, c. 1815–18, gouache and watercolour, 10.5 × 16.2 cm (4⅛ × 6⅜ in.), New Haven CT, Yale Center for British Art, W628 [pl. 62]

56. *Caley Hall*, c. 1818, watercolour and bodycolour, 30.2 × 42.7 cm (11⅞ × 16¾ in.), Edinburgh, National Galleries of Scotland, W612 [pl. 64]

57. *Lake Tiny, with Alm's Cliff in the distance*, 1818, watercolour and bodycolour, 33 × 43.9 cm (13 × 17¼ in.), Hereford Museum and Art Gallery, Herefordshire Heritage Services, W607 [pl. 66]

58. *Huntsmen in a Wood*, c. 1820s, pen and sepia ink and wash, 19.4 × 26.3 cm (7⅝ × 10⅜ in.), London, Trustees of the British Museum, [pl. 65]

59. *Farnley Hall from above Otley*, c. 1815, watercolour, 28 × 39.8 cm (11 × 15⅝ in.), Amsterdam, Rijksmuseum, W613 [pl. 67]

60. *London, from the windows of 45 Grosvenor Place*, ?1820, watercolour, 25 × 39 cm (9⅞ × 15⅜ in.), private collection, c/o Robert Holden Ltd, W498 [pl. 69]

Watercolours commissioned for engraving for *Picturesque Views on the Southern Coast of England*, listed in the order in which they were engraved, which is also largely the order in which they were painted

61. *Falmouth Harbour, Cornwall*, c. 1812–13, watercolour, 15.2 × 22.9 cm (6 × 9 in.), engraved 1816, Port Sunlight, Lady Lever Art Gallery, Board of Trustees of the National Museums and Galleries on Merseyside, W455 [pl. 77]

62. *Plymouth, with Mount Batten*, c. 1814, watercolour, 14.6 × 23.5 cm (5¾ × 9¼ in.), engraved 1817, London, Victoria and Albert Museum, W457 [pl. 79]

63. *Bow and Arrow Castle, Island of Portland*, c. 1815, watercolour, 15.2 × 23 cm (6 × 9 in.), engraved 1817, University of Liverpool Art Collections, W459 [pl. 81]

64. *Rye, Sussex*, c. 1823, watercolour, 14.5 × 22.7 cm (5¾ × 9 in.), engraved 1824, Cardiff, National Museums and Galleries of Wales, W471 [pl. 83]

65. *St Mawes, Cornwall*, c. 1822, watercolour and scraping out, 14.1 × 21.7 cm (9½ × 8½ in.), engraved 1824, New Haven CT, Yale Center for British Art W473 [pl. 82]

66. *Hythe, Kent*, c. 1823, watercolour, 14 × 22.9 cm (5½ × 9 in.), engraved 1824, Guildhall Art Gallery, Corporation of London, W475 [pl. 86]

67. *Boscastle, Cornwall*, c. 1824, watercolour, 14.1 × 23 cm (5½ × 9 in.), engraved 1825, Oxford, Ashmolean Museum; presented by John Ruskin, 1861, W478 [pl. 80]

Engravings

68. John Pye and Charles Heath after J.M.W. Turner, *Pope's Villa*, engraving after *Pope's Villa at Twickenham* (cat. 43), 1811, 17.5 × 22.9 cm (6⅞ × 9 in.), Birmingham Museums & Art Gallery [pl. 60]

69. George Cooke after J.M.W. Turner, *Land's End, Cornwall*, engraving after a lost original for *Picturesque Views on the Southern Coast of England*, 1814, 14 × 22 cm (5½ × 8⅝ in.), Birmingham Museums & Art Gallery [pl. 78]

70. Edward Goodall after J.M.W. Turner, *Rye, Sussex*, engraving after cat. 64 for *Picturesque Views on the Southern Coast of England*, 1824, 14.8 × 23.3 cm (5⅞ × 9⅛ in.), Birmingham Museums & Art Gallery [pl. 84]

71. George Cooke after J.M.W. Turner, *Hythe, Kent*, engraving after cat. 66 for *Picturesque Views on the Southern Coast of England*, 1824, 15.1 × 23.2 cm (6 × 9⅛ in.), Birmingham Museums & Art Gallery [pl. 85]

72. Attributed to J.M.W. Turner but possibly by Thomas Lupton, *Stonehenge*, mezzotint engraving, printed in sepia ink, working proof. Produced for the *Liber Studiorum* from a drawing of c. 1824, 19.2 × 26.2 cm (7½ × 10¼ in.) (image), Boston, Museum of Fine Arts; bequest of Francis Bullard [pl. 61]

CHAPTER III

Exhibited and commissioned oil paintings

73. *England: Richmond Hill, on the Prince Regent's Birthday*, exhibited RA 1819, oil on canvas, 180 × 334.5 cm (70⅞ × 131⅝ in.), London, Tate; bequeathed by the artist, 1856, BJ140 [pl. 106]

74. *Chichester Canal*, c. 1828, oil on canvas, 65.4 × 134.6 cm (25¾ × 53 in.), London, Tate; bequeathed by the artist, 1856, BJ290 [pl. 108]

75. *The Chain Pier, Brighton*, c. 1828, oil on canvas, 71.1 × 136.5 cm (28 × 53¾ in.), London, Tate; bequeathed by the artist, 1856, BJ291 [pl. 109]

76. *A Ship Aground*, c. 1828, oil on canvas, 70 × 136 cm (27½ × 53½ in.), London, Tate; bequeathed by the artist, 1856, BJ287 [pl. 110]

Watercolours commissioned for engraving

Subjects for *History of Richmondshire*

77. *Junction of the Greta and the Tees at Rokeby*, c. 1816, watercolour, 29 × 41.4 cm (11⅜ × 16¼ in.), engraved 1819, Oxford, Ashmolean Museum; presented by John Ruskin, 1861, W566 [pl. 90]

78. *Crook of Lune, looking towards Hornby Castle*, c. 1817, pencil, watercolour, bodycolour and chalk, 29 × 42.9 cm (11⅜ × 16⅞ in.), engraved 1821, London, Courtauld Institute Gallery, W575 [pl. 92]

79. *Simmer Lake, near Askrigg*, c. 1817, watercolour, 28.7 × 41.2 cm (11¼ × 16¼ in.), engraved 1822, London, Trustees of the British Museum, W571 [pl. 93]

80. *Lancaster Sands*, c. 1818, watercolour, 28 × 36.6 cm (11 × 14⅜ in.), not engraved, Birmingham Museums & Art Gallery; bequeathed by J. Leslie Wright, 1953, W581 [pl. 95]

Subjects for *History of Durham*

81. *Gibside, Co. Durham (SW view)*, 1817–18, watercolour, 26.5 × 44 cm (10½ × 17⅜ in.), engraved 1819, Barnard Castle, County Durham, Bowes Museum, W557 [pl. 96]

82. *Gibside, Co Durham (N View)*, 1817–18, watercolour and gum arabic, 27.5 × 45 cm (10⅞ × 17¾ in.), not engraved, Barnard Castle, County Durham, Bowes Museum [pl. 97]

Subjects for *Rivers of England*

83. *Dartmouth Castle, on the River Dart*, 1822, pencil and watercolour, 15.9 × 22.4 cm (6¼ × 8⅞ in.), engraved 1824, London, Tate; bequeathed by the artist, 1856, TB CCVIII-D W737 [pl. 99]

84. *Okehampton Castle, on the River Okement*, c. 1824, pencil, watercolour and bodycolour, 16.3 × 23 cm (6⅜ × 9 in.), engraved 1825, London, Tate; bequeathed by the artist, 1856, TB CCVIII-E W738 [pl. 100]

85. *The Mouth of the River Humber*, c. 1824, watercolour, 16.5 × 24.3 cm (6½ × 9½ in.), engraved 1826, London, Tate; bequeathed by the artist, 1856, TB CCVIII-R W743 [pl. 9]

Subjects for *Views in London and its Environs*

86. *Old London Bridge and Vicinity*, also known as *The Port of London*, 1824, watercolour, 29.2 × 44.5 cm (11½ × 17½ in.), engraved 1828, London, Victoria and Albert Museum, W514 [pl. 102]

87. *View of London from Greenwich*, 1825, watercolour, 21.3 × 28.4 cm (8⅜ × 11⅛ in.), not engraved, New York, Metropolitan Museum of Art; bequest of Alexandrine Sinsheimer, 1958 [pl. 104]

88. *St Paul's from the Thames*, ?1820s, pencil, 12.8 × 20.8 cm (5 × 8¼ in.), Cambridge MA, Fogg Art Museum, Harvard University Art Museums; bequest of Mrs. Alfred Mansfield Brooks [pl. 103]

Subjects illustrating the works of Sir Walter Scott

89. *Tantallon Castle*, 1821, watercolour, 17.5 × 25.4 cm (6⅞ × 10 in.), engraved 1822 for *Provincial Antiquities of Scotland*, Manchester City Galleries, W1067 [pl. 107]

90. *Carlisle*, c. 1832, watercolour with scratching out, 8.3 × 14.2 cm (3¼ × 5⅝ in.), engraved 1834 for *Scott's Poetical Works*, New Haven CT, Yale Center for British Art, W1070 [pl. 105]

Engravings

91. Henry le Keux after J.M.W. Turner, *Simmer Lake, near Askrigg*, engraving after cat. 79 for *History of Richmondshire*, 1822, 19 × 26.7 cm (7½ × 10½ in.), Birmingham Museums & Art Gallery [pl. 94]

92. Edward Goodall after J.M.W. Turner, *Old London Bridge and Vicinity*, engraving after cat. 86 for *Views in London and its Environs*, 1828, 17.5 × 26.5 cm (6⅞ × 10⅜ in.), Birmingham Museums & Art Gallery [pl. 101]

93. Edward Goodall after J.M.W. Turner, *Carlisle*, engraving after cat. 90 for *Scott's Poetical Works*, 1834, 8.3 × 14.3 (3¼ × 5⅝ in.), Birmingham Museums & Art Gallery [not illustrated]

CHAPTER IV

Watercolours commissioned for engraving for *England and Wales*,
listed in the order in which they were engraved, which is also largely the order in which they were painted

94. *Bolton Abbey, Yorkshire*, c. 1825, watercolour, 28 × 39.4 cm (11 × 15½ in.), engraved 1827, Port Sunlight, Lady Lever Art Gallery, Board of Trustees of the National Museums and Galleries on Merseyside, W788 [pl. 118]

95. *Lancaster, from the Aqueduct Bridge*, c. 1825, watercolour, 28 × 39.4 cm (11 × 15½ in.), engraved 1827, Port Sunlight, Lady Lever Art Gallery, Board of Trustees of the National Museums and Galleries on Merseyside, W786 [pl. 6]

96. *Lancaster Sands*, c. 1826, watercolour, 27.8 × 40.4 cm (11 × 15⅞ in.), engraved 1828, London, Trustees of the British Museum, W803 [pl. 116]

97. *Okehampton, Devonshire*, c. 1826, watercolour, 28.5 × 41.1 cm (11¼ × 16⅛ in.), engraved 1828, Melbourne, Australia, National Gallery of Victoria; Felton Bequest, 1905, W802 [pl. 117]

98. *Louth, Lincolnshire*, c. 1828, watercolour, 28.5 × 42 cm (11¼ × 16½ in.), engraved 1829, London, Trustees of the British Museum, W809 [pl. 113]

99. *Stamford, Lincolnshire*, c. 1828; watercolour, bodycolour and scratching out, 29.3 × 42 cm (11½ × 16½ in.), engraved 1830, Lincoln, Usher Gallery, Lincolnshire County Council, W817 [pl. 115]

100. *Pembroke Castle, Wales*, c. 1830, watercolour, engraved 1831, 29.8 × 42.6 cm (11¾ × 16¾ in.), Bath, The Holburne Museum of Art, W832 [pl. 10]

101. *Gosport, the Entrance to Portsmouth Harbour, Hampshire*, c. 1829, watercolour, 29.2 × 43.2 cm (11½ × 17 in.), engraved 1831, Portsmouth City Museums and Records Service, W828 [pl. 130]

102. *Kenilworth Castle, Warwickshire*, c. 1830, watercolour and bodycolour, 29.2 × 45.4 cm (11½ × 17⅞ in.), engraved 1832, Fine Arts Museums of San Francisco, Achenbach Foundation for Graphic Arts, Gift of Osgood Hooker, 1967, W842 [pl. 122]

103. *Warwick Castle, Warwickshire*, c. 1830, watercolour, 29.7 × 45.1 cm (11⅝ × 17¾ in.), engraved 1832, University of Manchester, The Whitworth Art Gallery, W841 [pl. 126]

104. *Chatham, from Fort Pitt, Kent*, 1831, watercolour, 28.2 × 45.7 cm (11⅛ × 18 in.), engraved 1832, private collection, W838. Photograph courtesy of Richard Green Gallery, London [pl. 4]

105. *Plymouth Cove, Devonshire*, c. 1829, watercolour, 28 × 41.2 cm (11 × 16¼ in.), engraved 1832, London, Victoria and Albert Museum, W835 [pl. 119]

106. *Castle Upnor, Kent*, c. 1831, watercolour, 28.6 × 43.5 cm (11¼ × 17⅛ in.), engraved 1833, University of Manchester, The Whitworth Art Gallery, W847 [pl. 131]

107. *Dudley, Worcestershire*, c. 1833, watercolour, 28.8 × 43 cm (11⅜ × 17 in.), engraved 1835, Birmingham Museums & Art Gallery, W858 [pl. 120]

108. *Kidwelly Castle, South Wales*, 1835, watercolour, 28.9 × 44.5 cm (11⅜ × 17½ in.), engraved 1837, Preston, Harris Museum and Art Gallery, W870 [pl. 132]

109. *Richmond Terrace, Surrey*, 1836, watercolour, 28 × 43.5 cm (11 × 17⅛ in.), engraved 1838, Port Sunlight, Lady Lever Art Gallery, Board of Trustees of the National Museums and Galleries on Merseyside, W879 [pl. 128]

110. *Mount St Michael, Cornwall*, 1836, watercolour, 30.5 × 43.9 cm (12 × 17¼ in.), engraved 1838, University of Liverpool Art Collections/Bridgeman Art Library, W880 [pl. 129]

Engravings

111. Robert Wallis after J.M.W. Turner, *Dudley, Worcestershire*, engraving after cat. 107 for *England and Wales*, 1835, 23.8 × 43 cm (11⅜ × 17 in.), Birmingham Museums & Art Gallery [pl. 121]

112. James T. Willmore after J.M.W. Turner, *Richmond Terrace, Surrey*, engraving after cat. 109 for *England and Wales*, 1838, 16.3 × 25 cm (6⅜ × 9⅞ in.), Birmingham Museums & Art Gallery; presented by Charles Willmore, 1940 [pl. 127]

Sketchbooks from the 1830 Midlands tour and related material

113. 'Kenilworth' sketchbook, 1830, 11.4 × 18.9 cm (4½ × 7½ in.), London, Tate; bequeathed by the artist, 1856, TB CCXXXVIII [pl. 123]

114. 'Birmingham and Coventry' sketchbook, 1830, 6.4 × 10.5 cm (2½ × 4¼ in.), London, Tate; bequeathed by the artist, 1856, TB CCXL [pls. 7, 8, 124]

115. *St Mary's Church, Warwick, from below Hill Wootton*, formerly known as *Gloucester Cathedral*, ?1830, watercolour, 23 × 30 cm (9 × 11¾ in.), London, Tate; bequeathed by the artist, 1856, TB CCLXIII 307 [pl. 125]

116. *Birmingham Society of Arts Exhibition 1829*. Catalogue of the exhibition in the Society's rooms in New Street, with a letter published in the *Birmingham Journal*, 12 December 1829, Birmingham Libraries, Local Studies Department, L54.61 (see Appendix I, p. 196) [not illustrated]

CHAPTER V

Oil paintings

117. *'Death on a Pale Horse'*, 1831–32, oil on canvas, 60 × 75.5 cm (23⅝ × 29¾ in.), London, Tate; bequeathed by the artist, 1856, BJ259 [pl. 142]

118. *The Fighting 'Temeraire', tugged to her Last Berth to be broken up, 1838*, exhibited RA 1839, oil on canvas, 91 × 122 cm (35⅞ × 48 in.), London, National Gallery, BJ377 [pl. 151]

Watercolours

119. *Wycliffe, near Rokeby*, c. 1816–20, from the *History of Richmondshire* series, watercolour, 29.2 × 43 cm (11½ × 16⅞ in.), engraved 1823, Liverpool, Walker Art Gallery, Board of Trustees of the National Museums and Galleries on Merseyside, W568 [pl. 141]

120. *Sidmouth, Devon*, 1825–27, from the *Ports of England* series, watercolour, 18.4 × 26.3 cm (7⅛ × 10⅜ in.), engraving begun in 1828, published 1856, University of Manchester, The Whitworth Art Gallery [pl. 137]

121. *Colchester, Essex*, c. 1825, from the *England and Wales* series, watercolour, 28.8 × 40.7 cm (11⅜ × 16 in.), engraved 1827, London, Courtauld Institute Gallery, W789 [pl. 139]

122. *Salisbury, from Old Sarum*, c. 1828, from the *England and Wales* series, watercolour, 27.2 × 39.5 cm (10¾ × 15½ in.), engraved 1830, Salisbury and South Wiltshire Museum, W836 [pl. 136]

123. *Blenheim House and Park, Oxfordshire*, 1830–31, from the *England and Wales* series, watercolour, 29.6 × 46.8 cm (11⅝ × 18⅜ in.), engraved 1833, Birmingham Museums & Art Gallery; bequeathed by Sir Edward E. Parkes, 1920, W846 [pl. 138]

124. *Nottingham, Nottinghamshire*, 1832, from the *England and Wales* series, watercolour, 30.5 × 46.3 cm (12 × 18¼ in.), engraved 1833, Nottingham Castle, City of Nottingham Museums and Galleries, w850 [pl. 134]

Engravings

125. John Pye after J.M.W. Turner, *The Birthplace of John Wycliffe (The Morning Star of Liberty) near Rokeby, Yorkshire*, engraving proof after cat. 119, with inscription [transcribed in the Appendix], 1823, London, Trustees of the British Museum, [pl. 140]

126. James T. Willmore after J.M.W. Turner, *Destruction of both Houses of Parliament by Fire Oct. 16, 1834*, engraving for *The Keepsake*, 1835, 10.6 × 8.7 cm (4⅛ × 3⅜ in.), Birmingham Museums & Art Gallery; presented by Charles Willmore, 1940 [pl. 148]

Historical Vignettes and *Fairfaxiana*

127 (i–xvii). Maroon leather-bound volume, blind-tooled and gold-stamped, with a brass clasp fitted centrally along leading edge and key on green ribbon. Inscribed: "HISTORICAL VIGNETTES/ AND/ FAIRFAXIANA/ BY/ J.M.W. TURNER R.A." At lower edge: "FARNLEY HALL, OTLEY/ YORKSHIRE". Inside front cover stamped at lower edge: "BOUND BY ZAEHNSEDORF 1912". Maroon watered-silk lining on back and front inside covers, 49.5 × 39 × 6.4 cm (19½ × 15⅜ × 2½ in.), private collection

Inside are two guard pages, a title page (text as cover), three further guard pages, then the following images, in pencil and watercolour with some collaged material. Some are interleaved with guard pages. All works are in pencil and watercolour, and date to between 1815 and the mid-1820s. All dimensions given are sight size, taken from inside existing mounts. In the following catalogue HV signifies *Historical Vignettes* and F signifies *Faifaxiana*.

i. Two coronation chairs in Westminster Abbey. The "Stone of Scone" (thus inscribed) lies under the right-hand throne. Both thrones have graffiti on their backs, much of it illegible, except (on left-hand throne) "WALTER" and "Abbott slept in this chair". Within the design are the crown, mace, sword; the quartered coats of arms of England and France; spurs, and parchment documents inscribed: "Norman Dynasty", "Plantagenet House of Anjou Dynasty", "Coronation Oath of England – by Edward Confessor", 30.7 × 22 cm (12⅛ × 8⅝ in.), HV [pl. 144]

ii. "A Gold Coin/ found at Agincourt/ presented to Walter Fawkes Esq by Majʳ Genˡ Sir Edward Barnes KCB/ 1823".

Shown are two figures, labelled (left): "The Armour of Sir/ Rᵈ de Vere Earl of Oxford/ 1416"; (right): "Gilt Armour/ of King Henʸ yᵉ Vᵗʰ 1415". Each carries an emblazoned shield. Above are flanking arms of France and England, with a study of the coin, obverse and reverse, with inscription: "Arms Side/ Carolus D Gracia Francorum Rex/ Reverse/ P. C. Regnat Imperat P. C. Vincit". Below is a red silk bag, empty, which once held the coin, 30.8 × 22.5 cm (12⅛ × 8⅞ in.), HV [pl. 144]

iii. Luther's Bible, dated on title page "MDXLI" with illegible German inscription, and signed on the facing page "Martinis Luther 1542"; figure with imploring hands burning at the stake. Twin towers of an abbey behind. Documents: "List of Abbeys/ Suppressed by Order York/ Canterbury/ Westminster/ Bristol/ Peterboro/ Lincoln/ Crowland/ Ely/ Wells/ Osney/ Tewkesbury/ Gloucester/ Worcester/ Netley/ Tintern/ Margam/ Merton/ Land ... "; "Henry VIII Proclamation", with ink pot and two quills; "REFORMATION". Pencil inscription at bottom edge: "The Lord is my Shepherd I shall want nothing/ who could better if he would rest sound and secure as Sheep of the faithful/ Shepherd who giveth his life for the flock. Wo [*sic*] to the shameful calumnation/ who does not follow such a Shepherd but rather suffers himself to be devoured by/ the wolf of Eternal Death Psalm 23", 32.6 × 20.2 cm (12⅞ × 8 in.), HV [pl. 144]

iv. King Charles's coffin, purple, studded with gold, with inscribed plate: "CAROLUS I/ obit/ Janʸ xxx 1648". On the coffin are the king's feathered hat, cloak, Garter Star, mace, a bloody axe, fasces and sword, with St George's Jewel on a blue ribbon, 22.7 × 16.2 cm (9 × 6⅜ in.), HV [pl. 144]

v. Inscribed: "Bad Advisers/ Arbitrary Measures/ Forced Loans/ The King's Will/ The Law/ FIRST PERIOD". Above, a drawn sword supporting a balance, with a cap of "Liberty" being weighed light against a crown inscribed "Perogative" [*sic*]. Right: money bags, with an elegant hand fondling the coins, and (left) masks. Documents: "Arbitrary Arrestm[ent?] Imprisonment", "Benevolence/ By the King", and an open book: (left page) "Fear God/ Honour/ the/ King"; (right page) "THE/ Kings/ Word/ LAW/ 1626", 27.8 × 18.8 (11 × 7⅜ in.), HV [pl. 145]

vi. A parchment inscribed "Ship Money &c/ The King vs Hampden/ Guilty", lying over a 'painting' of Marston [Moor] in a frame, is stuck over an engraved portrait of John Hampden; "John Hampden – Petition of Right". Above: Parliamentarians' hands with swords and flags. Red hat of liberty held aloft on staff. Below: shackle with lock, and inscription "SECOND PERIOD", 28.7 × 20 cm (11¼ × 7⅞ in.), HV [pl. 145]

vii. Tumbling castle tower, opposing armies; left: "For the King", and right: "Commonwealth" and "My Trust/ is in/ God". Cannon being lit by two hands holding flaming rolls of paper marked "Manifestoes", "Covenents". Inscribed, "Civil War"/ "THIRD PERIOD", 28.7 × 20 cm (11¼ × 7⅞ in.), HV [pl. 145]

viii. "Oʳ Cromwell/ Protector" (on paper obscuring a gold framed picture);, "RUIN/ of the Royal Cause". Scroll: "MARSTON/ MOOR/ TADCASTER/ NEWBURY/ NASEBY/ EDGEHILL", with swords and bloody axe above. Flag with hound wearing crown being chased by five other hounds, all barking "PYM PYM PYM". "Death Warrant" (signed by regicides), "WARRANT/ FOR/ EXECUTION [of]/ KING COMMITAL/ to/ CARISBROOK/ CASTLE". Black-framed painting of Whitehall and scaffold on central painting, itself covering up a panel edged in red, and part-obscured by the warrant. Inscribed "FOURTH PERIOD", 29.6 × 20 cm (11⅝ × 7⅞ in.), HV [pl. 145]

ix. "OLIVER CROMWELL" (inscribed frame awaiting engraved portrait). Banner above inscribed "THE COMMON WEAL", signed "Oliver P", swords, parliamentary mace, 32.2 × 20 cm (12⅝ × 7⅞ in.), HV [pl. 145]

x. "RICHARD CROMWELL" (inscribed frame awaiting engraved portrait). Above: crown, garter and cloak, sword, parchment inscribed "R. Cromwell", 32.2 × 20 cm (12⅝ × 7⅞ in.), HV [pl. 145]

xi. Two volumes of Book of Statutes (facing volume is Vol. II) with the Crown Jewels atop; three documents, inscribed "King William's/ Declaration/ for restoring the Liberties/ of England/ Elections ought to be Free/ To be made with an entire/ Liberty without any sort/ of Force or the requiring/ the Electors to Chuse/ such persons as shall/ be named to them./ vide the declaration/ of King William with state [...]."; "Magna Carta"; "Bill of Rights", 21.3 × 15.5 cm (8⅜ × 6⅛ in.), HV [pl. 145]

xii. Eight banners, and Fairfax's pale leather feathered hat, breastplate and pike. Clockwise from top, banners read: "TRUTH and PEACE"; "QUI NON: EST: HODIE: CRAS: MINUS: APTUS: ERIT"; "REX IN POTESTATUM SUI PUGNANS"; "GOD IS MY STRENGTH"; "QUI ADMITTIT SERVAT"; "DIVINIS PRO HUMANIS VIM. VI"; "QUOUSQUE TANDEM ABUTERIS PATIENTIA NOSTRA" (with hounds barking "PYM PYM PYM" and "KIMBOLTON", and chasing a larger hound); "VIRTUTIS COMES IVIDIA"; "OZA et PUDNA FURAT et Juraliit Jehoveh", 20.2 × 16.3 cm (8 × 6⅜ in.), HV [pl. 145]

xiii. Breastplate, helm and crossed spear and pike. Breastplate inscribed: "FAIRFAXIANA/ or/ Portraits &c &c illustrative/ of the part/ which/ THOMAS LORD FAIRFAX/ took/ in the defence/ of the Liberties of his/ Country". (A title page to the *Fairfaxiana* section of the volume.), 23.2 × 15 cm (9⅛ × 5⅞ in.), F [pl. 146]

xiv. Parliamentarian helmet, sword (inscribed "ANDREA FERARA" on blade) and drum, inscribed on corbelled wall-plaque: "Helmet Sword and Drum/ of Sir Thomas afterwards Lord Fairfax/ with Shot and bullets found at Marston Moor/ In the possession of Walter Fawkes Esqᵣ of Farnley", 27.5 × 19.3 cm (10⅞ × 7⅝ in.), F [pl. 146]

xv. Lord Fairfax's three-wheeled chair (as also appears in Turner's watercolour of the Oak Room at Farnley, W593), with sword and mace. Inscribed "FAIRFAXIANA", 20.9 × 15 cm (8¼ × 5⅞ in.), F [pl. 146]

xvi. "CAUSE and EFFECT 1642–1648", "John Lambert" (signature under his hat). Three swords piercing three documents. Main document: "BY THE KING", dated "12 day of May 1626". Sig "Ja. Wyllie", Document (left) signed: "O Cromwell";, (right) signed: "Thos Fairfax", 27.8 × 18.8 cm (11 × 7⅜ in.), F [pl. 146]

xvii. Oak cupboard with two opening doors, two drawers below, and ball feet; large pedimented overmantel. Inside, under gothick arch: "FAREFAXIANA" [sic]. Upper level: Swords of Cromwell, Fairfax and Lambert, and three portraits: Fairfax centre, Cromwell and Lambert flanking left and right. Lower level: Mug, pair of candlesticks, portrait of Oliver Cromwell, hat, and book inscribed "Oliver Cromwell/ Protector/ Sidney Coll/ Cambridge", 34 × 26.6 cm (13⅜ × 10½ in.), F [pl. 147]

The album ends with four guard sheets. On the outside cover is the Fawkes family coat of arms and motto "A DEO ET REGE".

128. *A Frontispiece (at Farnley Hall)*, 1815, pen and ink, pencil and watercolour with scratching out, 17.8 × 24.2 cm (7 × 9½ in.), Oxford, Ashmolean Museum, W582. A view of the east gate and entrance of Farnley Hall, with a tomb chest in the foreground. This is topped with an armour helm, a mug bearing a Parliamentarian coat of arms, and numerous documents. Among these are a Fawkes family tree, emblazoned with coats of arms; a document headed "BY THE KING"; another signed "Thos Fairfax"; and a third signed "O Cromwell". Also, behind, banners of "CROMWELL" and "Commonwealth" and, in front, a banner of "FAIRFAX"; a pike, sword and breastplate [pl. 143]

CHAPTER VI

129. *The New Moon; or, 'I've lost My Boat, You shan't have Your Hoop'*, exhibited RA 1840, oil on panel, 65.5 × 81.5 cm (25¾ × 32 in.), London, Tate; bequeathed by the artist, 1856, BJ386 [pl. 153]

130. *Morning after the Wreck*, 1840s, oil on canvas, 38 × 61 cm (15 × 24 in.), Cardiff, National Museums and Galleries of Wales, BJ478 [pl. 154]

131. *Off Deal*, 1840s, oil on paper on millboard, 24.5 × 32 cm (9⅝ × 12⅝ in.), Stockholm, Nationalmuseum, BJ483 [pl. 158]

132. *The Falls of the Clyde*, 1840s, oil on canvas, 89 × 119.5 cm (35 × 47 in.), Port Sunlight, Lady Lever Art Gallery, Board of Trustees of the National Museums and Galleries on Merseyside, BJ510 [pl. 155]

133. *Landscape with river and distant mountains*, 1840s, oil on canvas, 92 × 122.5 cm (36¼ × 48¼ in.), Liverpool, Walker Art Gallery, Board of Trustees of the National Museums and Galleries on Merseyside, BJ517 [pl. 156]

134. *Rough Sea*, 1840s, oil on canvas, 91.5 × 122 cm (36 × 48 in.), London, Tate; bequeathed by the artist, 1856, BJ471 [pl. 159]

We should like to thank the private collectors and the directors and staff of the following museums and galleries (works are referred to by catalogue number):

Amsterdam, Rijksmuseum 59
Barnard Castle, County Durham, Bowes Museum 81, 82
Bath, The Holburne Museum of Art 100
Bedford, Trustees of the Cecil Higgins Art Gallery 4
Birmingham Libraries, Local Studies Department 116
Birmingham Museums and Art Gallery 14, 32, 68–71, 80, 91–93, 107, 111, 112, 123, 126
Birmingham, University of Birmingham, The Barber Institute of Fine Arts 20
Boston, Museum of Fine Arts 72
Bristol Museums & Art Gallery 5
Cambridge MA, Harvard University Art Museums, Fogg Art Museum 6, 7, 8, 22, 29, 88
Cardiff, National Museums and Galleries of Wales 15, 64, 130
Coventry, Herbert Art Gallery and Museum 21
Dunedin Public Art Gallery 24
Edinburgh, National Galleries of Scotland 56
Herefordshire Museum and Art Gallery, Hereford Heritage Services 57
Leeds City Art Gallery 36
Lincolnshire County Council, Usher Gallery 26, 99
Liverpool, Board of the National Museums and Galleries on Merseyside: Lady Lever Art Gallery, Port Sunlight; Walker Art Gallery 19, 31, 61, 94, 95, 109, 119, 132, 133
Liverpool, University of Liverpool Art Collections 63, 110
London Borough of Hounslow, Local Studies Collection, Chiswick Library 1
London, Trustees of the British Museum 16, 54, 58, 79, 96, 98, 125
London, Courtauld Institute Gallery 78, 121
London, Guildhall Art Gallery, Corporation of London 66
London, National Gallery 118
London, Royal Academy of Arts 25
London, Tate 3, 23, 27, 35, 41, 45–49, 73–76, 83–85, 113–15, 117, 129, 134
London, Victoria and Albert Museum 2, 10, 33, 62, 86, 105
Manchester City Galleries 89
Manchester, The Whitworth Art Gallery, University of Manchester 11, 17, 103, 106, 120
Manchester, University of Manchester, Tabley House Collection 44

Melbourne, National Gallery of Victoria 97
New Haven CT, Yale Center for British Art 12, 55, 65, 90
New York, Metropolitan Museum of Art 87
Nottingham, City of Nottingham Museums and Galleries 124
Oxford, Ashmolean Museum, University of Oxford 9, 28, 37–39, 42, 50–53, 67, 77, 128
Plymouth City Museums and Art Gallery 30
Portsmouth City Museums and Records Service 101
Preston, Harris Museum and Art Gallery 108
Private collection 60, 104, 127
Salisbury and South Wiltshire Museum 34, 122
San Francisco, Fine Arts Museums of San Francisco 102
Sheffield Galleries and Museums Trust 40
Stockholm, Nationalmuseum 131
Sudeley Castle, Gloucestershire, Trustees of the Walter Morrison Picture Collection 43
Wolverhampton Art Gallery 13
York Museums Trust, York Art Gallery 18

Index